The Layman's Manual on Christian Apologetics

The Layman's Manual on Christian Apologetics

Bridging the Essentials of Apologetics from
the Ivory Tower to the Everyday Christian

Brian G. Chilton

Foreword by Gary R. Habermas

Preface by Daniel Merritt

RESOURCE *Publications* · Eugene, Oregon

THE LAYMAN'S MANUAL ON CHRISTIAN APOLOGETICS
Bridging the Essentials of Apologetics from the Ivory Tower to the Everyday Christian

Copyright © 2019 Brian G. Chilton. All rights reserved. Except for brief quotations in critical publications or reviews, no part of this book may be reproduced in any manner without prior written permission from the publisher. Write: Permissions, Wipf and Stock Publishers, 199 W. 8th Ave., Suite 3, Eugene, OR 97401.

Resource Publications
An Imprint of Wipf and Stock Publishers
199 W. 8th Ave., Suite 3
Eugene, OR 97401

www.wipfandstock.com

PAPERBACK ISBN: 978-1-5326-9710-4
HARDCOVER ISBN: 978-1-5326-9711-1
EBOOK ISBN: 978-1-5326-9712-8

Manufactured in the U.S.A.   OCTOBER 7, 2019

Unless otherwise noted, all Scripture quotations are taken from the Christian Standard Bible®, Copyright © 2016 by Holman Bible Publishers. Used by permission. Christian Standard Bible® and CSB® is a federally registered trademark of Holman Bible Publishers.

Scripture marked ESV comes from the *English Standard Version* (Wheaton, IL: Crossway, 2016).

Scripture marked NIV comes from the *New International Version* (Grand Rapids: Zondervan, 2011).

Scripture marked KJV comes from the *King James Version*.

Dedicated to my family. To Jennifer, my wife; Grayson, my son; Dennis and Gail Chilton, my parents; and to Virginia Church and Dan Talley.

Also, I would like to dedicate this book to my professor Gary Habermas, to the late Norman Geisler, and to the apologists everywhere whom God has used to strengthen my faith to what it is today.

CONTENTS

Foreword by Gary R. Habermas | ix
Preface by Daniel Merritt | xiii
Introduction | xv

Unit 1   Prolegomena—Apologetic Methodologies and the Nature of Truth | 1

  Chapter 1   What is Apologetics? | 3
  Chapter 2   What is Truth? | 16
  Chapter 3   The Role of Logic and Truth | 25

Unit 2   The Existence of God and Theological Objections | 31

  Chapter 4   God, His Attributes, and Seven Major Worldviews | 33
  Chapter 5   Classical Arguments For The Existence of God (Part 1) | 44
  Chapter 6   Classical Arguments For The Existence of God (Part 2) | 52
  Chapter 7   Morality and The Moral Argument for God's Existence | 62
  Chapter 8   Do Miracles Occur? | 68
  Chapter 9   Theodicy | 75

Unit 3   The Historicity of Jesus and the Veracity of Scripture | 89

  Chapter 10   Historicity of Jesus's Resurrection | 91
  Chapter 11   Manuscript Evidence | 100

Chapter 12   Rules of Canonicity, Fake Gospels, and the Uniqueness of
             Christianity | 111
Chapter 13   Archaeological Evidence for the Bible | 118
Chapter 14   Biblical Authority | 130
Chapter 15   Messianic Prophecy | 144
             Postlude | 165

Appendix 1   *Theodicy Centered in the Cross* by Daniel Merritt | 169
Appendix 2   *Thirty-Three Logical Fallacies Everyone Should Know* | 173
Appendix 3   *Responding to Four Apologetic Objections* | 182
Bibliography | 187

FOREWORD

Brian Chilton begins his volume *The Layman's Manual on Christian Apologetics* by framing his text against what increasingly looks like a coming time of struggle for believers in yet another new cultural revolution, similar in some ways to what transpired in the wake of the 1960s revolution. Depending on how the existing situation proceeds and works out, the field of Christian apologetics could face yet another incredible new challenge in addition to several others during the last few decades. The potential trials can only be imagined at present.

Allow me to explain. In 1977, I sent two completely different manuscripts on the subject of Jesus' resurrection to four leading publishers. All four rejected the manuscript they had received. One influential Managing Editor kindly sent me a long, detailed letter that is still in my files. Basically, he told me that apologetics was just about dead—it did not sell well anymore because the U.S. ethos had changed significantly post-1960s. Few folks, it seemed, liked to tell someone to their face that they were missing out on eternal life, or conversely, to always be arguing to prove their faith. It was not that I was wrong to head in this direction, only that apologetics was not selling well, so was forced to reject his manuscript. I really appreciated his honesty and we subsequently struck up a 40-year friendship!

Then, just a few years later, a Managing Editor at another major company wanted to know what I could write for them, because in this short time, he told me that apologetics had become the hottest subject in publishing! It was not that the two presses were that much different. But by this time, apologetics seemed to be a hot commodity at many presses, as I was to find out subsequently.

What had happened? Well, about the same time that these four refusal letters were arriving, the New Age Movement and its general mystical ethos had sprung up in many quarters. God could be anywhere, everywhere, or nowhere, depending on your own thoughts and feelings—follow your own heart! Over the next two decades or so, the New Atheism seemed to pop up out of nowhere. (Isn't that always the way it seems with what appears to be new movements?) Additionally, post-modern ideas (however those were defined!) was ravaging university campuses, but now was reaching full swing into popular, everyday issues, including permeating the church.

Whoa! These ideas had exploded in a couple of short decades? During this time, a popular author contacted me because he was writing about apologetics in a unique way. His new book was named, *Who Made the Moon?* (Thomas Nelson, 2008). In the flyleaf of this book, Sigmund Brouwer intriguingly wrote, "I began the journey that led to this book because, as a father, I want to see my daughters in heaven." That sentence stuck in my mind and has not left since then, for his daughters were very young at that time. What in the whole world could be more important to a father?

In my opinion, these ideas just might fit together. When I received those four rejection letters, I wondered if I would ever write another thing—500 pages simply took too much time! (By the way, both of those resurrection books were eventually published!) But the encouragement just a few short years later to write more apologetics awakened me! Then with that line regarding his concern for his young daughters, Brouwer's comment haunted me. Now it seemed like a natural: nobody was ready to talk evidence *until* certain ideas had entered their own homes! Only then did the alarm sound!

So how does a Christian parent respond when they first find out that their teenage son or daughter has been entertaining several New Age ideas, or atheism, or the post-modern urge to define truth with a small "t"? Or, how about the challenge to demonstrate that Jesus ever existed in the first place without using the "prejudiced" Bible located in your home? What if another family member or friend revealed that they were thinking about walking away from their faith? Good answers were now needed. How did Mom and Dad respond? I'm sure some did quite well; others, not so much!

Unfortunately, at this point, some believers conclude falsely that apologetics is unbiblical or that it contradicts faith. But such a criticism ignores literally dozens of biblical passages. Apologetic evidences may help minister to people in at least three distinct ways. First, apologetics can strengthen the faith of believers, as when Jesus answered John the Baptist's doubts by pointing him to His many miracles (Luke 7:18-23). If this was all apologetics accomplished, it would be worth its weight in gold. Second, the Holy Spirit may use evidence to bring unbelievers to faith in Jesus Christ, such as John's comment that Jesus' miracles were recorded for this very purpose (Jn 20:30-31). Third, evidences may also challenge unbelievers by simply making them think, even when they disagree or do not want to listen. Jesus reported to unbelievers that his resurrection would be the sign that his teachings were true (Matt. 12:38-40). After Paul provided resurrection evidence and argued that this event demonstrated the truth of his message, some Greek philosophers came to faith while others were challenged (Acts 17:30-34).

Amazingly, Paul even commented that our faith is vain apart from the resurrection (1 Cor. 15:1-11, 14, 17). Good books can help equip us to defend our faith in a biblical, meaningful, and even practical way. Enter Brian Chilton's work, *The Layman's Manual on Christian Apologetics*. Don't miss the subtitle, directed *"from the Ivory Tower to the Everyday Christian."* Someone may be thinking, "Right! That's the connection I needed." As the title and Contents indicate, this book was written to provide evidences and good answers to tough issues for lay people who now want the resources. Brian is finishing his PhD in Theology and Apologetics, so he has the "apologetic chops" as we might say, to produce great responses. But Brian is also a pastor who has been in the trenches for almost 20 years—enough time to see many ideas come and go, sometimes invading families. Practical challenges and concerns need to be tested and Brian has helped others do just that.

Note, too, that Brian didn't get one of my rejection letters. The time has now come. People today need honesty and real-world answers. Check out Brian's volume and see if it helps to build bridges where and how they are needed most.

—**Gary R. Habermas, PhD**
Research Professor
Liberty University

PREFACE

A farmer would never go into the field to labor without a proper understanding of the basic laws of nature and without the proper tools needed to experience a harvest. A soldier would never venture onto the field of battle without an understanding of his enemy and armed with the proper ammunition which will result in conquest. An athlete would never enter the arena of competition without a good grasp of their opponent and the proper equipment necessary which will lead to victory. Likewise, every Christian should strive to avail themselves of the proper tools which will enable them to gain an understanding of Christian truths which will allow them to confidently defend with assurance the "faith once delivered unto the saints" (Jude 3).

The book you hold in your hands, *The Layman's Manual on Christian Apologetics,* is a tool that will give the Christian a greater understanding of the glorious truths of the reality of the Gospel of Jesus Christ. We are living in a world that is growing increasingly hostile to the Christian faith, and it behooves those who embrace the truths of Christianity to be prepared to defend with confidence the one true reality that determines one's eternal destiny. Peter reminds believers to "sanctify the Lord God in your hearts: and *be* ready always to *give* an answer to every man that asks you a reason of the hope that is in you with meekness and fear" (I Peter 3:15). The Greek word translated as "give an answer" is *apologian,* from the root word *apologia*. *Apologia* is the source for the terms "apologetics" and "apologist," which refer to a rational defense of the Christian faith. And believers are exhorted to be ready to give an "answer back" or a reasoned explanation for the hope that is in the heart.

It has been this writer's privilege to have read Brian Chilton's *The Layman's Manual on Christian Apologetics* and I excitedly endorse this "tool" as a must for any Christian seeking to obtain a reasoned defense of the faith. Brian, in an orderly and uncomplicated manner, communicates glorious biblical and spiritual truths that are both rational and logical in their presentation. This will be a book you will refer to again and again for two reasons: it will strengthen the believer as well as prepare the believer to confidently "give an answer" in defense of the faith. This is a book you will be glad you read.

As you absorb the truths found within these pages, it is Brian's prayer that when you have the opportunity to "give an answer" to a searching soul, that the divine light of the Gospel will brightly illuminate the path that leads that searching one to the foot of the Christ of the cross where alone is found eternal life.

—**Daniel Merritt, Ph.D.**
Director of Missions Surry Baptist Association

INTRODUCTION

As Bob Dylan quipped in 1963, "the times, they are a-changin.'" I have been in the gospel ministry for close to twenty years. The ministry today is far more challenging than it was in mid-nineties when God first called me. My grandfather was in the ministry. The challenges he faced in the seventies and eighties were far different than they are now. The advent of the internet and the creation of social media have exposed individuals to questions previously asked only in the ivory towers of academia. In addition, an increasingly secularized culture has created a greater spirit of skepticism in American culture. The challenges facing the modern church are more complex, more challenging, and greater in scope than they were in previous generations.

The Slow Death of Cultural Christianity in American Culture

The primary problem the church is facing is the demise of *cultural Christianity*. What is cultural Christianity? *Culture* is defined by the *Merriam-Webster's Collegiate Dictionary* as "the set of shared attitudes, values, goals, and practices that characterizes an institution or organization."[1] When Christianity is added, one speaks of the shared attitudes, values, goals, and practices of society developed around the Judeo-Christian worldview.

For instance, when cultural Christianity was prevalent, individuals knew that worshiping God and being in church were admirable things. I remember going to the drive-in theater in Mount Airy, North Carolina with my parents as a child. The better movie (the A-movie) was played first. Before the second movie was played—which was generally a lesser known

1. Merriam-Webster, *Merriam-Webster's Collegiate Dictionary*, Logos Bible Software.

movie and more cheaply made (the B-movie),² the theater had an intermission. This allowed individuals the opportunity to leave their vehicles to head over to the snack shop in the back building. Clips on the screen with talking cartoon tacos, hot dogs, popcorn, drinks, and fries encouraged individuals to quench their thirst with an ice-cold Pepsi or fill their hunger with a scrumptious hamburger or butter drenched popcorn. The commercials were enough to clog a person's arteries by viewing them alone.

In addition to the food commercials, the intermission also featured a promo encouraging individuals to attend church the following Sunday. The slide would read, "See you in Church Sunday! When you attend church, it's not an ordinary act, it is something worthwhile. When you attend church, you come to God's house to adore, to worship, to praise. See you in Church Sunday!"³ This generation assumed that people knew that they needed to be in church as seen by shows like the *Andy Griffith Show* and even *The Twilight Zone*. It was assumed that everyone at least respected the Christian worldview.

During the sexual revolution of the sixties and seventies, the culture began shifting away from its Judeo-Christian roots. The internet certainly sped up the process of secularization in the mid-nineties, especially with social media and chat boards which exposed the underlying cynicism and skepticism already taking root in Americana. It may surprise you to discover that the process had begun far before the sixties.

In fact, the argument about where truth is found goes back to debates held in ancient Athens. Protagoras of Abdera (c. 490–c. 420 BC) is quoted as saying, "man is 'the measure of all things, of the existence of the things that are and the non-existence of the things that are not.'"⁴ Protagoras suggests that truth is dependent upon each person. Truth is made by the person observing it. Thus, truth is different for each person. One can readily note from Protagoras's worldview that the ideals of secularism are anything but new.

In stark contrast, Socrates of Athens (c. 470—399 BC) argued that truth was not found within each person but was transcendent. Socrates says,

> Let us stick close to the statement we made a moment ago, and assume that nothing exists by itself as invariably one: then it will be apparent that black or white or any other color whatsoever is

---

2. These movies were often kung-fu movies which featured the late, great martial artist Bruce Lee. I loved them. My mom, not so much.

3. For an example, at the 4:40 mark, see "Drive-In Movie Ads: Drive in Intermission 1960's, YouTube (August 6, 2009), https://www.youtube.com/watch?v=26pQNKEOXjo.

4. Plato, *Theaetetus* 152a, Logos Bible Software.

the result of the impact of the eye upon the appropriate motion, and therefore that which we call color will be in each instance neither that which impinges nor that which is impinged upon, but something between, which has occurred, peculiar to each individual.[5]

In other words, truth exists outside of the individual. Otherwise, each person would only know what was perceived by oneself. Actual truth could never be fully known. Seeing that Socrates believed in God, in a manner of speaking, the philosopher contended that truth is found in the transcendent God and is discovered by the process of learning.[6] Thus, the contention between Protagorean and Socratic philosophy is quite vast. For Protagoras, humanity sets its own standards. For Socrates, God has established the standards for all creation. So, how did we as a Western civilization move from a Socratic viewpoint of truth grounded in a Judeo-Christian worldview to a secularist Protagorean viewpoint of truth grounded in secular humanism?

The shift away from the Judeo-Christian worldview in the Western world began with the Enlightenment of the seventeenth and eighteenth centuries. The dawning of the American experiment came during the midst of this Enlightenment era. This is not to say that the United States was not built upon Christian principles. Rather, it originated within the time frame of the Enlightenment period.

While the Enlightenment was not necessarily bad in and of itself, it did create a movement that placed more emphasis on human reason than traditional beliefs which led to a more Protagorean construct. Traditional beliefs often need to be challenged. But writers of the Enlightenment—secularists such as David Hume, John Locke, Voltaire, and Baruch Spinoza—pushed the envelope farther than most. Hume would deny that miracles could be proven. The God of Voltaire and Spinoza was not one who interacted with the world but was largely hands off. This led to the concept of deism, a belief that would influence some American founders as James Madison, Thomas Jefferson, and Benjamin Franklin. Spinoza's biblical criticism and Immanuel Kant's ideology would influence German theologian Rudolf Bultmann who held that enlightened Christians should demythologize the Bible. Bultmann, an influence on many critical scholars, wrote,

---

5. Ibid., 153e–154a.

6. Socrates also notes, "Look round and see that none of the uninitiated is listening. The uninitiated are those who think nothing is except what they can grasp firmly with their hands, and who deny the existence of actions and generation and all that is invisible." Ibid., 155e. That is, some truths exist beyond the capacity of the senses to detect.

> Can the Christian proclamation today expect men and women to acknowledge the mythical world picture as true? To do so would be both pointless and impossible. It would be pointless because there is nothing specifically Christian about the mythical world picture, which is simply the world picture of a time now past which was not yet formed by scientific thinking. It would be impossible because no one can appropriate a world picture by sheer resolve, since it is already given with one's historical situation.[7]

Skepticism already took root before the sixties and seventies. The development of the television, radio, and especially the internet in the nineties and beyond brought these ideas which were previously discussed in the halls of academia into the forefront of popular discourse. The problem is that traditional scholars who were trained in these areas did not pushback on the thoughts of guys like Bultmann as fiercely as progressive theologians were promoting their own. Many in the church today are faced with the same kinds of questions, but problematically they often lack the training needed to combat secularist philosophies.

Responses of the Church to the New Demand

It should be noted that cultural Christianity and authentic Christianity are two different things. Even at the peak of cultural Christianity, many individuals claimed to be Christian because it was the hip thing to do. Like most trends, when Christianity was popular, everyone claimed to be a Christian. It is much like a child who says to his mother, "Ma, everyone else is a Christian. So, why shouldn't I be one, too?" In turn, mothers everywhere know the response that follows. "If everyone jumped off a building, would you jump, too?" Thus because of the popularity of Christianity, some individuals were part of the authentic church while other Christians were believers in name only.

The response of the modern church to the growing threat of secularism has been mixed. Some in the church choose the *ostrich response* which is to *deny* that there is a problem. These individuals claim that the problem is not as bad as some suggest so they continue their lives in a delusional utopia. This thinking has given rise to conspiracy theories where anyone who holds a different perspective is viewed with suspicious eyes. It is amazing the lengths some people will go to justify their own denial. Some individuals would rather adhere to ludicrous claims of some Orwellian conspiracy in

---

7. Rudolf Bultmann, *New Testament Mythology and Other Basic Writings* IV.2.2, 3.

the medical community rather than accepting the fact that the person or the person's family has a disease that needs to be treated.

In like manner, advocates of the ostrich response will hold that the problem is not as bad as people think. Others will justify their denial with the belief with the notion that ideas travel in cyclical patterns, so we are just in a bad phase of the cycle right now. The question is, do we have a problem with doubt and a lack of faith in the modern church? The increasing decline of church attendance and the exodus of youth should serve as red flags that we do have a major problem.

Others have chosen to respond with the *Amish response* which is the response of *isolation*. Like the Amish, these individuals isolate themselves to their Christian communities and do not engage the culture. Worse yet, they may become hermits. When I lived in Southport, North Carolina—a coastal region in southeast North Carolina—I was told about a man who lived on a small island off an inlet at the intercoastal waterway. He had no electricity and no plumbing. The only way to get to his shack was by boat. As for finances, he would fish and gather oysters to make any money he required. The hermit had no contact with the outside world except for selling seafood at an occasional market. If this is the response we take, what impact will we make on society? None!

Those who take the Amish response intentionally become naïve to the problems of the world and lose interest in evangelism because evangelism would require them to leave their safety net. Their mantra is "ignorance is bliss." Unfortunately, this response has led many well-qualified Christians to take themselves out of the public sphere. I believe that this response is partially responsible for the secularization of former Christian universities like Princeton, Harvard, and Yale. When Christians are uninvolved with the world, they essentially leave a dark world with no light. Thus, they leave no impact. How can a light shine in the darkness if there is no light to shine? A Christian must ask oneself whether God has called the Christian to evangelize? If so, how can a Christian evangelize if all one surrounds oneself with are other Christians? It is a nonsensical strategy. I also realize that parents want to protect their children. However, if a parent is not engaging their child and challenging them to analyze false ideas, then the child is left helpless against false philosophies when they enter the real world. The child will become easy prey for the secularist predators who desire to lead him away from the Christian worldview. Let me state that even though my son is in the public-school system, I am for homeschooling if it is where the parents can do so.[8] However, homeschooling parents must educate their children

---

8. We are blessed to live in an area where teachers are compassionate and largely

about the ideas of the world in order to show them the problems of opposing worldviews. That way when they enter the secular world, they will not be taken by surprise and will have a response to worldviews that are opposite of their own.

A third response came to me in a moment of inspiration at the proverbial eleventh hour in preparing this book. It is a response that is crippling the church, quite frankly. It is the *scapegoat response* which *blames others* for the current conditions. Because many congregants do not know how to respond to the changing demands threatening the church, they lash out at anyone or anything that might seek to change the status quo. Political candidates may become their scapegoat. Pastors and church staff may become their scapegoats of choice. Missionaries or other church members may receive their judgmental eye. In many churches across the nation, this response takes shape in generational wars. Older congregants fear the latest ideas from younger congregants falsely ascribing them to New Age or, worse yet, liberal ideologies. So, they will blame the younger generation for the current state of the church because they seem to be out-of-touch with the way the church works. Younger congregants ascribe the declining church to the older generation's obstinate idolatry which is set on traditions and methodologies that are as old as Methuselah. Thus, the older generation is blamed for the problems of the modern church because they seem to be out-of-touch with the way the world works. Such mindsets quickly escalate into turf wars if left unresolved. Let it be said, when congregants employ the scapegoat response, not only will they not make an impact in society, they will quickly implode what impact was being made in their churches.

The better response is the *shepherd response* which *deals and engages* with the problem. Shepherds were similar to modern mixed martial artist fighters for good reason. They had to be willing to fight for the protection of their sheep. Predators and thieves may try to kill or steal their sheep. However, a good shepherd was willing to deal with the threats that endangered one's flock. In similar manner, those individuals who accept the shepherd response will take seriously the task of evangelism. In addition, they desire to make an impact in the culture. Such thinking can actually bring about a solution to the problem. Rather than putting a band-aid on a deep wound, it adds balm to the wound and stitches it from the inside out. Ultimately, this response brings healing to the church and evangelizes the lost. Lastly, the shepherd response is the only healthy response that one can take. Across the nation, it is estimated that between 6,000 and 10,000 churches will close their door each year with the numbers expected to escalate unless something

---

hold traditional views in most matters.

is done to change the trend.⁹ That's something like 100 to 200 churches each week! Apologetics is not only beneficial for evangelism and discipleship, it can also serve as a means to help dying churches.

If dealing with the issue is the response you choose to take, then welcome to the world of Christian apologetics! If you want to simply hide you head in the sand and pretend that there is no problem. Put this book down now and go purchase an emotionally driven devotional. Then, go join a commune and sing *Kumbaya* while dancing around a campfire. But, don't blame anyone if your loved ones are taken astray by false ideologies.¹⁰ In contrast, if you are ready to make a defense for the faith, then welcome aboard. Apologetics is the defense of the Christian faith. It is not a new concept. In fact, as you will discover in this book, apologetics has a rich history dating back to Jesus himself.

Even though you may be pumped to begin the study of apologetics, it must be admitted that many who have not been trained in seminary are threatened by apologetics and for good reason. Part of the problem that laypersons face is that the concepts that were at one time discussed in the halls of the ivory towers of academia have trickled down into the streets of the common person. Academic Christians in seminary possess training on how to deal with certain concepts that others do not have. While this book cannot provide all the tools that one needs to maneuver through the murky waters of academia, it is possible to make the material accessible to the laity so that they can feel more confident in sharing their faith with the majority of people on the street. That is the purpose behind this book, to make the most important material in Christian apologetics accessible so that anyone can engage their doubting friend or family member. Perhaps, this book will help you deal with your own personal doubts.

Personal Testimony

Before we begin the book, I would like to share why this book is so important to me. I was saved at an early age and entered the ministry at the tender age of 16. In the late nineties, I started having doubts after reading a book by the Jesus Seminar titled *The Five Gospels: What Did Jesus Really Say*. The

---

9. Thom S. Rainer, "Hope for Dying Churches," *Facts & Trends* (January 16, 2018), https://factsandtrends.net/2018/01/16/hope-for-dying-churches/.

10. Even if you have some answers to the challenges, you may lose some of your loved ones to the pressing secularist worldviews that has captivated our society. But having no responses will most certainly leave your loved ones helpless against the attacks that arise against their faith.

book presented the four Gospels of the New Testament along with the Gospel of Thomas. The Seminar had gauged the teachings of Jesus according to what they thought were the most authentic sayings of Jesus. If they believed the words were authentic, they colored the words in red. If they thought the words were most likely Jesus's, they colored the words pink. If they thought that the words had some root in Jesus's teaching but was reworded by the writer, they colored the words in gray. Statements that were not Jesus's own words, but the writer's invention were colored in black. They deemed that only 14 percent of the statements ascribed to Jesus were ascribed to him as authentic. This caused a great deal of doubt for me in my young ministerial career. How could I tell people to trust a book which I was finding increasingly inauthentic?

I asked some leaders of the church. When I did, I was scorned and told that the Bible was true because it is the Bible and that I should not be asking questions like that. When I noticed that those same Christians were not living up to their own convictions, I became an agnostic. It was not something that I wanted to happen. I agonized and shed many tears during the process. I nearly had a nervous breakdown during the transition. But I found no help from the church. None. I only found scorn and shame.

Fast-forward five years. By 2005, I had married my wife and worked at a textile industry by this time. On a hot day in the summer of 2005, I was driving down Hanes Mall Boulevard in Winston-Salem, North Carolina when something told me that I should go to the local Lifeway Christian Bookstore. I had no clue why, but I did. While I was there, I picked up a copy of Josh McDowell's *Evidence that Demands a Verdict* (the old copy) and Lee Strobel's *The Case for Christ*. These books led me to the works of Gary Habermas and William Lane Craig. I found in these books the answers to the questions that had troubled me. I discovered that faith is based on fact. That truth completely changed me and strengthened me to a greater faith than I had before encountering my doubts.

What to Expect

This book cannot provide an exhaustive treatment of apologetics. Each one of the chapters in this study could have its own graduate level course. This book is built so that the layman can understand apologetic principles and will provide a winsome defense for the faith. However, some issues are complex by their very nature. While the book has tried to simplify the issues, some may find that certain aspects of the book will require more attention than others. Don't become discouraged. If you have questions, ask! Seek out fellow apologists and theologians. The only dumb question is the question not asked.

This book will be broken down into three major units. The first unit will discuss the nature of truth and apologetic methodologies. This unit could potentially be the most complex due to the nature of logic, reasoning, and the epistemological[11] philosophy behind truth itself. The second unit will examine the evidences for the existence of God and will probe into some of the major questions concerning him. The third and final unit will discuss the historical basis for Christianity in the resurrection of Jesus and the authenticity of the Scriptures. The first unit is philosophical, the second unit is theological, and the third unit is historical.

I hope this book will not only be enjoyable for you but will provide you the tools you need to encounter the challenges that the church faces today. I also hope that the book will whet your appetite for the issues so that you will deepen your knowledge, strengthen your faith, and impassion your desire to share Christ with a lost and dying world.

---

11. *Epistemology* is a philosophical study about how a person can know something is true. In contrast, *ontology* is the study of how a person can know that someone or something exists.

UNIT 1

Prolegomena— Apologetic Methodologies and the Nature of Truth

Before the task of apologetics is conducted, some preliminary remarks are necessary. We must first define what is meant by apologetics and how a person can know what is true. The term *prolegomena* comes from two Greek terms: *pros* meaning before and *legein* meaning to say. The term literally means "to say beforehand." Charles Ryrie defines *prolegomena* as "prefatory or preliminary remarks."[1] Unit 1 consists of chapters 2–4. Chapter 2 will define what is meant by the term *apologetics* and will show the need and the methodologies employed. Chapter 3 asks the same question that Procurator Pontius Pilate posed to Jesus as it seeks to define truth. How do we know what is true? Is truth obtainable? Chapter 4 will examine the role that logic plays in one's quest for truth. The student will find chapter 4 very helpful as it will provide them, what I call, an instant bologna detector. So now, without further ado, let's begin our journey into the world of apologetics.

1. Charles Caldwell Ryrie, *Basic Theology: A Popular Systematic Guide to Understanding Biblical Truth*, 12–13.

Chapter 1

WHAT IS APOLOGETICS?

What Is Apologetics?

Without fail, when an apologist mentions apologetics to individuals in their congregations or to loved ones, the inquirer asks, "Why do you want to apologize for being a Christian?" Luckily, apologists do not apologize for their faith. The term *apology* holds at least two meanings in the English language. It can be meant to offer an acknowledgement of an offense. But the older meaning of the word means something quite different, it means to offer a defense for a person's belief as a lawyer would defend his case in a court of law.

In Christian apologetics, the term *apology* is used from the Greek definition of the term from which it is derived. The Greek term *apologia* (apologia) means "to defend" or to "clear oneself from false accusations." *Apologia* is a compound word stemming from the terms *apo* which means "from" and *logos* meaning "word, reason, or logic." Literally, *apologia* is translated "from logic." The *Oxford Dictionary of the Christian Church* defines apologetics as "The defence [sic] of Christian belief and of the Christian way against alternatives and against criticism."[1] The term *apologia* is found in 1 Pet. 3:15 where the aged apostle writes, "but in your hearts regard Christ the Lord as holy, ready at any time to give a defense (*apologia*) to anyone who asks you for a reason for the hope that is in you" (1 Pet. 3:15).[2] The apostle Paul uses the term in Acts 22:1 when he asks the brothers to listen to his defense. The

---

1. F. L. Cross and Elizabeth A. Livingstone, eds., *The Oxford Dictionary of the Christian Church*, 87.

2. Unless otherwise noted, all quoted Scripture comes from the *Christian Standard Bible* (Nashville: Holman, 2017).

term *apologia* is also used in Acts 25:16; 1 Corinthians 9:3; 2 Corinthians 7:11; Philippians 1:7, 16; and 2 Timothy 4:16. Simply put: The Christian apologist is a defender of the Christian faith.[3]

The Need for Apologetics

Some individuals may inquire why there is a need for apologetics. Some will hold that God does not need defending. Granted, God is far more powerful than anyone could hope to be. But by using that same logic, why would anyone need to evangelize? God could simply lead a person to faith, couldn't he? He doesn't need to use people to bring others to faith. But... HE DOES! Likewise, when a believer sees his or her faith attacked, does it not behoove the believer to at least clear the air concerning what the faith holds? It is fascinating to me that the same people who claim that Christianity does not need defending will also spend three hours defending why their chosen sports team is the best. So, why is it that a sports team is worth defending and the Christian worldview isn't? In reality, apologetics is necessary for modern evangelism. Investigating the issue further, I contend that there are three reasons why a person should be an apologist.

Biblical Reasons

First, the student of Scripture will note multiple biblical reasons for why a person should defend the faith. Beginning with the most important reason, Jesus was himself an apologist. Jesus gives a bold word to the Jewish individuals who trusted in him at the temple. He said, "If you continue in my word, you are really my disciples. You will know the truth, and the truth will set you free" (John 8:31–32). Note three things about Jesus's teaching in John 8:1. The disciple is to continue in Jesus's word—this does not mean that a person stops studying the truths of Christianity after accepting them; 2) truth is knowable—it is something that can be attained; and 3) the truth has a freeing capacity to it. If this is the case, then why would a Christian want to settle for ignorance?

One of my favorite examples of Jesus's apologetic ministry was when John the Baptist sent his disciples to Jesus asking him if he really was the anticipated Messiah. John the Baptist found himself in a prison cell for

---

3. For that reason, many apologists use the logo of a Crusader's shield. See Josh McDowell and Sean McDowell, *Evidence that Demands a Verdict: Life-changing Truth for a Skeptical World*, xxxii.

preaching the truth. John was anything but politically correct. He realized that he would be executed soon.

In a moment of doubt, John the Baptist sent his disciples to make absolutely certain that he had identified the correct person as the Messiah. By the way, if John the Baptist had doubts, don't beat yourself up if you find that you have doubts, too. Luke recounts a spectacular event. When the disciples asked Jesus about his messianic identity, Jesus "at that time healed many people of diseases, afflictions, and evil spirits, and he granted sight to many blind people.

He replied to them, 'Go and report to John what you have seen and heard: The blind receive their sight, the lame walk, those with leprosy are cleansed, the deaf hear, the dead are raised, and the poor are told the good news, and blessed is the one who isn't offended by me'" (Luke 7:21–23). Jesus performed miracles before the very eyes of John's disciples and sent them back to John to reveal to him all the things that they had seen. Jesus did not perform miracles to put on a show. Rather, his miracles were used to back up his messianic and divine claims.

Not only was Jesus an apologist, Peter was also. As noted earlier, Peter gives what has been adopted as the apologetic banner. The apostle said,

> But even if you should suffer for righteousness, you are blessed. Do not fear what they fear or be intimidated, but in your hearts regard Christ the Lord as holy, ready at any time to give a defense to anyone who asks you for a reason for the hope that is in you. Yet do this with gentleness and respect, keeping a clear conscience, so that when you are accused, those who disparage your good conduct in Christ will be put to shame (1 Pet. 3:14–16).

Peter teaches three important points concerning the use of apologetics.

1. The apologist gives a defense for one's hope. You say you have hope. Well and good. Why do you have hope?
2. The apologist gives a defense with gentleness and respect. Apologetics is not meant to engage in obnoxious argumentation. Rather, apologetics should be done in love.
3. The apologist gives a defense for Christ and not for oneself. Apologetics is not to show off your intellectual prowess. It is not about becoming a rock star. Apologetics should point a person to Jesus.

As an additional example, Peter used apologetics in Acts 2. On the Day of Pentecost, God used Peter to lead three thousand people to faith in Jesus Christ. Although the reason for this mass conversion can be contributed to the pouring out of the Holy Spirit upon all who were in attendance, it should be noted that Peter preached an apologetic sermon to the crowd on this day. Throughout his sermon in Acts 2, Peter presents a three-fold testimony of evidence in order to convince his listeners that Jesus is God.

1. He appeals to the miracles of Jesus as proof that he was from God (v. 22).
2. He appeals to fulfilled prophecy as proof that Jesus was the promised Messiah (vv.25–31).
3. He appeals to eyewitness accounts of Jesus's post-resurrection appearances as proof that he was God (v. 32).

The result of Peter's "apologetic sermon" was the addition of three-thousand souls won to the kingdom. It must be remembered that the goal of the apologist is not to win arguments. The goal is to win souls into the kingdom and to strengthen the faith of those who have become weak. Apologetics is never about proving how intelligent you are. In reality, while working on a PhD in Theology and Apologetics at Liberty University, I have discovered that the more I have learned about God and how to defend the faith, the more inadequate I sometimes feel. Why? I have learned that the more I learn about God, the more I realize that I don't know about him. I also realize that there are many things about God that I may never understand.

Understand, it is okay if you do not have all the answers. Your willingness to investigate the doubter's objections is most important. Also remember that the apologetics task is about networking with others working in different areas. Some apologists specialize in investigations of the soul through neurology. Other apologists are specialists in science. I am trained more in historical and philosophical apologetics. The point is, apologetics is not about being the smartest, biggest, and the brightest. Apologetics is about working together to find answers to life's most important questions, strengthening those who have become weak in the faith, and offering compelling reasons to those who have not believed. This is what Peter teaches us in the previously mentioned verse.

Third and finally, Paul the apostle often used apologetics in his ministry. Consider the following teachings of Paul.

> 2 Cor. 10:4–5. *"Since the weapons of our warfare are not of the flesh, but are powerful through God for the demolition of strongholds. We demolish arguments and every proud thing that is raised up against the knowledge of God, and we take every thought captive to obey Christ."*

Notice that apologetics enters the spiritual warfare arena. God is unable to lie (Titus. 1:2) and Satan is the father of lies (John 8:44). Thus, defending the truth is to demolish the lies of Satan and to proclaim the truth that God has given. Why on earth would any Christian be content with allowing the lies of Satan to spread without at least attempting to teach others the truth of God? By not doing anything, the Christian supports the lying campaign of the devil.

> Phil. 1:7. *"Indeed, it is right for me to think this way about all of you, because I have you in my heart, and you are all partners with me in grace, both in my imprisonment and in the defense and confirmation of the gospel."*

Apologists uphold their brothers and sisters in the faith as they confirm the gospel message. We need not compete with one another to get the message out. We must prayerfully lift up one another and use our collective talents for the glory of God. You may want to become an expert in philosophy. That's great! But don't downplay the role of historical apologetics in the process of promoting philosophical apologetics.

> 1 Tim. 6:20–21. *"Timothy, guard what has been entrusted to you, avoiding irreverent and empty speech and contradictions from what is falsely called knowledge. By professing it, some people have departed from the faith. Grace be with you all."*

Apologists have been entrusted with the truth of Christ. It is our job to preserve the truth for future generations and to boldly proclaim it to the world. We have joined a great lineage. The Christian movement began with Jesus of Nazareth. He passed on his teachings to the early apostles. In turn, they passed on the information they had to the patristic writers, who passed them along to the Byzantine generation, who passed them along to the medieval Christians, who passed them along to generation after generation, until it has now reached us. Modern Christians have been entrusted with the truth of Christ. We now have the baton. What will we do with it? Will it be passed along to the next generation?

> 1 Cor. 15:17–18. *"And if Christ has not been raised, your faith is worthless; you are still in your sins. Those, then, who have fallen asleep in Christ have also perished. If we have put our hope in Christ for this life only, we should be pitied more than anyone."*

Paul contends that Christ's resurrection is based on a true historical event. If Christ has not been raised from the dead, then we shouldn't be Christians. We are lost in our sin and our preaching is void. But if Christ really did rise from the dead, then our task as believers is the most important thing anyone can do. It holds eternal significance. Christianity begins and ends with the literal, bodily resurrection of Jesus. The resurrection is the linchpin to the entire worldview.

While on his second missionary journey we find Paul preaching an apologetic sermon to the people at Mars Hill (Acts 17:22-34), using the following approach:

1. Paul found common ground with his audience—they all believed in some form of religion (vv. 22-23). He started with what the people knew. He met them where they were. There is a great lesson in Paul's tactic.
2. Paul argued based on facts that could be investigated (vv. 24-28). People could verify the claims that Paul was making.
3. Paul stated that Jesus' historicity, particularly the resurrection, is the foundation of Christianity (vv. 30-31). Again, he pointed to a real person, at a real time, and in a real place.

Paul's apologetic arguments won some to the Lord and resulted in others rethinking their positions. Even though everyone didn't come to the Lord that day, Paul was successful in what he had accomplished for Christ.

Philosophical Reasons

The second reason to do apologetics is philosophical. Philosophy concerns itself with the search for truth. As you will discover when we discuss logic in the fourth chapter, truth demands that there is a right and a wrong. People hold erroneous notions concerning philosophy due to a misinterpretation of Paul's teaching on philosophy. Paul writes, "Be careful that no one takes you captive through philosophy and empty deceit based on human tradition, based on the elements of the world, rather than Christ" (Col. 2:8). But Paul does not say that philosophy is bad. For one reason, Paul would be using philosophy to combat philosophy if that were so, which would cause Paul to employ a self-defeating claim. Rather than arguing against philosophy, Paul is speaking against bad philosophy. As Douglas Groothuis notes,

> Jesus deftly employed a variety of reasoning strategies in His debates on various topics. These include escaping the horns of a dilemma, *a fortiori* arguments, appeals to evidence, and *reductio ad absurdum* arguments. Jesus' use of persuasive arguments demonstrates that He was both a philosopher and an apologist

who rationally defended His worldview in discussion with some of the best thinkers of His day. This intellectual approach does not detract from His divine authority but enhances it. Jesus' high estimation of rationality and His own application of arguments indicates that Christianity is not an anti-intellectual faith. Followers of Jesus today, therefore, should emulate His intellectual zeal, using the same kind of arguments He Himself used.[4]

Using philosophy, apologetics helps a person discover the truth. Either God exists or he doesn't. There can be no middle ground. Either Jesus is the Messiah, or he isn't. There can be no middle ground. Either Jesus rose from the dead or he didn't. Do I need to say it again? Here goes: There can be no middle ground. As Paul noted in 1 Corinthians 15, there can be no middle ground (four times for good measure). If Christianity is false, then no one should believe it. If it is true, then the Christian should boldly proclaim it. Norman Geisler adds, "God created humans to reason as part of his image (Gen. 1:27; cf. Col. 3:10). Indeed, it is by reasoning that humans are distinguished from "brute beasts" (Jude 10). God calls upon his people to use reason (Isa. 1:18) to discern truth from error (1 John 4:6) and right from wrong (Heb. 5:14)."[5]

Ministerial Reasons

The third reason to do apologetics is ministerial. Ministry in today's increasingly secularized culture demands an engagement with apologetics for two reasons. First, evangelism requires apologetics. Why? Individuals must be shown the validity of a worldview before giving it a fair hearing. This is nothing new. Augustine did the same in defending Christianity against Roman misconceptions in his book *City of God*. In this book, he shows there are two cities—the city of God and the city of the world. When Rome was sacked by the Visigoths in 410 AD, many had thought that the Roman gods had struck back. Numerous individuals thought that the world was coming to an end. They were the ones holding signs saying, "Repent! For the end is near!" At least they didn't hold signs that said "The Roman gods hate this or that" as some modern movements do using God as the subject. Augustine calmly reassured everyone that the most important citizenship was the one found in the kingdom of God.

4. Douglas Groothuis, "Jesus: Philosopher and Apologist," *Christian Research Journal* 25, no. 2 (2002): http://www.equip.org/article/jesus-philosopher-and-apologist/.

5. Norman L. Geisler, "Apologetics, Need For," *Baker Encyclopedia of Christian Apologetics*, 38.

Justin Martyr is another example of an apologist who evangelized by using apologetics. Justin Martyr defended the faith against the polytheism of his day in his book *Dialogue with Trypho*. Throughout the text, Martyr argues with a Jewish man named Trypho as he contends for the validity of the Christian faith by way of fulfilled prophecy, the superior philosophy of the Christian worldview, and the new law of grace found in Christ.

Second, apologetics is needed for discipleship. Said another way, Discipleship in ministry requires apologetics as believers have many questions that they are afraid to ask. One of the greatest and most challenging questions I have ever been asked was from a 75-year-old woman who had attended the church where I served for years. She wanted to know what evidence there was for heaven and what she could expect. She had feared that heaven would be boring as she thought that singing hymns was the only activity in heaven. While she enjoyed singing, she was afraid that she would quickly grow bored. She told me she had been afraid to ask anyone, especially a preacher, for fears that she would be deemed a heretic. After our conversation, she was freed from the doubts that had plagued her for years. I was later told that when she died, that she was not afraid as she once was. She had a newfound faith because of our apologetic conversation.

Not only is apologetics important for our senior citizens, it is especially important for our younger generations. Our youth are bombarded by a plethora of attacks against their faith from the media, television, and internet communities. An apologist friend of mine noted that the questions that had been asked in graduate school started to drift down to the undergraduate level around the eighties. By the late nineties and early two-thousands, those questions began to be asked by high school students. In the mid-to-late two-thousands, those questions began surfacing in middle school. Now, there's evidence that elementary school students are asking complex questions about the existence of God and the legitimacy of the Bible. We CANNOT be like the proverbial ostrich with its head in the sand. We must, as Peter tells us, be willing to give a defense for the hope that we have within us (1 Pet. 3:15). So, how do we do apologetics?

Apologetic Methodologies

Before departing from this chapter, a few words need to be said about apologetic methodologies. An *apologetic method* is how the apologist conducts his or her task. In the book *Five Views on Apologetics*,[6] five different approaches to apologetics, as the name implies are described. It is important to note

---

6. Stanley N. Gundry and Steven B. Cowan, eds, *Five Views on Apologetics*, 15–20.

that the starting point marks the greatest difference between the apologetic methods. Where does the apologist begin? Where does the conversation begin? That's the question.

Classical Approach

The *classical apologetic method* gets its name due to the numerous apologists who have utilized the method throughout history. It is the oldest version of apologetics. Classical apologists begin their defense by appealing to the evidence for God's existence before defending the historicity of Jesus's resurrection. For this reason, the classical approach is called the "two-step approach." The first step defends God's existence and the second defends Jesus's messianic claims. While it is called the two-step approach, many classical apologists may use far more steps than these. Norman Geisler has used as many as twelve steps to argue for the Christian faith.

This book utilizes the classical approach to provide a full survey of apologetic issues. It could be said that the book uses a three-step approach: 1) the nature of truth; 2) arguments for God's existence; and 3) the historical truth for Christianity.

Some famous classical apologists include Justin Martyr, Thomas Aquinas, Augustine, Origen, Tertullian, Duns Scotus, William of Ockham, Anselm of Canterbury, Blaise Pascal, and more recently C. S. Lewis, G. K. Chesterton, Norman Geisler, Ravi Zacharias, William Lane Craig, Dinesh D'Souza, R. C. Sproul, Lee Strobel, John Lennox, J. P. Moreland, Hugh Ross, Frank Turek, and Greg Koukl.

Evidentialist Approach

The *evidential apologetic method*, or *evidentialism*, begins with the historical data pertaining to the resurrection of Jesus and branches out from there. Evidentialists hold that if one can demonstrate Jesus's resurrection to be true in light of his claims to divinity, then one can automatically prove the existence of God. The rationale is if Jesus is claiming that it is by God's power that he is risen from the dead and he is risen exactly as he prescribed, then a rational person would hold that a divine force was behind the resurrection of Jesus.

Because of the immediate discussion of Jesus and his resurrection, evidentialism is called the "one-step approach" because it does not begin with arguments for God's existence. However, evidentialists hold that if it is necessary to defend God's existence, it comes after the resurrection is set in place. Evidentialism is somewhat better than the classical approach in apologetic discussions because it gets to the gospel much quicker. The reason being that an evangelist may only have the time that it takes to take an elevator to reach a higher floor to share the gospel message. When pushed for time, evidentialism delivers the core message of the gospel backed with evidence in the briefest manner available. It is not bogged down with complex philosophical syllogisms. The presentation is simply an evidence backed gospel message.

Famed evidentialists include Gary Habermas, P. T. Forsyth, Josh McDowell, John Warwick Montgomery, Clark Pinnock, and Wolfhart Pannenberg.

Presuppositionalist Approach

One of the more controversial apologetic methodologies is the *presuppositional apologetic method*. By and large, those of the Calvinist persuasion gravitate toward presuppositionalism far more than non-Calvinists mostly because of their views on natural theology.[7] Calvin was not as opposed to natural theology than more hardline Calvinists are.[8] Nevertheless, since hardline Calvinists highly emphasize special revelation and diminish the usefulness of natural revelation, the use of presuppositionalism is the apologetic methodology of choice.

---

7. *Natural theology* denotes the truths about God that can be revealed through nature and not by special revelation. Hardline Calvinists hold that human beings can know nothing about God without God revealing it to them. Calvin holds, "Mingled vanity and pride appear in this, that when miserable men do seek after God, instead of ascending higher than themselves as they ought to do, they measure him by their own carnal stupidity, and neglecting solid inquiry, fly off to indulge their curiosity in vain speculation. Hence, they do not conceive of him in the character in which he is manifested, but imagine him to be whatever their own rashness has devised." John Calvin and Henry Beveridge, *Institutes of the Christian Religion*, vol. 1, 59. However, Calvin was not as adamantly against natural theology as some Calvinists are. He did hold that people can measure the heavens and do all manners of science. He says, "In attestation of his wondrous wisdom, both the heavens and the earth present us with innumerable proofs, not only those more recondite proofs which astronomy, medicine, and all the natural sciences, are designed to illustrate, but proofs which force themselves on the notice of the most illiterate peasant, who cannot open his eyes without beholding them . . . Can any thing be more detestable than this madness in man, who, finding God a hundred times both in his body and his soul, makes his excellence in this respect a pretext for denying that there is a God?" Ibid., 66, 68. In the end, Calvin believes that only special revelation can lead someone to faith. This has been misconstrued by more hardline Calvinists.

8. See previous footnote.

Presuppositionalism argues for faith on the basis that reason can come only by the Christian faith. The ability to reason demands God's existence according to the presuppositionalist. Truth can never be fully known unless it is revealed. Presuppositionalist John Frame states that "presupposition is therefore our ultimate criterion of truth."[9] Norman Geisler defines the system as "the apologetic system that defends Christianity from the departure point of certain basic presuppositions. The apologist presupposes the truth of Christianity and then reasons from that point. One basic presupposition is that the non-Christian also has presuppositions that color everything he or she hears about God."[10]

Presuppositionalism may be helpful when speaking to a person who holds a strong bias against God and supernaturalism. It may help in casting doubt upon the unbeliever's presuppositions. However, the system is not as strong when engaging individuals who desire evidence for the Christian worldview. The greatest weakness of presuppositionalism is that it often commits the logical fallacy of circular reasoning.[11] For this reason, presuppositionalism is often unconvincing for the evidence-based skeptic. Famous presuppositionalists include John Frame, Karl Barth, Cornelius Van Til, Gordon Clark, Edward J. Carnell, Carl F. H. Henry, and Greg Bahnsen.

Cumulative Approach

The *cumulative apologetic methodology* is one that combines several of the other methods to build a cumulative case for the Christian faith. The approach does not specialize in one area but is more a generalist in scope. This approach may be useful as it gleans the best tools from various approaches. But the downside is that it may never give a detailed treatment in any one area. Famous cumulative case apologists include Basil Mitchell, C. S. Lewis,[12] Francis Schaeffer,[13] and Douglas Groothuis.

---

9. John Frame, "Presuppositional Apologetics," *Five Views on Apologetics*, 209.

10. Geisler, "Presuppositional Apologetics," *Baker Encyclopedia of Christian Apologetics*, 607.

11. This is a logical fallacy where the conclusion is built in the argument. The person essentially argues in a circle. For example, the claim "all men are short because I am a man who is short" is guilty of circular reasoning. The claim, "The Bible is true because it says it's true" is also guilty of circular reasoning. The assumption that the Bible is true is built into the presupposition that the Bible is true. No evidence is given for the Bible's truthfulness in this case.

12. C. S. Lewis was a classical apologist earlier in his career and leaned towards the cumulative case approach later in life.

13. Some hold that Schaeffer was a presuppositionalist while others hold that he

Reformed Epistemological

The *Reformed Epistemological apologetic method* (REM) is somewhat like the presuppositional method. The main difference is that the REM is far more open to evidences than its presuppositional sibling. REM is based on the works of famed theologian and philosopher Alvin Plantinga. Plantinga held that certain beliefs were *warranted beliefs*—beliefs that were so evident that they required no evidence for their existence.[14] Plantinga held that belief in God was a warranted belief. Thus, REM operates much like presuppositionalism. The key difference is that REM holds that a belief in God is properly basic, meaning that the belief is justified through logic and reason. Famous REM advocates include Kelly James Clark, Alvin Plantinga, William Alston, and Michael C. Rea.

Here are a few tips to consider when it comes to apologetic methodologies.

1. Don't become obsessed over one methodology. Each apologetic method is useful in its own way. Sometimes it may be necessary for a person to use multiple approaches. It is an embarrassment to the Christian apologetic community when apologists argue more for an apologetic method than they do for the truths they are trying to defend.

2. Each person you encounter is different. Use the method that will best help the person with whom you are speaking. Sometimes, it may be necessary to use various methods with an individual as the conversation progresses.

3. All the methods have their strengths and weaknesses. No apologetic method is perfect. Each has its own merit. Each has its own set of problems. Be willing to use whichever method is most suitable. Often, it may be that the apologetic evangelist needs to employ more than just one method depending on the person and on the situation. In my ministry, I normally begin with the evidential approach, but sometimes have to use presuppositional apologetics if the person is resistant to the evidence. No matter what method you choose, we must be defenders standing for the truth of God!

---

observed multiple disciplines.

14. See Alvin Plantinga, *Warranted Christian Belief*, vii–xiv.

Conclusion

Apologetics is the defense for the Christian faith. It does not indicate that the Christian is apologizing for his or her faith, quite the opposite. The Christian has every reason to defend the faith for biblical, ministerial, and philosophical reasons. The apologist must choose the method one desires to use but be adaptable depending on the situation and the person to whom they speak.

Some may contend, "Why does God need defending?" Well and good. Well, let me pose this question. Why does your favorite football team need defending? I am a Green Bay Packers fan. I could list several reasons why I love the Packers. But at the end of the day, the data that really matters is their number of championships. How is it that a person could go on and on defending their favorite team but not defend the One to whom they have devoted their deepest faith? In such cases, one must ask what holds the greatest importance to such a person.

Chapter 2

WHAT IS TRUTH?

Truth: What Is It and Can It Be Known?

Socrates once said that "The unexamined life is not worth living for a human being."[1] While on trial, the great philosopher Socrates chose death over exile as he contended that the pursuit of truth is a pursuit of oneself. What are the biases that one holds? Why does a person believe what one does? If it is true that an unexamined life is not worth living, then it is also true that an unexamined faith is not worth holding. If we cannot know that our faith is true, then why possess it? I had rather live with the discomfort of truth than with the vain pleasures of a lie.

One question that must be asked is one that Pontius Pilate posed to Jesus, "What is truth?" (John 18:38). Anyone who watches the news and peruses social media knows how segmented and distorted ideas can become. Conservative news agencies will present an event in a completely different light than what their progressive counterparts do. To get at the truth, one must often purge through the biases of the reporters. So before looking at the nature of truth, it would prove profitable to look what truth is not.

1. *Truth is not a matter of personal opinion.* What you think is still wrong if it is not in accordance with reality. Personal opinions that are not based on truth are called delusions. For example, stealing could be wrong in one person's opinion but right in another person's opinion. It cannot be both wrong and right at the same time. It must be one or the other. The thief may enjoy theft, but the victim will not. If truth is left

---

1. Socrates, *The Apology* 38b, retrieved June 25, 2019, http://www.sjsu.edu/people/james.lindahl/courses/Phil70A/s3/apology.pdf.

to individual opinions, then truth can never be known as it changes from person to person.

2. *Truth is not a matter of individual preference.* Truth is not ice cream. It is not something that is chosen. Rather, it is something that is discovered. Every person has different preferences. Truth loses its transcendent nature if it is left to individualism. If truth were a matter of individual preference, then one person couldn't say that another was "right" or "wrong" about a particular matter. Proponents of political correctness espouse such an idea because the view dilutes the nature of truth. Luckily, truth is transcendent and does not depend on individual whims and fancies.

3. *Truth is not simply whatever works.* Pragmatism has its place. But, truth is not merely something that practical. It is true no matter if it works for a certain situation or not. Christianity may not work for someone who wants to ignore the needs of others. But, the truth of Christianity is based on the resurrection of Jesus. The resurrection of Jesus is not based on what suits one person's pragmatic approach to life. It is true regardless of whether its philosophical stance on life works for a person or not. For instance, lies and deception can work for a while, yet this does not mean that they are true.

4. *Truth is not what makes people feel good.* You've probably heard the phrase "the truth hurts." So often, that is the case. If a person has a disease, the news of having the disease is not going to make the person feel good. However, if left untreated, the reality of the disease will make the person feel much worse. Bad news can be true and may not make one feel good. Lies may bring about a "feel good" result, yet it is still an untruth. Truth is not based on "feel good philosophies."

5. *Truth is not based upon emotions.* Like the fourth statement, truth is not an emotional pursuit. If there is one thing I have learned in life, it is that a person cannot trust one's emotions. Our emotions can easily lead us astray depending on each moment. Since emotions constantly change and differ depending upon the individual, this would mean that truth would then be ever-changing according to one's emotional state. Depending on a person's EQ (emotional quotient), that could lead to scary results.

6. *Truth is not what the majority says is true.* Truth is not a matter of popular opinion. It may very well be true that the majority of people believe a lie. Truth is not discovered by a vote. Truth is not a democracy. It is what is in accordance with the way things really are. The

majority of Nazis said it was ok to murder six million Jews, yet regardless of the atrocious acts the majority was wrong. Governmental authorities pass laws that may be unethical and lead to false truths. Truth may not be found in what the majority believes, but it is found in what is actual and factual.

7. *Truth is not what is comprehensive.* Just because something a comprehensive does not mean that it is true. Good liars will elaborate good stories. A lengthy, appealing, detailed explanation can still be false. A good example of this is found in the exploits of a family member. A member of my family pulled a prank as a kid that fooled everyone. He claimed that he had broken his arm at school. He had it bandaged and in a sling. He told the elaborate story of how he broke his arm and the things that happened leading up to the break. When other members of the family called later in the evening to check on him, his father informed us that he had not broken his arm at all. This member of our family could have won an academy award for that performance. He had us all fooled. But at the end of the day, the truth surfaced. His arm was not broken. So, comprehensive stories may merely be comprehensive lies.

8. *Truth is not what is understandable or coherent.* Something can be true and still remain confusing, and something can be false and be completely understandable. A group of people can collectively determine what makes the most sense and still be wrong. For instance, higher mathematics has always intrigued me. Primarily because I have never been a math whiz. I was better at geometry than algebra. Just because I often could not find the missing "x" did not mean that there wasn't a solution to find it. The truth can become complicated. Thus, the nature of truth is not found in its level of complexity or simplicity.

9. *Truth is not merely what is believed.* Explorers centuries ago believed that the earth was flat; did that make it true? Absolutely not! People believe false things all the time. A group of people hold that the moon landing was an elaborate hoax rather than an actual occurrence. Just because a conspiracy theory is believed does not indicate the truthfulness of the claim.

10. *Truth is not based on what is politically correct or socially acceptable.* What a hostile world in which we find ourselves! Now, if a person disagrees with your stance, you may be called a host of names. But, if it is politically and socially acceptable to legalize drugs or sexual perversion, does such behavior then become morally right? Just as truth is

not found in popular opinion, truth is not found in what is deemed politically correct or socially acceptable. What is deemed taboo yesterday may be deemed a practiced tradition tomorrow. Trends always change. Truth does not.

Having looked at what truth is not, how would one define truth? The best definition of truth is this: *Truth is what exists in reality.* Truth is in accord with the way things really exist in space and time. Three comments can be made about truth.

First, truth is personal. True events impact a person's life either good or bad. Tremendous positive true events leave lasting fond memories with an individual, whereas horrific and traumatic negative events lead to deep emotional scars and post-traumatic stress disorders (PTSD). Stewart E. Kelly lists five practical ways that truth matters:

I.   Truth matters for daily life.
II. The pursuit of truth is correlated with happiness.
III. Science is a truth-seeking enterprise.
IV. Knowledge is a veritistic (verifiable) enterprise.
V.   Truth is intrinsically valuable.[2]

While individuals may come to love fictional stories, true events make the person who they are.

Second, truth is practical. Truth helps us know what is real from what is fantasy. I must confess that I am a comics nerd. I grew up watching Christopher Reeves as Superman and Bill Bixby and Lou Ferrigno as Bruce Banner/Incredible Hulk. Today, CGI makes these characters come to life in a dramatic fashion in the Marvel movie franchise. Yet, at the end of the day, when someone is robbed, a person does not really anticipate an alien dressed in blue with a red cape to come flying to his or her rescue. While a person who is bullied may want to turn into a massive green monster, one knows that he or she cannot. Rather than calling Superman or the Incredible Hulk, the person will call the police or EMS. Why does the person call 911 rather than Superman? It is because the person knows fact from fiction. Prayer is practical only if there is someone listening on the other side of our prayers. The same is true for faith in general. Why do we do what we do? We do it because of the truth we come to discover and know.

Third, truth is engaging. In order for a person to come to faith, they need to believe the truthfulness of the view. Truth is something one must

---

2. Stewart E. Kelly, *Truth Considered and Applied: Examining Postmodernism, History, and the Christian Faith*, 262–267.

encounter. If a person faces some true obstacle, he or she must deal with the situation. If God truly exists and if Jesus truly is his Son, then each person must decide what they are going to do with such truths. Truth must eventually be engaged. It cannot be left alone.

The Knowability Of Truth

A common objection that is frequently given is the idea that truth can never be known. People will say, "What's true for you may not be true for me." But, is that true for everyone? It is quite amazing that such objections are presented in the realm of religion and philosophy but not in the area of science and mathematics. Hardly anyone would deny that 10^2 equals 100 or that square root of 81 is 9. So why would other truths be denied? Truth is knowable for three reasons.

First, truth is known because of reality. When I was in elementary school, I was called into the principal's office. She asked, "Are you Brian Chilton?" I said, "Yes, ma'am. I am." She said, "Okay, now what can you tell me about your situation in the gymnasium this morning?" I said, "I don't know. I wasn't in the gymnasium." She said, "Well, I have it on good account that a boy by the name of Brian Chilton was in the gymnasium this morning and was involved in an incident." I nervously replied, "Ma'am, I don't know what you're talking about. I was in class all morning." She said, "Aren't you F. Brian Chilton?"[3] I said, "No, ma'am. I am Brian G. Chilton." She retorted, "Wait! There are two of you?" She apologized and sent me back to class.

Why did it matter if she had the right Brian Chilton? It mattered because F. Brian was in the gymnasium and not Brian G. Chilton. The principal could decipher who was the guilty person and who was innocent based on the reality of what actually happened and who was present and who was absent. That reality was truth. Police and detectives base their cases on identifying what occurred and who committed the crime. If truth did not exist, or better yet, if truth was not decipherable, then there is no way that law enforcement could do their job. Crimes would go unpunished. Anarchy would rule the day in a truthless society.

Second, truth is known because of logic. God gave human beings a mind. The trouble is, many human beings do not use the mind God gave them. Logical truths and strategies provide a basis for individuals to know truth from fiction. This topic will be discussed in length in chapter 4. But before leaving the topic, the issue of scientism must be addressed.

---

3. The name was changed to protect the identity of the other Brian Chilton.

Scientism is the belief that science is the only method to discover truth. The problem is that science is incapable of explaining and deciphering all truth. Apologist Frank Turek rightly states, "Science doesn't say anything, scientists do. To say that a scientist can disprove the existence of God is like saying a mechanic can disprove the existence of Henry Ford."[4] People must investigate the data rather than accepting only the scientist's interpretation. An example of this problem is found with cosmologist Lawrence Krauss. Krauss, himself an atheist, claims that the universe came from nothing. Many would accept his claims at face value unless one were to investigate what Krauss means by "nothing." Rather than no-thing, Krauss uses a physical process known as a quantum vacuum for his idea of nothing. Krauss's nothing is actually something.[5]

Science cannot prove everything. William Lane Craig in a debate with Peter Atkins lists five things that science cannot tell us.

1. Science cannot prove logical and mathematical truths (it assumes certain presuppositions).

2. Science cannot prove metaphysical truths (other minds, past not created five minutes ago).

3. Science cannot prove ethical beliefs (science cannot condemn Adolf Hitler's actions).

4. Science cannot prove aesthetic judgments (what is beautiful and what is not).

5. Science cannot justify science itself (i.e., special theory of relativity and the assumption of the speed of light).[6]

Science is most certainly helpful. But science is not the end all method to discover truth. Logic must be included as science is based on logic. Furthermore, science would be impossible if God did not exist. As Turek notes, "Atheists can do science only by stealing several immaterial realities from God. These include orderly natural laws, the laws of logic, the laws of mathematics, the laws of morality, our ability to reason, etc."[7]

Third, truth can be known because of first principles. First principles, as Josh and Sean McDowell denote, are "fundamental principles that we

---

4. Frank Turek, *Stealing from God: Why Atheists Need God to Make Their Case*, 145.

5. See Lawrence M. Krauss, *A Universe from Nothing*, 141–152.

6. "What Science Can't Prove: Dr. William Lane Craig explains to Dr. Peter Atkins," YouTube video (October 18, 2010), https://www.youtube.com/watch?v=BQL2YDY_LiM.

7. Turek, *Stealing from God*, 175.

use in the demonstration of further principles. They provide the basis for all the conclusions drawn in any area of knowledge, whether in science or philosophy."[8] First principles are the starting points for all of truth and knowledge. First principles contain the following elements:

1. *They are self-evident.* These principles are evident in the world. A good example would be the existence of gravity. Because people remain on earth and do not float off to space, one can naturally agree that gravity exists.
2. *They are derived from reality.* The first principle exists in space-time. Everyone can know its existence.
3. *They are undeniable.* To discredit a first principle leads to utter nonsense. To deny a first principle would be considered delusional or insane. An example of this is seen in the flat earth movement. Though everyone can observe the circularity of the earth, the moon, the sun, and the planets, those in this camp contend that the earth is flat regardless.
4. *They are demonstrably true.* That is, they are so self-evident that they do not need proof[9].[10] The laws of logic in chapter 4 are examples of first principles. They are so commonsensical that to deny them would be absurd.

The Theories of Truth

Three theories on truth exist. While others exist, these three constitute the most important of the theories. Each theory evaluates truth from different angles.

Coherence theory of truth. Millard Erickson defines this theory as one that says, "propositions are true if they agree with, or cohere with, other propositions."[11] McDowell and McDowell note that this theory holds that something is true if "it coheres internally . . . if it fits together or does not contradict itself."[12] In this model, truth is internally coherent. If something

---

8. McDowell and McDowell, *ETDAV,* 623.

9. This is similar to Alvin Plantinga's *warranted belief.* This is a belief that is so self-evident that it does not require evidence although evidence does exist. Planginga, *Warranted Christian Belief,* vii–xiv.

10. McDowell and McDowell, *ETDAV,* 623

11. Millard J. Erickson, *Christian Theology,* 3rd ed., 38.

12. McDowell and McDowell, *ETDAV,* 615.

is not coherent, then it must not be true. However, some arguments can be constructed and are coherent but false. For example, some people claim that Elvis still lives. They hold that an aged person resembling Elvis has been seen so it must be him. The argument goes that Elvis faked his death because he didn't like the limelight. There is nothing incoherent about this claim just as there is nothing incoherent in the claim that the earth is flat. But the problem comes when the theory is tested. Elvis's body could be exhumed which would put to death this claim–literally and figuratively. The world has been viewed and is circular. Thus, the coherence theory of truth is not the best model. Also, as the McDowell's note, both the theistic worldview and the atheistic worldview are coherent, but both cannot be true.[13] As was mentioned earlier, just because something is comprehensive does not mean that its true.

Pragmatic theory of truth. The pragmatic theory of truth "states that truth is what works."[14] If something works out practically, then it must be true. The problem with pragmatism is asking for whom the system works. One person may say that it's true for them that stealing another person's wallet or purse is beneficial. But for the one who had their wallet or purse stolen, he or she may have a very different view of how useful the practice was for him or her. Equally troubling in this view is that there is no transcendent framework of operation in pragmatism. That is, there is no way to gauge truth for everyone. The pragmatist could only say what was true in his or her little part of the world.

Correspondence theory of truth. The correspondence theory of truth identifies a person, place, thing, or event as it happens in reality. According to the theory, truth corresponds with reality. Millard Erickson notes, "The *correspondence* view says that propositions are true if they correctly describe things as they are."[15] Or worded another way, truth is what it is. This theory works for three reasons.

1. *This theory works because truth corresponds with reality.*[16] Truth is not a matter of personal opinion; it is a matter of what exists in accordance with reality.
2. *This theory works because truth is logical.*[17] To know anything, truth must be in accordance with logic. Otherwise, nothing could ever be

---

13. Ibid., 616.
14. Ibid., 617.
15. Erickson, *Christian Theology*, 38.
16. McDowell and McDowell, *ETDAV,* 608.
17. Ibid., 611.

known. Logic is a great benefit in discerning truth claims. This is not to say that something could not be logically sound and still false. Nonetheless, truth is discernable by logic.

3. *This theory is most in line with the Bible.* Scripture indicates that truth is knowable and true for everyone. Jesus said, "You will know the truth and the truth will set you free" (John 8:23). In Greek, the term *aletheia* (αλη;θεια) is translated as "truth." *Aletheia* "indicates the quality or state of being real or genuine—often in the sense of visible and verifiable reality, demonstrated by facts, actual events, or proven character."[18] In other words, it indicates something as it exists in reality.

Conclusion

Truth is what exists in reality. Truth is personal, practical, and engaging. Truth is known because of reality, logic, and the existence of first principles. Of the three theories on truth (coherence, pragmatist, and correspondence), the correspondence theory of truth best coheres with reality, logic, and Scripture. Truth is knowable. Its existence is the basis not only for the enterprise of apologetics, but for all of knowledge. Much, much more could be said concerning the nature of truth. Suffice it to say, this area is one that deserves a lot of attention. Hopefully, you see by now that claims like "What's true for you may not be true for me" holds little ground when the nature of truth is anchored.

---

18. Douglas Mangum, "Truth," in *Lexham Theological Wordbook*, Logos Bible Software.

Chapter 3

THE ROLE OF LOGIC AND TRUTH

Logic and Truth.
Three Primary Laws of Logic and Its Exclusivity

Earlier, we learned about first principles—common sense truths that serve as a launchpad to discover truth. First principles are so steadfast with the way the world operates that they are beyond dispute. This is not to say that some haven't tried. But upon further study, first principles are steadfast in their validity. The laws of logic are examples of first principles. While the laws might sound odd at first glance, you should see the undeniable wisdom found in its principles. When you learn these laws, they become like second nature.

The Law of Identity (b = b)

The *law of identity* states that a thing's identity is what constitutes its essence. If a person says, "There's an oak in the front yard," then it can be assumed that a large tree is in front of the person's house as an oak is known to be a tree. The McDowells note that "Identity is the relation that everything has to itself."[1] As John Fox, former coach of the Carolina Panthers, used to say when his team lost, "It is what it is." Something is what it is found to be in reality. The first established law of logic leads to the second.

---

1. McDowell and McDowell, *ETDAV,* 627.

The Law of Non-contradiction (b ≠ ~b)

The *law of non-contradiction* holds that a thing cannot be what it is not. As Thomas Aquinas notes, "The first demonstratable principle is that the same thing cannot be affirmed and denied at the same time, which is based on the notion of being and not-being: and on this principle all others are based."[2] Going back to the illustration of the oak tree, the law of non-contradiction states that the oak cannot be at the same time a tree and a cat. There could be a cat in the tree, but the tree is not the cat, and the cat is not the tree. To look at the issue another way, I previously told the story about F. Brian Chilton and myself (Brian G. Chilton). I am Brian G. Chilton and not F. Brian Chilton. Because the principal had Brian G. Chilton, they had the wrong person since Brian G. Chilton is not F. Brian Chilton. We could not be the same person at the same time even though we had very similar names. Following the first and second laws of logic, the third naturally flows.

The Law of Excluded Middle (b V ~b)

The final major law of logic is called the *law of excluded middle*. This law states that either something is what it is, or it is not what it is, but it cannot be both. The oak tree cannot at the same time be a tree and be something else. It must be one or the other. I am Brian G. Chilton and not F. Brian Chilton. I cannot be two different people. The principle either looked for Brian G. Chilton, F. Brian Chilton, or both of us. But Brian G. was not F. Brian, and vice versa.

Using another example, either 2 + 2 = 4 or 2 + 2 = 5 but it cannot be both. One student may say the answer is 4 and another may say 5. One is correct and one is wrong. This is not something in which people find comfort. It is not easy to tell someone that he or she is wrong. But that is the problem with truth, it is exclusive. It makes discernable claims.

Self-defeaters

When evaluating truth claims, the apologist does well to identify what is known as *self-defeaters*. Self-defeating claims are those that cannot stand up to the statement's own scrutiny. Worded another way, a self-defeating claim defeats the statement it purports by the very wording of the sentence. The following are examples of self-defeaters:

---

2. Thomas Aquinas, *Summa Theologica* 94.2, 628.

1. "I cannot speak a word of English." (Really? Then how did you just construct a seven-word sentence in English?)
2. "I cannot type a single word on my computer." (Really? Then how did the sentence appear on this page?)
3. "There is absolutely no such thing as truth." (Do you know that absolutely? If it's true that truth does not exist, then the statement cannot even be true. But if truth does exist, then we can know that the statement "truth does not exist" is false.)
4. "Anyone who mentions God is an idiot." (You just mentioned God. So, that must mean that you're . . . forget it. I need to be polite.)
5. "You absolutely must not force your religion on me." (Aren't you trying to force your religion on me? By forcing me to remain silent, you in turn are forcing your set of religious beliefs on me. This is a tactic used in modern society quite a bit.)
6. "You're judgmental! You should never judge someone!" (Really? Did you not just judge me?)
7. "History cannot be known." (Okay. This one will need some work. By the time you make this statement, it will have been in history. So, can I know that you just said "History cannot be known" if history cannot be known?)
8. "History is only known by the rich and powerful." (Okay, this again will need to be unpacked. Are you rich and powerful? If not, then can I know that what you just said came from your mouth? If so, then history can be known by those who are not rich and powerful. If you are rich and powerful, then I (the listener) am not. I still know that you said, "History is only known by the rich and powerful." So, a poor and unpowerful person like myself can still know historical truth.)
9. "The scientific method is the only way you can prove something to be true." (Really? Did you prove your statement to be true using the scientific method? If not, then how do we know that what you said is true?)
10. "Philosophy is dead."[3] (With all due respect to the late Stephen Hawking, was that not a philosophical statement? So, how can philosophy be dead when you are espousing a philosophical claim to proclaim its demise?)

---

3. Stephen Hawking and Leonard Mlodinow, *The Grand Design*, 5.

As an experiment, pick up a copy of your local newspaper or watch a newscast. See how many self-defeaters you can find. You will be surprised at how often people use self-defeaters without consciously thinking through their statements. Atheism is notoriously known for self-defeating claims as the atheist must hold omniscient knowledge to make the claim that God cannot exist. The atheist would, in essence, need to be God to say that God does not exist. The atheist appeals to a moral lawgiver when admonishing others for bad moral behavior. The self-defeating nature of atheism will become more prevalent as the book proceeds.

Logic, Theology, and Exclusivity

How many of you have heard someone say, "All religions essentially teach the same thing"? It is understandable such a claim would be desired. It is not considered nice in polite society to tell someone that their religious beliefs are wrong. However, the nature of truth in addition to a study of world religions teaches that not all worldviews can be correct especially when applying the laws of logic.

In logic and philosophy, we discover the truth about theology and worldviews. If God exists, then atheists, agnostics, and Buddhists are wrong. If God doesn't exist, then atheists and Buddhists could be correct in their assessment.[4] If there is one God, then Mormons, Hindus, and pagans cannot be right in their beliefs.[5] If there are many gods, then Jews, Muslims, and Christians are wrong. If God reveals himself and performs miracles in the world, then deism is false. If he doesn't, then deism is true. If God revealed himself through the lineage of Abraham, Isaac, and Jacob, then Islam cannot be true. If God revealed himself through Abraham, Ishmael, and Muhammed, then Christianity and Judaism cannot be fully true. If Jesus of Nazareth was and is the promised Messiah who rose from the dead, then the modern non-messianic versions of Judaism are incorrect. If he was and did, then Christianity is the only viable worldview. Truth is exclusive. Because of that, there cannot be multiple paths to God. Since this is true, New Age versions of Christianity are also inherently false because some versions claim that there are multiple ways to reach God.

---

4. Buddhism is largely agnostic.

5. Although Hinduism largely believes in one God who is manifested in different avatars.

Evaluating Arguments from Logic

Before closing this chapter and the unit, let us look at one more way that a person can evaluate truth claims. A logical argument normally exists in the form of a *syllogism*. A syllogism consists of two statements called *premises* and a third line which holds the *conclusion*. A syllogism looks like the following:

1. All birds have wings. (Premise #1)
2. Cardinals have wings. (Premise #2)
3. Therefore, cardinals are birds. (Conclusion)

A person needs to evaluate syllogistic arguments to see if it is valid. Almost any argument from a movie, a book, or article can be constructed as a syllogism for testing. This should be done because we live in a world inundated with fake news online, over the air, and in print. In his book *Socratic Logic*, Peter Kreeft provides three ways a person can evaluate syllogistic claims to see if they hold.[6]

First, *define the terms*. Look at the words in each statement. The terms are either clear or unclear. Say a person uses the term "bank." Is the person describing a financial institution, an inclined piece of land near a river, or the tilt of an airplane? If the terms are unclear, ask the person to clarify what he or she means by the term. If you are reading an article, look through the article to see how the term is used. Be suspicious of overly shady terminology.

Second, *test the statements*. The statements are either true or false. Look at the following syllogism.

1. An oak has leaves.
2. Leaves are grass.
3. Therefore, oaks are grass.

The argument seems silly at first glance. The first statement is true. But the problem comes with the second statement. Leaves are not grass. Leaves may fall on the grass, but leaves are not grass. Already the argument fails because the second statement is false. The conclusion does not follow.

Third, *evaluate the argument*. If the terms are clear and the statements are true, then evaluate the argument to see whether the argument is valid or invalid. The following syllogism holds two statements that are true, but the conclusion does not follow. Look to see if you can discover why.

---

6. The following information taken from Peter Kreeft, *Socratic Logic: A Logic Test Using Socratic Method, Platonic Questions, and Aristotelian Principles*, 26–34.

1. Brian Chilton is a man.
2. Brian Chilton is short.
3. Therefore, all men are short.

At first glance, the syllogism seems to hold. However, the conclusion does not follow with reality and does not follow through with its own structure. Brian Chilton is a man. Standing at 5'8" on a good day, I readily admit that I (Brian Chilton) am short. But is every male human being on planet earth Brian Chilton? Thank the Lord, no. Brian Chilton is not indicative of every male who has ever walked the earth. The argument fails because it is invalid.

Conclusion

Truth is knowable due to the laws of logic. The three laws of logic are the law of identity, the law of non-contradiction, and the law of excluded middle. Self-defeating statements are a clear giveaway that a person is not speaking truth. Truth is exclusive and indicates that not everyone can be correct, and this is especially true when it comes to worldviews. When presented with a syllogistic argument, remember the three ways to test an argument. Define the terms—are they clear or unclear. Test the statements—are they true or false. Evaluate the argument—is it valid or invalid.

Before beginning the next unit, try answering the following objections. How would you respond?

a. What's true for you may not be true for me?
b. Truth is relative for each person. So how can you know your beliefs are true?
c. All religions are essentially true and teach the same thing.
d. Truth cannot be known so how do you know your Jesus is true?

UNIT 2

The Existence of God and Theological Objections

The first unit discussed the essence of truth and how truth is knowable. Now that truth has been shown to be a reality (something that exists and is knowable), it is time to investigate one of the oldest questions in history. Does God exist? This unit will deal with the most pressing issues related to God's existence.

Chapter 5 will describe whom we are discussing when we speak of God. Many confuse the Christian's description of God with that of other worldviews. Some confuse God's nature with popularized depictions of God in the media. Thus, it is important to describe the God of whom the Bible speaks.

Chapters 6 and 7 discuss the classical arguments for God's existence. Chapter 6 discusses the cosmological and ontological arguments for the existence of God. Chapter 7 investigates the teleological (design), the aesthetic, the information argument (one I especially promote), and the argument from consciousness.

Chapter 8 deals with the moral argument for God's existence. Furthermore, the issue of morality and ethics must be discussed in the chapter as morality is often described as a personal rather than a transcendent concept.

Chapter 9 discusses why the apologist can believe in and promote God's miraculous works. This section will describe the various types of miracles that Jesus performed, evaluate the challenges that David Hume presented, and the miracles that continue to occur today.

Chapter 10 will be the most emotionally charged chapter in the book. Chapter 10 discusses how a person can believe in a good and powerful God while living in the midst of such evil. How does the believer deal with moral and natural evil and still hold to God's goodness?

Chapter 4

GOD, HIS ATTRIBUTES, AND SEVEN MAJOR WORLDVIEWS

What Do We Mean by "God?"— God and His Major Attributes

As we discuss the existence of God, one must first ask, what do we mean when we refer to God? The god of Deism is a god who is inactive in the world, whereas the god of Hinduism is a god who is so interconnected with nature that creation is part of god's existence.[1] The god of Islam is transcendent but not personal, while God in the Judeo-Christian worldview is both transcendent and personal. What do Christians mean when they say they believe in God? As we learned in the previous unit, defining terms is of vital essence when deciphering truth. Hence, we must first examine what Christians mean when they speak of God.

Theologically, believers can know certain aspects of God by his attributes. *Attributes* are characteristics that describe the person or being in question—the Being here being God. The attributes of God are typically separated into two categories: non-communicable and communicable. *Non-communicable attributes* are characteristics that God alone possesses. He does not share these attributes with anyone. That is, non-communicable attributes are traits that God alone holds. It is impossible for a human being to be omnipresent (in all places at one time) since a person only occupies one place at a time. Despite the popular myth that many churchgoers hold, not even pastors can be in multiple places at one time. Believe me, I've tried

---

1. The lower-case *god* is used to describe gods of other religions. The upper-case *God* is reserved for the personal God the Christian worships.

with not so great success. Pastors are also not omniscient; they don't know when people are in the hospital if they are not told. I hate to be the mythbuster that bursts your bubble. But these are traits that God alone possesses which means that they are non-communicable. As much as we pastors may want to hold the following attributes, they are only held by God and God alone. The following are some of God's non-communicable attributes.

Non-Communicable Attributes

First, God is *omnipotent*. This means that God has power to do anything power can do, he is all-powerful. (Matt. 19:26; Isa. 40:28; Jer. 32:15–17). Philosophers have posed the question, asking if God could create a stone too heavy that he could not lift it. Many have pondered the idea. But, further evaluating the question, it is seen to be nonsensical. It is like asking if God can create a married bachelor. A married man is not a bachelor. A bachelor is an unmarried man. So, it is impossible for God to create a married bachelor because it is nonsensical. Likewise, it is nonsensical to think that God could create a stone too heavy for him to lift it because it holds that omnipotence has limitations. The question confuses terms. Thus, when understanding God's omnipotence, one defines divine omnipotence as God possessing the power to do anything that is logically possible for power to do.

Second, God is *omniscient*. This means God knows all there is to know (Ps. 147:4; Rom. 11:33). God created all the laws of mathematics and the laws of nature. He knows them better than anyone could. Consider this: All the sciences that are studied are the result of what God already established and knows. All our discoveries are impressive, but they are of things that God knew in the ancient past. God is the ultimate scientist and mathematician. He knows all there is to know about all there is to know. God is also unlimited in his knowledge of future events and future decisions before they are freely made. In Exodus, God knew the actions that Pharaoh was going to make before Pharaoh made them. David notes that before a word comes to our tongues, God already knew what the word was going to be (Ps. 139:4). God knew that you were going to buy this book before it was even published.

As a word to the wise, don't play chess with God. How do you suppose you can defeat someone who already knows all the moves you are going to make before you make them? It's worse—prepare yourself. God knows the reactions to the moves he makes before he makes the move. He also knows your response to the reactions to the moves he made before he makes the move. Okay, so what if you called an audible? What if you changed your move to trick God? Omniscience means that God knows that you would know that he knows what you would know, and that you would choose to choose differently before you ever chose to choose differently. Try saying that three times fast. Wow! What knowledge! So, don't play games with God. Because there's no way to defeat someone with that kind of knowledge.

Third, God is *omnipresent.* This means that God is in all places in all points at all times (Ps. 139:7–12; Acts 17:24–25). No mountain is too high, no ocean is too deep, no valley is too wide, and no galaxy is too far that God's presence is not found there. Again, God is in all places at all times. If you were to take the 40-year trek to the planet Mars, you would find that God was already on Mars before you ever departed Earth. God is with all people at all times and at all places. This also indicates God is neither Russian nor American. God is not exclusive to any nationality. God is not tied to any political party. God is neither Democrat nor Republican. So, stop trying to put God in a box because he will escape every time.

Fourth, God is *omnisapient.* This means that God is all wise (1 Cor. 1:21; 2:7; Luke 11:49; Exod. 35:31). God knows how to apply his knowledge to make the right decisions. His wisdom is certain and is best. While we may not always understand why God does what he does, we must trust that he knows how to work in the appropriate fashion. If God knows all there is to know and God is loving and kind, then God is someone who could be trusted. Romans 8:28 takes on a new meaning when we understand that God will take all the things of our lives and make something great out of them.

I have a quick story that I would like to share at this point. When I was a little boy, I stayed with my grandparents while my parents were at work. Even when I was big enough to go to school, I would ride the bus to my grandparents' house and stay with them until my parents arrived from work. My grandmother was the late Eva Chilton. I called her "Grandma Chilton." After getting off the bus, I asked Grandma if I could have a drink of milk. She said I could. I poured the milk in a glass and took a big gulp. I said, "Grandma, there's something wrong with your milk!" She said, "There shouldn't be. I just bought it yesterday." I took another gulp. It was nastier than the gulp before. I said, "Grandma, there is something bad wrong with your milk." She came into the kitchen and looked at the label. She replied, "Brian, honey, there's nothing wrong with this buttermilk." "Buttermilk?" She said, "Yes, I use buttermilk in my biscuits."

Buttermilk was nasty by itself. But I sure did love my grandma's buttermilk biscuits. She took the dough, the buttermilk, and other ingredients to make some of the most mouth-watering biscuits a person could ever taste. God's omnisapience is much like that. Divine omnisapience helps us realize that he takes all the things in our lives—both good and bad—and has the wisdom to bring forth something great in the end. Romans 8:28 only makes sense if the believer accepts the omnisapient nature of God.

Fifth, God is *eternal* and *infinite*. This means that God is beyond time as time has no bearing on God. He is eternal, without beginning and without end (Ps. 90:2; Deut. 33:27; Isa. 40:28; 2 Cor. 5:1). God never dies and never ages. He is not bound by the limitations of time that human beings are. God is in eternity past, in eternity present, and in eternity future. Time is a creation of God, thus God is unrestricted by time.

Sixth, God is *immutable*. This means that God's essential attributes never change. He is always the same all the time (Num. 23:19; Jas. 1:17; Heb. 13:8). Societies change, governments change, politicians, and theologians change, but God never changes. This doesn't mean that God doesn't begin new relationships with people at a real point in space and time. Rather, immutability notes that God's essential attributes and nature never changes. He is a steadfast anchor in the midst of a turbulent sea. You may have had some relationships that soured over time. Marriages fall apart because one or both people claim that they changed and fell out of love with the other party. However, God is steadfast. He never changes. He is always the same—perfect, good, and holy.

Seventh, God holds both the traits of *aseity* and *transcendence*. God's transcendence indicates that he is self-existent and is beyond the scope of creation. This means that God is not bound by anything in creation. Creation is upheld by the sovereign power of almighty God. God's aseity indicates that God depends on nothing, yet everything depends on him (Exod. 3:14; John 5:26). The personal name of God (Yahweh) means that God is who he is. Or, he will be who he will be. He is self-existent and self-sufficient. There is nothing that you could ever give God that he does not already possess. God does not need air to breath, blood to pump, or water to drink. God needs nothing. But everything is dependent upon the transcendent God.

Eighth, God is *sovereign*. God is in control of all things (Eph. 1:11). This does mean nor does it indicate that people do not have freedom of the will. Rather, this means that God oversees creation and even the direction of history. How God's sovereignty corresponds with human freedom is another debate for another time.[2] Nevertheless, no person, no place, no

---

2. There are multiple views on this issue. Determinists believe that God is completely sovereign and that human beings have no freedom. Calvinists hold a strong view of God's sovereignty with a limited view of human freedom. Thomists and Molinists hold to a balanced view of God's sovereignty and human freedom. Molinists emphasize what Luis de Molina called *middle knowledge*—that is, that God knows what free creatures would choose given certain circumstances. Wesleyans and Arminians hold a

electron, no quark, no drop of water, fish of the sea, star in a galaxy, nor any thing that exists that is outside of God's knowledge and control. When combined with God's divine omnisapience, Romans 8:28 brings great hope when considering the sovereign power of Almighty God.

Ninth, God is *triune*. God is one God, but manifested in three persons—Father, Son, and Holy Spirit (Matt. 3:16–17). The trinity of God is mysterious, but it is not paradoxical. That is, God's triune nature is not contradictory when properly understood. The baptism of Jesus clearly shows the Father, Son, and Holy Spirit working harmoniously to bring about our salvation. God planned our salvation, the Son accomplished it, and the Spirit applies it to our lives. All three essences of God were vital in bringing about a person's salvation.

Tenth, God is *spirit*. God is spirit and is not physical. *Spirit* implies a personal, eternal, energy like wind or electricity. Seeing that the word *pneuma* can mean either wind or spirit, I think a good definition for spirit is a conscious, personal, energy. A spirit is conscious meaning that it has a mind, will, and emotions. So, a spirit is not like mere electrical energy which flows according to the way it was created. Rather, the spirit is a personal, sentient being. The Spirit of God is a person and not a thing. A spirit is personal, meaning that it can relate to the world and other beings. Finally, a spirit is energy. As such, it may not hold a physical body, but moves and interacts with creation. While God may not be physically visible, when he is fully manifested in creation, the elements will melt at his presence (John 4:24; 2 Pet. 3:10–13). That's incredible power and energy!

Eleventh, God is *creator*. God created all that exists from nothing but his spoken word. (Gen. 1:1; Col. 1:15–20). This means that God created all scientific laws, all mathematical formulations, and every speck of matter even in the quantum world. Everything we learn about the universe is a result of what God has already made and established. God is not only the Lord of lords; he is the Scientist of scientists. This also indicates that if God were to remove his presence from the universe, the universe could not continue to exist as it is. He is the Creator and Sustainer of all things.

---

strong view of human freedom with God limiting his interactions with human choices. While all views have their strengths and weaknesses, I contend that Thomism and Molinism offer the best perspectives. A hybrid view of Molinism known as Congruism espoused by Francisco Suarez is especially interesting. It combines traits of Thomism and Molinism. For more information on Molinism, see Kenneth Keathley, *Salvation and Sovereignty: A Molinist Approach*, 16–41.

Communicable Attributes

God's communicable attributes are characteristics God shares with other beings. These attributes describe God's moral nature, or how he relates to other beings and to creation itself. Scripture ascribes the following nine communicable attributes to God.

First, God is *holy*. God's holiness indicates that he is both completely unique and absolutely pure. He shares his holiness with us after salvation, calling us to be holy as he is holy (Lev. 22:32; Ps. 105:42; Num. 20:6–13; Isa. 6:1–4; 1 Pet. 1:1–16). God's holiness illustrates the supreme nature of his goodness. Holiness can also indicate something that is set apart. Just as God is set apart from the modern world, believers are to be set apart in their actions and beliefs.

Second, God is *righteous*. We have a saying at church where we say, "God is good, all the time, and all the time, God is good!" Scripturally and philosophically, God is the absolute good (Gen. 18:25; Ps. 19:7–9). God is morally upright and in him exists no evil at all. He shares his righteousness with us upon our salvation. The Christian is called to righteous living only because of the righteousness of God imputed to the believer. The believer is not bound to sin any longer.

Third, God is *just*. God punishes sin and upholds what is right. This stems from his righteous nature (Gen. 2:17; Rom. 6:23; Ps. 73). As God's people, we should seek justice for those whom are weak and oppressed (Amos 5:12–15; Jas. 2:9). The defender of the faith upholds God's justice as the person stands against false accusations and philosophies waged against the truth of Christ. Furthermore, the apologist should stand up for the least in society, those who cannot defend themselves, and those who are the most vulnerable. If injustice bothers you, understand that it bothers God infinitely more.

Fourth, God is *truth*. God always speaks the truth. He cannot lie because it would oppose his perfect moral nature (Titus 1:2; John 17:17–19). Likewise, we are called to live in truth and oppose ideas and thoughts that reject or deny God's principles. We should strive to always speak the truth. By standing for the truth, we stand for God's truthful nature and strengthen those who have adopted lies into their philosophical outlook on life. We encourage those who believe that they are defeated and worthless. Since God is truth, Christians should always seek to speak the truth in love, meaning that speaking the truth does not justify a person to be a jerk.

Fifth, God is *faithful*. Flowing from God's immutability, love, and truthfulness, God will always be faithful to what he promises (Matt. 28:20; Lam. 3:23–24; 1 Thess. 5:24). God never reneges on a promise he has made.

Likewise, we are to be faithful to God and to the promises we make. Christians should be the most trustworthy people around since God has been faithful to them. "Should" is the operative word. Christians should be so trustworthy that businesses and corporations from across the spectrum desire to hire Christians because of their honesty.

Sixth, God is *loving* (omnibenevolent). God is love and loves all people. God is a loving father (Matt. 5:45), cares like a loving mother (Isa. 49:14–16), and lovingly disciplines his own (Heb. 12:6). He seeks the very best for his people (Jer. 31:3; John 3:16) and initiates this love towards us (1 John 4:7–8). Likewise, we are to love others the way God has loved us. Love does not mean that a person seeks what he or she can get out of another person. This Godlike love indicates a volitional choice on the part of the lover, who chooses to love the beloved no matter what may come. Others may have stopped loving you, but God never will (Rom. 8:31–39).

Seventh, God is *graceful*. This has nothing to do with God walking around with a book or plate on his head trying not to tip it over. Rather, his grace is defined as God sharing his grace to us even though we did nothing to deserve it. Because of God's amazing love, he has chosen to share his goodness. He bestows his love towards us, giving us things that we do not deserve (Eph. 1:7; 2:8; Titus 3:4–7). We should aspire to bestow grace to others, as well.

Eighth, God is *merciful*. Similar to grace, God's amazing love is given to undeserving sinners. Unlike grace, mercy is God's withdrawal of punishment towards those who deserve to be punished (Rom. 2:4; 2 Pet. 3:9). At the heart of mercy is forgiveness. Christ calls us to forgive even as God has forgiven us. That is one way a person can demonstrate mercy. How horrible it is for a person to receive God's forgiveness yet cling to past hurts, denying another the gift of forgiveness. I have experienced tremendous hurt in life. Ironically, that hurt has often come from fellow believers. I have learned that holding grudges hurts no one except the grudge bearer. Forgiveness is a gift. It places the burden upon God and releases it from the person. Life is too short to carry bitterness. Thankfully, God has shared his merciful nature to his children.

Ninth, God is *immanent*. God is actively involved in creation, even upholding creation (Col. 1:17). Likewise, we should be actively involved in the world and should seek to make the world a better place. God is not a deadbeat dad as the model presented in deism. Rather, God is actively involved in creation and in the believer's life. As such, God performs miracles as he pleases since he is not bound by the laws of creation. If a person believes in the continuous power of God, then this divine intimacy continues throughout all eternity.

Now that the biblical attributes of God have been given, we need to consider how other people from other worldviews perceive God. The next section will discuss seven major worldviews.

Seven Major Worldviews

A *worldview* is the way a person understands the world around them. Norman Geisler defines a worldview as "how one views or interprets reality."[3] A person's worldview includes the way a person understands God, the world, sin, humanity, and truth. The globe's major worldviews can be condensed into seven categories. Understanding these categories will help the apologist know at what point they need to engage the person to whom they are speaking.

Atheism

The first worldview is *atheism*. The term *atheism* comes from two Greek terms: *a* which describes a negation of something (i.e., no, not); and *theos* which is the Greek term for "God." Atheists do not believe in the existence of God. Atheists do not claim ignorance concerning God's existence, rather they are adamant that God doesn't exist. For this reason, most atheists are actually practicing agnostics as atheism would require the atheist to possess absolute knowledge of all things at all times. Modern atheists include Richard Dawkins, Lawrence Krauss, Bill Maher, Daniel Dennett, and Sam Harris.

Agnosticism

The term *agnostic* comes from two Greek words: *a* meaning the negation of something and *gnosis* meaning "knowledge." The agnostic literally claims to have no knowledge of God's existence. Agnosticism is broken into three sectors:

1. *Atheist-leaning agnostics* hold that God probably doesn't exist, but they could be wrong. Many atheist-leaning agnostics may call themselves atheists, but when pressed on the issue, they will admit to their agnosticism.

---

3. Norman L. Geisler, "Worldview," *Baker Encyclopedia of Christian Apologetics*, 785.

2. *Neutral agnostics* hold that God could exist, but they are not sure if a person could ever know for sure that God actually does exist. Neutral agnostics may delve into the area of New Age philosophies and Eastern religions that do not require a firm belief in a transcendent God.

3. *Theistic-leaning agnostics* hold that God probably exists in some form, but no one religion has the fullness of God's identity. Theistic leaning agnostics can include individuals who seek to combine religious principles across the spectrum such as Unitarians and adherents to the Bah'ai faith.

Some modern famous agnostics at the time of this writing include famed astrophysicist Neil deGrasse Tyson, New Testament scholar Bart Ehrman, actor Brad Pitt, actor Leonardo DiCaprio, actor Zac Efron, actress Uma Thurman, actress Carrie Fisher, and former CNN host Larry King.

Pantheism

Pantheism is constructed of two Greek terms: *pan* meaning all, and *theos* meaning God. Pantheists hold that everything is God. This is a unique perspective that is held in Buddhism and many pagan beliefs. In pantheism, God is not a personal being but rather an impersonal force. Pundits of pantheism may not claim that God is God, but rather call God the "universe." A good example of this tactic is found in nature shows where the universe is said to create and do things that only intelligence could do. In pantheism, God is not personal. The concept of God is viewed as an impersonal entity. As noted earlier, Buddhists are pantheists or agnostics, but this also includes wiccan, and many pagan religions. Another good way to think about pantheism is to consider the idea of the Force in the *Star Wars* movies. The Jedi hold to a Good Force and the Sith use a Bad Force. Either way, they are not calling upon a divine entity, but rather an impersonal force that holds all things together. This is the general idea behind pantheism.

Panentheism

The term *panentheism* comprises three Greek words: *pan* meaning "all," *theos* meaning "God," and *en* meaning "in." Literally, panentheism is defined as "God in all." Unlike pantheism, panentheists believe in a personal God. But panentheists believe that God is in everything and that everything contains the essence of God. For the panentheist, God is a spirit and the universe is his physical body. Hindu and New Age philosophies hold to a panentheist worldview. The Hindu would readily admit that he or she believed that Jesus is God. But they would also say that they were God, you are God, and the mosquito you killed is God. Some Eastern religions do not allow a person to swat a mosquito because to do so would mean that you are potentially killing your long-lost aunt! Some wear cloths over their mouths to keep from swallowing gnats because they view even the accidental consumption of a gnat to be equivalent to murder.

Concerning Hinduism, it is important to note that the majority of Hindus believe in one God. However, they believe that God manifests himself in various avatars. So, a person may worship one of a multiplicity of gods and goddesses, but the person still worships the same God. That comes from a panentheist worldview—that the one God is manifested in all things and that all things constitute his physical body.

Polytheism

The term *polytheism* comes from the Greek words *poly* meaning "many" and *theos* meaning "God." Polytheism is the belief that creation was developed and is maintained by multiple gods and goddesses. Ancient Greek and Roman religions believed in the existence of multiple gods including Zeus (Jupiter, Roman equivalent), Aries (Mars, Roman equivalent), and so on. It may surprise you to discover that Mormonism is a polytheistic religion. Mormons hold that a Heavenly Father and a Heavenly Mother procreated to have spirit children. Jesus and Lucifer were the first spirit children. The belief is often held that couples who wed in a Mormon temple anticipate the time when they will become the gods and goddesses of their own celestial planet. Nevertheless, the heart of our study at this point is the acceptance of a multiplicity of gods and goddesses. Thus, the religion is polytheistic in nature. Contrast that with the Shema of Deuteronomy 6:4 which emphasizes the oneness of God.

Deism

Deism derives its name from the Latin term *deus* which means "God." Deists hold to the existence of a transcendent God. However, they do not believe that the transcendent God concerns himself with the everyday workings of the world. Essentially, it is as if God wound up a clock and lets it tick to its finality without any interaction. The deist would not accept special revelation, the existence of any miracle, or a person having a personal relationship with God through the Holy Spirit. Meditation is the preferred method of prayer for the deist. Famed deists include Benjamin Franklin, Thomas Jefferson,[4] and Stephen Hopkins.

Theism

After now, a person would not be surprised to learn that the term *theism* comes simply from the Greek term *theos* meaning "God." Classical theists hold to both the transcendence of the one God and the immanence of God working in creation. In contrast with pantheists, theists hold that God is personal and possesses a mind, will, and emotions. In contrast with panentheists, theists hold that God and creation are two distinct entities, that creation flowed from God, but creation is not God. In contrast with deists, theists contend that God is active in creation, but he is not restrained by creation. Christians, Jews, and Muslims are considered classical theists.

Conclusion

When the Christian apologist refers to God, the theistic understanding of God is being advocated. God's non-communicable attributes reference those attributes that God alone possesses. God also possesses communicable attributes which are the ways that God interacts with other beings and may share those attributes. Theists contend that one God exists beyond the scope of creation while working in creation as opposed to deists, polytheists, panentheists, pantheists, agnostics, and atheists.

Biblical illiteracy is rampant in the church. Unfortunately, many good meaningful Christians have no clue what the Bible teaches about the intrinsic nature of God. Hopefully, this brief theological exercise has defined more clearly what is meant by God. If you are still unsure about the nature of God, invest in a good theology book before proceeding. It is critical for the apologist to know what is meant by God. Otherwise, the God the apologist may be defending may be foreign to what orthodox Christians actually accept.

---

4. Jefferson is known to have cut passages of Scripture out to create his own Bible.

Chapter 5

CLASSICAL ARGUMENTS FOR THE EXISTENCE OF GOD (PART 1)

Cosmological and Ontological Arguments

The last chapter described the nature of the God as found in Christian theology. Now the apologist must concern oneself about examining the arguments for God's existence. Does one have good reasons for believing in God's existence? The evidence for God's existence is so vast that three chapters are required to cover the arguments with any reasonable effort. This chapter will cover the cosmological and ontological arguments for God's existence. Chapter 7 will cover the design argument and other compelling arguments for God's existence. Chapter 8 will contend for the moral argument.

Cosmological Argument for God's Existence

The *cosmological argument* argues that God is the best explanation for the origin of the universe's existence. Something must have brought the universe into being. The universe is not an answer for its existence in and of itself. The Bible begins with the words, "In the beginning God created the heavens and the earth" (Gen. 1:1). The phrase *heavens and earth* relates to the entirety of the universe. All of the universe came about because God created it. The universe's dependence upon God evident due to its contingent nature. The psalmist notes that the "fool says in his heart, 'There's no God'" (Ps. 14:1). Scripture indicates that creation demands a Creator. Paul contends that God's "invisible attributes, that is, his eternal power and divine nature, have been clearly seen since the creation of the world, being understood through what he has made. As a result, people are without excuse" (Rom. 1:20). Something greater than the universe must exist.

Two forms of the cosmological argument are most popular: Thomas Aquinas's argument from first causes, and William Lane Craig's kalam cosmological argument.

Thomas Aquinas's First Cosmological Argument from First Causes

Thomas Aquinas (1225–1274) is perhaps one of the greatest theologians in all of church history. Aquinas was an Italian, Dominican priest who became a Doctor of the Church in theology. Aquinas was greatly influenced by the Greek philosopher Aristotle. Like Aristotle, Aquinas was interested in natural theology which is what a person can know about God by nature.

In his massive book *Summa Theologia*,[1] Aquinas offers five reasons to believe in God's existence—known as the "Five Ways." The five ways are listed as follows:

1. *Argument from motion (cosmological).*
2. *Argument from causation (cosmological).*
3. *Argument from contingency (cosmological/ontological).*
4. *Argument from degree (ontological).*
5. *Argument from final cause (design).*

Aquinas's first two ways could be considered cosmological because they deal with first causes. The third way will be incorporated into the section on the ontological argument as will the fourth. The fifth will be mentioned in the section devoted to the design argument.

Aquinas's first way is the argument from motion. Aquinas holds that "whatever is in motion is put in motion by another, for nothing can be in motion except it is in potentiality to that towards which it is in motion; whereas a thing moves inasmuch as it is in act."[2] Think of it this way: When playing billiards (a.k.a., pool), the cue ball (white ball) strikes the yellow 1 ball, causing the yellow 1 ball to strike the purple 4 ball, which banks off

---

1. Latin for "A comprehensive treatise of theology."
2. Thomas Aquinas, *Summa Theologica*, in *A Summa of the Summa: The Essential Philosophical Passages of St. Thomas Aquinas' Summa Theologica*, 59.

the tan 7 ball, causing the tan 7 ball to enter the corner pocket of the billiard table. The series of motions leading to the tan 7's entry into the corner pocket was started by the initial first cause—a person striking the cue ball with a cue stick. Likewise, Aquinas argues that the series of events leading to the creation of the universe began with a Creator who created all things and set all things into motion. Eventually, something must be eternal—either God or the universe. The universe is finite, so something beyond the universe must have brought it into being. The universe is shown to have a starting point which cosmologists call a *singularity*. Because of this, Aquinas's argument holds more weight than his opponents readily admit. If the universe is not eternal, then something . . . or Someone set the universe into motion at the creation event.

Aquinas's second way coincides with the first. The argument from causation, or *efficient cause,* holds that a thing can in no way "be the efficient cause of itself; for so it would be prior to itself, which is impossible."[3] In other words, nothing can be the cause of its own self. For instance, this writer was born in 1977. Prior to 1977, Brian Chilton did not exist. It would be impossible for Brian Chilton to claim that he created Brian Chilton. Biologically, the necessary cause for Brian Chilton is his parents—Dennis and Gail Chilton. Without the existence of Dennis and Gail Chilton, the existence of Brian Chilton would be impossible. Likewise, the universe could not create itself. Therefore, the universe must have an explanation for its existence beyond the universe itself. Just as the necessary cause for Brian Chilton's existence is his parents—Dennis and Gail Chilton—so the necessary cause for the finite universe is an eternal God. The best explanation for the universe's efficient cause is the same given in Genesis 1:1. That is, an eternal, powerful, intelligent Being created all that exists in the universe. That Being is God.

William Lane Craig's Kalam Cosmological Argument

Another cosmological argument that has gained a lot of attention in modern times is one posed by theologian and philosopher William Lane Craig. Craig promotes a cosmological argument which he calls the *kalam cosmological argument*. The argument holds three tenets:

1. Whatever begins to exist has a cause.
2. The universe began to exist.

---

3. Ibid., 60–61.

3. Therefore, the universe has a cause.[4]

The first statement coincides with Aquinas's argument from efficient cause. Nothing can be the cause of its own self, so it stands to reason that whatever begins to exist has a cause for its beginning. That is, something must explain the existence of something created. A painting does not paint itself. Rather, the efficient cause of the painting is the painter.

The second statement is nearly universally accepted in the scientific community. That is, the universe began to exist. While it has received bad press in many Christian communities, the scientific theory known as *the Big Bang Theory* helps our case.[5] The theory notes that the universe has a starting point. Before that starting point, nothing physical existed in the universe because the universe did not exist. The laws of nature, the laws of physics, and even time itself did not exist. At one dramatic moment, the universe exploded onto the scene. Thus, the universe is not eternal. It had an initial starting point. This information strengthens the case for the kalam argument.

The conclusion follows from the first two premises. If it is true that whatever begins to exist has a cause for its existence and that the universe began to exist; then the universe demands a cause for its existence. The cause must be something . . . or Someone that is an eternal, powerful, intelligent Being. That Being we know to be God.

B.R.I.C.K.

Before leaving the cosmological argument, an acronym that I developed in a paper may prove beneficial. The acronym is *B.R.I.C.K.*

B = BGV theorem.

Three leading cosmologists named Arvind Borde, Alan Guth, and Alexander Vilenkin discovered a mathematical theorem that contends that all physical universes have a starting point. Some atheist cosmologists hold that a multiverse (a universe which contains mini universes) may be the

---

4. William Lane Craig, *On Guard: Defending Your Faith with Reason and Precision*, 74.

5. It may surprise you to know that the Big Bang Theory was developed by a Christian. Father Georges Lemaitre developed the theory when he observed the redshifting of spiral nebulae. *Redshifting* means that the nebulae were drifting farther apart. *Blueshifting* means that astronomical bodies drift toward one another.

cause behind this universe's existence. However, Borde, Guth, and Vilenkin—none of whom are Christian—contend that even a multiverse would demand a cause for its existence. All physical universes require a start point which coincides with what Aquinas and, especially, Craig have argued. Thus, the BGV theorem will help you if a person claims that a multiverse is the explanation for this universe's existence. You can simply point out that the multiverse, if it exists, would also require a starting point which puts you right back in the situation in which you initially started—a situation that requires a Creator.

R = Right conditions.

Life requires the perfect conditions to exist. This will be covered with the design argument. Nevertheless, life requires numerous conditions which must be met before life is possible or sustainable.

I = Information.

The information argument will be discussed later in this book. Suffice for now, the account of information is an important aspect in providing a case for the existence of God. As the universe holds data, processes, and procedures; it demands that Someone programmed the information that it holds.

C = Compassion and ethics.

This is the moral argument which will be discussed later in the study. Anytime a skeptic appeals to morality, the skeptic appeals to the existence of God. In a universe without God, nothing has any value. Thus, morality cannot exist if God does not exist.

K = Kalam cosmological argument.

The kalam argument will prove beneficial due to its simplicity and ease of memory. It is clear, precise, and quite useful.

Ontological Argument for God's Existence

The *ontological argument* for God's existence may take a little longer to absorb. Ontological arguments are deeply philosophical because they originate from the branch of philosophy known as *ontology*.[6] Geisler defines the ontological argument as proceeding "from the mere idea that God is an absolutely perfect or Necessary Being."[7] The essence of necessary beings is where the ontological argument finds its power. Going back to the previous illustration of Brian Chilton's existence and his dependence on his parents' existence—in this case, Brian's existence is said to be *contingent* (requiring a cause) upon the existence of *necessary beings* (not requiring a cause for the particular aspect being investigated). Brian's parents' existence is required to explain his existence. Likewise, the ontological argument will hold that in similar fashion, the universe's existence is contingent upon the existence of God, a necessary Being.

Aquinas's Ontological Argument

Aquinas's third way is the argument from contingency. Thomas Aquinas's third point is perhaps one of the more confusing aspects of his apologetic. The third way holds that nothing physical can create itself. There was a time when no physical thing existed. Thus, there must be an answer as to why anything exists. Essentially, as was mentioned in the previous point, something eternal must exist. One of two things must exist: Either an eternal physical universe exists; or an eternal, transcendent Creator exists. Seeing that the universe had a beginning, it is more rationale than ever before to hold that an eternal, transcendent Creator must exist.[8] The eternal exis-

---

6. *Ontology* is the study of being and how a person can know whether something or someone exists.

7. Geisler, "Ontological Argument," *Baker Encyclopedia of Christian Apologetics*, 554.

8. Aquinas's exact wording is as follows: "The third way is taken from possibility and necessity, and runs thus. We find in nature things that are possible to be and not to be, since they are found to be generated, and to corrupt, and consequently, they are possible to be and not to be. But it is impossible for these always to exist, for that which is possible not to be at some time is not. Therefore, if everything is possible not to be, then at one time there could have been nothing in existence. Now if this were true, even now there would be nothing in existence, because that which does not exist only begins to exist by something already existing. Therefore, if at one time nothing was in existence, it would have been impossible for anything to have begun to exist; and thus even now nothing would be in existence—which is absurd. Therefore, not all beings are merely possible, but there must exist something the existence of which is necessary."

tence of something is necessitated by the existence of the finite, physical universe. Ontologically, the very nature of God (his eternal Being) demands the reality of his existence.

Aquinas's fourth way is the argument from degree. This argument is extremely complex, at least in my mind. To simplify the fourth argument to its most basic form, there must be a highest good. The degradation of that which is good argues that there must be an ultimate good which one calls God. The fourth ontological argument of Aquinas is comparable to the moral argument which will be discussed in a future chapter. To simplify, God is the ultimate good and his goodness is anticipated from our moral depravity. Because we are so bad, there must be something that is the ultimate good from which we derived. God is that absolute good.

Anselm of Canterbury's Ontological Argument

When speaking of the ontological argument, it is necessary for us to mention, although briefly, the work of Anselm of Canterbury. Anselm of Canterbury was a Benedictine monk who was appointed as the archbishop of Canterbury in 1093. Anselm held that God was the greatest thing anyone could perceive. From that, he created an ontological argument that can be summarized as follows:

1. God is by definition that than which nothing greater can be conceived.
2. It is greater to exist in reality than to exist only in the mind.
3. Therefore God must exist in reality. If he didn't exist, he wouldn't be the greatest possible.[9]

Anselm says that God's existence is demanded by the essence of what would known to be God. Anselm's ontological argument is quite complex, nuanced, and may not be applicable in most modern discussions. Many even question the validity of Anselm's form of the ontological argument. Others argue that Anselm never intended his ontological argument to be used as an apologetic, but as a tool for devotion. Nevertheless, it is good to acknowledge his concept at the very least.

Aquinas, *Summa Theologica*, 67–68.
9. Geisler, "Anselm," *Baker Encyclopedia of Christian Apologetics*, 26.

Conclusion

The cosmological and ontological arguments both provide compelling cases for the existence of God. The necessity of God's existence is something, in my estimation, that is nearly impossible to get around. The universe is finite. Thus, the universe's existence demands something greater than itself to explain its existence. Ontological arguments further explore the idea of necessary things (things or beings whose existence is demanded) and contingent things (things or beings that require an explanation for their existence). Even if we only had these two arguments, we would have sufficient reason to believe in God. But the good news is, there's more to come!

Chapter 6

CLASSICAL ARGUMENTS FOR THE EXISTENCE OF GOD (PART 2)

Design, Aesthetic, Information, and Consciousness

In the last chapter, we uncovered two forms of argumentation for God's existence—the cosmological and the ontological arguments. Chapter 7 will add four additional arguments for God's existence. First, attention will be given to the design argument which holds that the universe is structured in such a way that shows evidence that a Designer designed it. Second, brief consideration will be given to the aesthetic argument for God's existence. Does anything hold beauty and/or purpose in a world without God? The aesthetic argument will contend that God must exist if anything is to have purpose. The information argument is one that I especially promote. It holds that if any system holds data, programs, and processes, a programmer must be necessary. Finally, this chapter will discuss the argument from consciousness. What is the mind? What does consciousness tell us about God's existence? What about near-death experiences? Because the study examines so many arguments, we cannot give a deep exploration of these arguments. But hopefully this chapter will encourage you to explore the arguments further.

Teleological (Design) Argument for God's Existence

The *teleological argument* gets its name from the Greek term *telos* which means "the goal or end of something . . . a point marking the end of a duration of time."[1] Thus, the teleological argument is one based upon the end goal of creation. From the end of something looking back, one can see marks of design in the universe which indicates that a Designer exists whom we know to be God. The teleological argument is often known as the *design argument*. Attention needs to be given to three forms of the argument.

Paley's Watchmaker Argument

William Paley (1743–1805) was an English apologist and archdeacon of Carlisle. Paley argued for the existence of God by the design argument using the illustration of a watch found on a shoreline. In his book *A View of the Evidences of Christianity* (1794), Paley notes the following:

> In crossing a heath, suppose I pitched my foot against a *stone* and was asked how the stone came to be there, I might possibly answer that for anything I knew to the contrary it had lain there forever . . ." But "suppose I had found a *watch* upon the ground, and it should be inquired how the watch happened to be in that place, I should hardly think of the answer which I had given before, that for anything I knew the watch might have always been there." He asks, "why is it not as admissible in the second case as in the first? For this reason, and for no other, namely, that when we come to inspect the watch, we perceive—what we could not discover in the stone—that its several parts are framed and put together for a purpose . . .[2]

Paley held that a person who discovered a watch would not say the same thing about its origins as one would a stone. The watch shows evidence of being created by its own design. The stone was there by happenstance. Ironically, while in Paley's argument the stone holds no inherent design, he would use his argument to note that if the universe showed evidence of design, the universe must hold the same design that the watch found on the shore would. The stone would have elements of design just as the watch. Since the universe shows obvious signs of design, then one would conclude that there must be a Designer—God.

Aquinas's Design Argument

Thomas Aquinas's fifth way is an argument from design. Aquinas holds that the natural bodies cannot be led by their own intelligence since they have

---

1. Rebecca Skaggs, "Time," *Lexham Theological Wordbook*, Logos Bible Software.
2. William Paley, *A View of the Evidences of Christianity*, 3

none. Inanimate things have no inherent intelligence within themselves. Thus, Aquinas notes that "whatever lacks intelligence cannot move towards an end, unless it be directed by some being endowed with knowledge and intelligence; as the arrow is shot to its mark by the archer."[3] Thus, the natural world cannot design itself. If the universe shows evidence of design, then it must be designed as the natural world by its own power cannot achieve anything.

Try this experiment when watching nature shows. See how many times the narrator must give signs of intelligence to nature. For instance, she may say, "Nature chose to produce the particle" or "The universe found a way to produce life." Can nature of its own power do anything? Can the universe produce anything in its own power? The answer in both cases is, no. Nature and the universe are inanimate things. Only intelligence can choose or produce anything. Thus, an overseeing Intelligence must be guiding and sustaining nature.

Intelligent Design

A new creationist movement has gained steam in recent years. It is known as the *intelligent design movement* (ID). Those in ID come from various backgrounds and consist of scientists from various fields who hold that the universe's design demands a Creator's existence. Even non-theists admit that the universe shows amazing traits of fine-tuning. One author makes the following observation:

> For the universe to exist as it does requires that hydrogen be converted to helium in a precise but comparatively stately manner—specifically, in a way that converts seven one-thousandths of its mass to energy. Lower that value very slightly—from 0.007 percent to 0.006 percent, say—and no transformation could take place: the universe would consist of hydrogen and nothing else. Raise the value very slightly—to 0.008 percent—and the bonding would be so wildly prolific that the hydrogen would long since have been exhausted. In either case, with the slightest tweaking of the numbers the universe as we know and need it would not be here.[4]

The universe demands design, but biological life does so even more. When considering all that is required to make life possible, it is amazing to

---

3. Aquinas, *Summa Theologica*, 69.
4. Bill Bryson, *A Short History of Nearly Everything*, 16.

think that anything is alive. For life to exist, the planet must be at the right distance from the sun. If we were any closer to the sun, the earth would be too hot for life and we would all be toast—literally. If we were any further from the sun, the earth would be too cold, and we would all be popsicles.

In the solar system, there must be an adequate number of large planets (like Jupiter and Saturn in our case) that holds enough gravity to ward off dangerous meteors. The solar system itself must be in the right place in the galaxy (2/3s away from the center) and have enough space between the galaxy's spiral arms. If the solar system is any closer to the galaxy's center, then the planet will collide into too much debris making life impossible. Think about driving in downtown New York City with all the traffic that's there. Now imagine if our planet were gliding along a heavily trafficked area. Collisions would be far more likely. If we were any further away from the galactic center, the planet would drift out of the galaxy's gravitational field and the planet would drift into the darkness of the universe.[5] If one would expect to find design in the universe, then more and more elements of design would be detected. Originally, scientists found only a few dozen elements of design. Now, the number of design cosmological constants is well over 180.

Aesthetic Argument for God's Existence

The aesthetic argument for God's existence could be constructed in multiple ways. At its core, the aesthetic argument emphasizes the purpose that can only be found in a universe created by God. A person only has meaning in a world that has been created by God. If all of life is nothing more than molecules in motion—individuals driven by the drums of their own DNA—then life ultimately has no meaning at all. Consider this: If life has no meaning, then all the scientific achievements of the past, present, and future have no relevance. The art of Leonardo da Vinci becomes nothing more than pigments on paper and the music of Beethoven becomes mere dots on a page. The sunflowers of the field are no more relevant than poison ivy and the sunrise over the ocean is no more picturesque than garbage lying in the midst of a slum. In a world like this, your life has no meaning. It does not matter if your children live or die. It does not matter if you live or die. Everything becomes meaningless. Pretty depressing, indeed.[6]

---

5. For more information concerning intelligent design, see Michael Behe's book *Darwin's Black Box*, 187–208.

6. Think of all the Christians who sacrificed their lives for Christ. If there is no God, then their sacrifices were note admirable. Rather, they were foolish. The lives of soldiers whose lives were sacrificed in the battlefields would not be heroic in an

However, if God exists, then God has given life purpose. Everyone's life holds meaning and value. Creation provides beauty for observers. In a purposeful universe; art finds value, and music holds a marvelous melody. For the purpose of this study—which only has purpose because intelligent minds gave it a purpose—one could summarize the argument presented as follows:

1. If anything holds value, it must have purpose.
2. Purpose comes from intelligence.
3. The universe holds purpose.
4. Therefore, the universe came from intelligence.

Information Argument for God's Existence

The information argument is one which I have adopted as a means to combat the idea that evolution disproves God's existence.[7] Skeptics have purported that the theory of evolution disproves the existence of God as the natural process would eliminate the need for God's involvement in creation. But is this true?

Information is described in three different categories. First, *specified order* is a string of repeating information that is found naturally in crystals or snowflakes.[8] Second, *unspecified complexities* are non-repeating, natural occurrences that one finds in the shape of natural objects. The third category is *specified complexities* which do not happen naturally and are non-repetitive and non-random.[9] A sculpture, painting, or computer program are examples of information that is a specified complexity. The way something is deemed specified complex is if its existence is contingent (or dependent) on a previously existing being. William Dembski holds that "Contingency is the chief characteristic of information."[10] That is, the sculpture only exists because of the sculptor's existence. The painting's existence is dependent upon the existence of an artist. When one begins to consider the great complexities of human DNA and irreducibly complex things, such as the eye

---

atheistic universe. They would be merely tragic.

7. I am not an evolutionist. However, the argument provided demonstrates that even if evolution *were* true, it would *not* disprove God's existence.
8. Doug Powell, *Holman QuickSource Guide to Christian Apologetics*, 57.
9. Ibid.
10. William Dembski, *Intelligent Design*, 160.

and a bacterium, the existence of a Designer is demanded. That Designer is who we know to be God.

The deeper one digs into the information argument, the more one finds that at the heart of all creation, everything becomes specified complexities. Where did the data contained within the physical laws of the universe arise? Did the laws of physics create themselves? What about mathematical theorems? Did the universal mathematical theorems construct themselves? As already noted, things cannot make themselves. To think that the information within the universe merely created itself would be comparable to Luigi telling Mario that the Super Mario Brothers game spawned naturally out of a random calculator.

Going back to the question of evolution, the skeptic must ask how it was that the process of evolution came to be. It could not have merely developed itself as it would require a programmer. Thus, evolution cannot disprove God's existence, rather it requires God. Evolution is not the failsafe theory that skeptics often purport it to be. It has major problems and is beginning to be doubted within the modern scientific community.[11] However, an understanding of the information argument would contend that any processes, procedures, and data require the prior existence of a Creator. The information argument can be summarized by the following:

1. Data, processes, and procedures are all forms of information.
2. Information is designed by intelligence.
3. The universe contains data, processes, and procedures.
4. Therefore, the universe was designed by intelligence.

Argument from Consciousness

One of the premiere apologetic fields of study pertains to human consciousness. First, one must ask, what is the soul? Scripture employs two terms to define the soul. The Old Testament uses the term *ruach* some 361 times. *Ruach* overlaps with another term used to describe the soul, *nephesh*. *Ruach* describes the notion of power or the ability to do something.[12] *Nephesh* indicates what J. P. Moreland calls a "substantial principle of life and ground of consciousness and personal identity that leaves, continues to exist after

---

11. See https://dissentfromdarwin.org/ for more details.
12. J. P. Moreland, *The Soul: How We Know It's Real and Why It Matters*, 49.

biological death, and that can return."[13] Genesis 35:18 and 49:15 indicate the soul's survival beyond physical death.

The New Testament also uses two terms to define the soul or human consciousness. *Pseuche* is one of the words used which, according to the *Lexham Theological Wordbook*, refers to a "person's inner life or to the life-principle."[14] *Pneuma* is another New Testament term for the soul which refers to the animating spirit of human beings and to the Holy Spirit. One could postulate that the soul is a personal, eternal, energy of sorts. Not an energy that is mindless, but rather the soul is a conscious energy that has a mind, will, and emotions.

Scripture indicates that the soul survives death which awaits the time of resurrection, a time when the body will be remade just as Christ's body was remade on the first Easter morning. In Matthew 22:23–33, Jesus argues that the soul survives death as he sides with the Pharisees' interpretation. He notes that God is "not the God of the dead, but of the living" (Matt. 23:32). Jesus also strongly implies that the soul survives death when he says to the criminal on the cross who asks for Jesus to allow him entrance into his kingdom, "Truly I tell you, today you will be with me in paradise" (Luke 23:43). Many ask, is the mind/soul separate from the brain? If the soul is separate from the brain, then a case is made for the spiritual dimension. Since God is said to be Spirit (John 4:24) and immaterial, the argument from consciousness contends for the existence of immaterial God. Are there reasons to believe that the mind and soul are different from the brain?

First, the existence of human free will illustrates the existence of a conscious soul. Atheists are often determinists who hold that DNA and the brain dictate what a person will decide to do and will become.[15] Christian theism holds that due to the person's soulish existence, he or she can choose to do x versus y. A person can choose chocolate ice cream or vanilla, and so on. Seeing that the body changes over time, if a person's total being was simply his or her physical makeup, then no one could be held accountable for a crime or moral indiscretion because they are physically a different person as time progresses. Since the body changes, the person who commits a crime in 1990 cannot be held accountable in 2020 because the person's physical makeup has changed. If a person is only their body, then we all become different people each year. Strange, huh? Moreland provides the following argument:

13. Ibid., 47–48.
14. Benjamin S. Davis, "Life," *Lexham Theological Wordbook*, Logos Bible Software.
15. Oddly, hardcore Calvinism and atheism both share a determinist viewpoint.

1. If I am a physical object (e.g., a brain or a body), then I do not have free will.
2. But I do have free will.
3. Therefore, I am not a physical object.
4. I am either a physical object or a soul.
5. Therefore, I am a soul.[16]

If anyone is able to consciously choose an option, then the person has free will which implies he or she has a soul. Your choice in reading this sentence illustrates your freedom. Your choice in reading this book illustrates this freedom. I am glad that you *chose* to do so.

Second, the ability to tell the differences between acts of the brain and acts of the mind indicate that the brain and the mind are not mutually exclusive. When I had to have my wisdom teeth extracted, the dentist provided a certain kind of anxiety medication which was to be taken an hour before the procedure. After taking the medication initially, it seemed as if nothing happened. However, after a few minutes, everything seemed to slow down. Even the limbs of the trees outside seemed grow larger. Even though the medication was affecting my brain, I consciously knew that what was taking place was an effect on my brain and did not represent reality. If all of life merely came from the brain, then such a distinction could not be made.

I can provide another illustration concerning this distinction. While pastoring a church in North Carolina, I visited a woman who was having several medical issues. The doctors had prescribed her to take medicine for her pain. However, the medicine was known to cause hallucinations. I rung her doorbell. She came to the door and said that she thought the doorbell was actually ringing this time. When I asked why she thought that it had been ringing before, she said it was a result of her medication. She said that the medicine was causing her to see snakes on the wall, but she knew that the snakes were not real. Despite the effects of her medication, she could tell the difference between reality and what was a hallucination.

Finally, near-death experiences serve as evidence for the consciousness of the human being. Here, the apologist is not trying to defend all the stories one hears about a person's experience beyond the grave. Proof cannot be found in what a person experiences in heaven or in hell. But the out-of-body experiences a person has while still on this side of eternity can be verified when there are other witnesses of events, or if physical objects are distinguishable. For instance, Gary Habermas and J.P. Moreland researched

---

16. Moreland, *Soul*, 128.

multiple accounts of near-death experiences in their book *Beyond Death*. The following are some of the stories verified in their book.

> Another young lady, who was in a hospital and near death, experienced herself leaving her body and visiting her relatives in another room. There she witnessed her brother-in-law saying that he was going to wait and see if she was going to 'kick the bucket' or not. Later after her recovery she confronted and shocked her relative by repeating his words to him![17]

This account is extremely fascinating because there were other witnesses who heard the brother-in-law speak about his sister-in-law "kicking the bucket." Since the woman was dead, there was no way she could have known about the experience unless she had consciously experienced the conversation while outside of her body.

Habermas and Moreland provide another fascinating story from Seattle, Washington. The account is told by Kimberly Clark Sharp.

> Maria, a victim of a heart attack, described an NDE in which she saw a number of items both inside and outside of Harborview Hospital in Seattle. Her report was later confirmed. But it was not this potential confirmation that interested Sharp at the time. Maria told Sharp that she especially concentrated on a single item in her line of vision—a tennis shoe. It was located out on the roof of the hospital ledge, around the corner of the building that she had entered and currently occupied. Maria revealed that the shoe was characterized by a worn little toe and the position of the lace, which was located under the heel. After unsuccessful attempts to find the object in the roof area indicated by Maria, Sharp finally located and retrieved the shoe.[18]

Interestingly, they recount another story like the one told in Seattle. A woman had died and floated above the hospital. She noticed a red shoe on the roof of the hospital. It was later found exactly where she described. She had never heard about the story in Seattle with the lacy, blue shoe.[19] These accounts defend the notion that the soul survives death. In turn, they prove that a spiritual dimension of reality exists beyond the scope of this mere physical reality. Spiritual beings exist. Furthermore, no physical explanation

---

17. Gary R. Habermas and J. P. Moreland, *Beyond Death: Exploring the Evidence for Immortality*, 158.
18. Ibid., 212.
19. Ibid., 214.

sufficiently describes why consciousness exists. Only God's existence solves the problem.

Before leaving near-death-experiences, I would like to add an additional thought. Many people have been guilty of proverbially throwing the baby out with the bathwater due to some faulty reports of NDEs. Other people are frightened by the thought that NDEs and OBEs[20] could be real. For some, these experiences leave the realm of comfort and enter the world of paranormal activity. But I have experienced death quite a bit in my ministerial career as a pastor. I have friends, such as Jason Kline, who work in hospice who have also witnessed interesting events as a person approaches death. On one such occurrence, I was by the bedside of a World War II veteran when he passed away. I had my hand on his shoulder and his son held him by the hand. At the moment that he died, we felt something leave his body. We believe it was his soul. The nurse verified that he had passed at the moment we felt his spirit leave his body. While NDEs are frightening for some, it might just be that God is allowing individuals to have these experiences as his own apologetic. Lives have been transformed by these amazing experiences. So, if God brings a person to faith by NDEs, why should we aggressively be against it?

Conclusion

The arguments presented in this chapter provide further compelling reasons to believe in God. It is quite interesting to me that while I am not an evolutionist, evolution is not the one-two punch that skeptics often claim it to be. Even an evolutionary process would require information to permit the process to take shape. Hence, God is still required. The aesthetic argument notes that nothing can have beauty or inherent value in a world without God. God's existence is necessary for anything to have value and worth. The argument from consciousness denotes that the free will, your distinction between the mind and the brain, and conscious experiences outside the body prove that humans hold a spiritual existence. That spiritual existence can only be explained by a Spiritual Divine Being which we know to be God. It was also noted that the design argument tracks the ways that the universe exhibits design. Design strongly implies that an Intelligent Mind was behind all that exists. The arguments tip the scales in favor of God's existence, but amazingly, there's even more to come!

---

20. OBEs are out-of-body experiences.

Chapter 7

MORALITY AND THE MORAL ARGUMENT FOR GOD'S EXISTENCE

Atheists and skeptics ascribe all kinds of misbehaviors to religious believers, especially Christians. Critics accuse Christians of misogyny, advocation of slavery, genocide, homophobia, homicide, and so on. In such cases, the antagonist will quickly mention the Crusades and the Inquisition to derail any form of moral ethic held by the believer. Some as, famed atheist Richard Dawkins, accuse God of being a moral monster. Dawkins wrote the following to describe the way he perceives Yahweh in the Old Testament:

> The God of the Old Testament is arguably the most unpleasant character in all fiction: jealous and proud of it; a petty, unjust, unforgiving control-freak; a vindictive, bloodthirsty ethnic cleanser; a misogynistic, homophobic, racist, infanticidal, genocidal, filicidal, pestilential, megalomaniacal, sadomasochistic, capriciously malevolent bully.[1]

While Dawkins's profound use of adjectives may be astonishing—I would hate to play him in a game of *Scrabble*—his diatribe against Yahweh fails at a critical juncture. Without God, there is no basis for morality. Any appeal to morality surprisingly requires a Creator in order for the appeal to hold. A moral Lawgiver is required if there is to be a moral code. Otherwise, everything is meaningless.

---

1. Richard Dawkins, *The God Delusion*, 52.

Kant and the Origins of the Moral Argument

Among the first to postulate the existence for God from a moral argument perspective was Immanuel Kant in 1724 to 1804. In the *Critique of Practical Reason*, Kant implies the evidence for God's existence and immortality based on moral reasoning and the reality of moral duties; a proof based on practical reasoning. Others such as Hastings Rashdall, W. R. Sorely, C. S. Lewis, Elton Trueblood, David Baggett, and Marybeth Baggett have expounded on the moral argument for God's existence. Some would hold that Kant arguably laid that the groundwork.

Kant reasoned that all people desire happiness. He contended that morality was ultimately a question of the duty of all humanity, and that duty is what we ought to do and in so doing happiness would be achieved. The greatest good, in Kant's reasoning, then, the merger of happiness and moral duty. While it was not Kant's sole purpose to argue for a proof of God's existence as such, he postulated that any moral system would necessarily deduce the existence of a God as the originator of moral absolutes. Kant argues that our innate knowledge of what we ought to do is acknowledgment that we live in a moral world. Second, the greatest good of each person is that we have happiness in conjuncture with harmony in moral duties. Since rational moral thought tells us we should aim for the highest good this must exist. Third, it is the moral obligation and duty of all persons to strive for the greatest good and they ought to do so. Fourth, Kant argues that perfect accordance to the will of the moral law is the supreme good and to do so would bring about the perfect proportion of happiness. Fifth, "the ought implies the can,"[2] because life is too short persons are not able to realize the greatest good in this life and do as they ought. Sixth, since persons are unable to realize the greatest good and achieve that balance between moral duty and happiness within the allotted span of this life, that innate longing "towards that perfect accordance is only possible on the supposition of an endless duration of existence."[3] And if there is an endless duration of existence it is only possible "on the supposition of a Supreme Being having a causality corresponding to moral character; [therefore] it is morally necessary to assume the existence of God."[4] Seventh, it is necessary, then, we must postulate there is a God and a future life in which the greatest good can be achieved. Since perfect accordance to the will of the moral law is not

---

2. Immanuel Kant, *The Critique of Practical Reason*, 218.
3. Ibid.
4. Ibid., 221–222.

possible on earth, God must exist and there must be a life after death where this balance between moral excellence and happiness exists.

In summary, while Kant held that we ought to pursue the greatest good, we are not capable of doing so perfectly in this life. If we have an innate duty which cannot be achieved in this life, there must be a solution. Kant reasoned, therefore, that God must exist, and there must be an afterlife. Without the existence of a Supreme Being, there can be no wedding of happiness and duty, the greatest good, since nothing would have purpose outside of God which is similar to the aesthetic argument mentioned earlier. Since we are incapable of achieving this on our own, Kant postulated a Supreme Being must exist who can bring perfect balance between the desire for happiness and the pursuit of duty.

The Moral Argument and the Necessity of a Moral Lawgiver

Morality requires a moral Lawgiver. Consider the following illustration. Imagine yourself driving down a highway. As you speed down the road, you notice a large white sign with the following written on it: "SPEED LIMIT 35." You look down at your speedometer noticing that you are driving 55 miles-per-hour. When you look in your rear-view mirror, you notice a white car with flashing blue lights. You realize you have broken the law and are being pulled over by your friendly, neighborhood police officer. Why do you know you broke the law? You realize you did because of the speed limit posted by the side of the road. Here's the good part. Who established that the speed limit was 35 miles per hour? It must have been by legislators. The existence of a speed limit demands the existence of lawgivers.

In a similar case, my wife and I were driving back home from our honeymoon. My wife was driving, apparently a tad too fast. A police officer pulled us over. My wife asked me if I was wearing my seat belt. I conferred that I was. She said, "Good, because we're about to be pulled over." The officer came up to our car and shook his head. He noticed the "Just married" paint on our rear window. He approached our car and smiled. He said, "Get out of here. Just drive slower!" The sign on our window helped our case. While we had a wonderful and gracious police officer who pulled us over, I would not advice young married couples to attempt this. Nevertheless, my wife knew the reason we were being pulled. We were traveling too fast. Why did she know this? It was because she knew the speed limit and the speed we were traveling and the two did not match. Laws come from lawgivers.

The previous experiment is but a microcosm of the greater reality of the moral code. If morality exists, then Someone must have established the morality that everyone accepts. While different cultures have differing practices, the moral codes of all civilizations become remarkably similar when discussing the practices done to those held most dear.[5] Nearly everyone accepts that it is evil to kill and abuse young children. Certain things cause great anger and despair. For instance, I become enraged when defenseless people are abused, especially when it comes to children and the elderly. Why? Because I realize they are often defenseless. It is wrong for them to be abused even more when they cannot defend themselves. But why does this bother me? Why are we enraged when injustice occurs? In our very essence, we are moral beings.

Morality's Failure without God

While Christians have been blamed for many things throughout the centuries by those who ascribe to a secular atheistic worldview, the most intriguing aspect of the conversation is that the atheist has no ground for calling anything good or evil. How so? If God does not exist, then there is no purpose to anything which also means that morality is merely an illusion. It does not matter whether a person finds a cure for cancer or kills hundreds of people in a mass shooting. There is no difference between Hitler and a loving grandmother. It's all the same in an atheistic world because there is no higher authority to claim something good from evil. Morality becomes relative to each individual.

Some would claim, "Yes, but governments dictate which laws should be followed." But if society establishes morality, then no one could claim that Nazi Germany was any worse than the republic of the United States. The standard to kill eleven-million individuals, mostly who were Jewish, was established by the Nazi society. But nearly everyone accepts that the Nazi German government was evil. Therefore, morality must have a higher standing than society alone.

God grounds morality and human worth. As David and Marybeth Baggett write, "Theism offers an account of human persons that permits the *irreducibility of human consciousness and purposes,* as a ground for human rights. According to the theist, God is personal and is the source of all value."[6] Without God, no one could call anything unethical. Governments

---

5. Even cannibalistic societies have a high moral code for those within their own community. Their disdain is held for those outside their group.
6. David Baggett and Marybeth Baggett, *The Morals of the Story: Good News about*

would have no philosophical basis for establishing laws. No one could theoretically be thrown in prison because there would be no basis for calling anything good or bad. God not only is the basis for morality, he is the lynchpin of stability for human civilization.

Furthermore, as Thomas Aquinas notes, "some intelligent being exists by whom all natural things are directed to their end; and this being we call God."[7] Aquinas's fifth and final way argues that God is the basis for all morality and the director of all human history. Without God, morality has no basis. Even the most progressive of all atheists lose their right to call anything good or evil because by rejecting God, the person has removed one's moral foundation.

The moral argument could be constructed as the following:

1. If God does not exist, then objective morality does not exist.

2. Objective morality does exist.

3. Therefore, God exists.

Conclusion

It is an absolutely fascinating concept to consider. Without God, nothing has any meaning or value. Therefore, morality cannot exist in a world where there is no meaning or value. Good can only be known in a world where people have meaning and value. Evil is the absence of the good. If nothing has meaning or value, then smacking a person would be the same as stepping on a worm. However, we know that human life does hold meaning and value. Why? It is because God has given everything meaning and value because he created it so. Thus, morality can only exist if God exists. God is the lawgiver who has established objective moral codes. Thus, the atheist can do good things in the world. But the atheist can only know good because of the value that God gives the atheist and the world. Thus, when an atheist charges a Christian for some indiscretion, he or she is actually unconsciously appealing to the existence of God.

Before we leave this chapter, let me just add the importance that meaning and value hold for a person which all the more shows the importance that morality holds. Viktor Frankl was a survivor of the Nazi concentration camps. He notes the importance that hope provided individuals in the camps. Frankl, in his book *Man's Search for Meaning*, states that the

---

a Good God, 129.

7. Aquinas, *Summa of the Summa*, 69.

"prisoner who had lost faith in the future—his future—was doomed. With his loss of belief in the future, he also lost his spiritual hold; he let himself decline and became subject to mental and physical decay."[8] He goes on to say that "those who know how close the connection is between the state of mind of a man—his courage and hope, or lack of them—and the state of immunity of his body will understand that a sudden loss of hope and courage can have a deadly effect."[9]

It is my opinion that life without God is not only dangerous eternally, but it is also dangerous in the here and now. A person without transcendence in one's life only holds on to the things of this life. Everything in this life changes and eventually decays. What hope is found in that? None. Not only are there intellectual reasons for believing in God, there are also psychological and emotional reasons for believing in God, as well. Without God, life holds no morality, but it also loses its hope.

---

8. Viktor E. Frankl, *Man's Search for Meaning*, 74.

9. Frankl also adds that his friend's death ultimately came because his anticipated liberation did not come as he expected. He lost hope and then died shortly thereafter. Ibid., 75.

Chapter 8

DO MIRACLES OCCUR?

Thus far, the second unit has described reasons for believing in God. However, the evidence thus far has not indicated whether the deist or the theist interpretation of God is correct. Remember the deist believes in God but does not accept that God is personal. That is to say, the deist does not think that God interacts with creation, thereby the deist does not believe in miracles. The deist's God is likened to a dead-beat dad who neglects humanity to the world of his own making. The deist's God may or may not correct moral injustices in the afterlife, but as far as it relates to the present universe, he has no interaction.

To decipher the existence of a theistic God—one that is both transcendent (separate) from the universe and immanent (involved) in the universe—the apologist needs to evaluate whether there are reasons to believe that God has interacted with the universe after creation. A good way to evaluate this issue is to explore whether God performs miracles in space and time.

For the sake of this book, the working definition of a *miracle* will be *a divine interaction with creation in a manner that does not correspond with the normal operation of events, which does not necessarily contradict the natural order*. Peter Kreeft and Ronald Tacille define a miracle as "*a striking and religiously significant intervention of God in the system of natural causes.*"[1] Thus, a miracle need not be a deed that always stands opposed to nature. Rather, it could very well be a work of God within the normal course of nature. Before looking at the kinds of miracles Jesus performed and modern

---

1. Peter Kreeft and Ronald K. Tacelli, *Handbook of Christian Apologetics: Hundreds of Answers to Crucial Questions*, 109.

examples of the miraculous, attention must first be given to the eighteenth century skeptic David Hume.

The Challenge of David Hume and His Bias

People have accepted the possibility of the miraculous for the vast majority of human history. Greeks, Romans, and Egyptians thought that the miraculous was possible. Magical incantations and divinations were how such feats were believed to occur.[2] In the Age of Enlightenment, emphasis was placed more on reason than divine or magical practices. David Hume took such skepticism a step further.

David Hume (1711–1776) was a Scottish philosopher and historian. It is unclear whether Hume was an atheist or a deist, but his writings tend to indicate the former—it is possible that he was an agnostic.[3] Nonetheless, Hume was highly skeptical of miraculous claims. He held that miracles did not exist and that miracles would require such overwhelming proof that could not deem them as defensible. Hume holds,

> A wise man . . . considers which side is supported by the greater number of experiments . . . A hundred instances of experiments on one side, and fifty on another, afford a doubtful expectation of any event; though a hundred uniform experiments, with only one that is contradictory, reasonably beget a pretty strong degree of assurance. In all cases, we must balance the opposite experiments . . . and deduct the smaller number from the greater, in order to know the exact force of the superior evidence.[4]

Hume argues that unless an event can be tested and experimented, the event cannot be known with any certainty. Thus, any aberration of history, which would certainly include miracles, must be tossed aside due to the person's knowledge of the ordinary course of events.

While Hume's argument may seem convincing at first, further investigation into Hume's claims reveals three major flaws with his logic. First, Hume holds that events that are known to a person but are unrepeatable cannot be accepted with any certainty. However, if this is true, this discredits all historical investigation. By all means, England was the strongest nation

---

2. This is comparable to what one finds in paganism. The thought is that the elements can be manipulated to bring forth certain blessings or curses.

3. During this era, it is sometimes difficult to decipher whether a writer was a deist or an atheist as deism was extremely popular at the time. Both the deist and atheist deny the involvement of God in human affairs.

4. David Hume, *An Enquiry Concerning Human Understanding*, 110–111.

in the 1700s. The American patriots should not have been able to defeat the "red coats" but they did. Should one dismiss the outcome of the Revolutionary War because it seems implausible that a ragtag group of farmers defeated the strongest military regime of the day? Certainly not! By Hume's logic, no one could know that I had bacon and eggs this morning for breakfast even though I did—or did I? It would be impossible to know since history is unrepeatable.

Furthermore, human experience can only measure reality on an extremely small scale according to Humeanism. I have not traveled but to a few states. One of my lifelong dreams is to travel out west to see the Rocky Mountains. Should the existence of the Rocky Mountains be denied based on my inability to view them? Certainly not! Yet, this is the rationale one holds with Hume's logic. Things that are not readily seen and repeatable cannot be believed.

Second, Hume is guilty of circular reasoning. *Circular reasoning* occurs when a person begins to argue with what they are trying to prove. The conclusion is built into the argument to the point that the person argues in a circle. For instance, claiming that the Bible is the Word of God because the Bible says it's the Word of God is an example of circular reasoning. The person has proven nothing. Claiming that one is right because he's never wrong is another example of circular reasoning.

Hume is guilty of circular reasoning because he says that miracles don't occur, therefore they cannot occur. Hume strongly holds that God, if he exists, does not interact with the world. Because God does not interact with the world, miracles cannot exist. Again, Hume has not proven that God has not interacted with the world. Even if it were shown that God did interact with the world, Hume would reject God's interaction with the world because he believes that God does not interact with the world. Therefore, miracles cannot happen because miracles are God's interaction with the world. Do you see how this is problematic?

Third, Hume has a major problem with bias. While listing all the cases of Hume's bias would cause this text to be far larger than necessary, suffice it to say, Hume does not believe in miracles which leads him to deny miracles. Hume has the right to reject miracles all he likes, just as a person has the right to deny the existence of Oreo milkshakes. However, a blind rejection of a thing does not mean that the rejection is based on evidence. One can deny the existence of Oreo milkshakes all one likes, but I appreciate the evidence for their existence by obtaining an Oreo milkshake anytime I come near a Cookout restaurant. The question exists: Have miracles occurred? Only one miracle is needed to debunk Hume's humanism.

The Kinds of Miracles Jesus Performed

The New Testament records numerous miracles. The Gospels are the epicenter of the New Testament as they record the life and ministry of Jesus of Nazareth. The Gospel writers, called *evangelists,* document numerous miracles associated with Jesus's ministry. The miracles of Jesus play such a prominent role in Jesus's life and ministry that, as Thomas D. Lea and David Alan Black denote, "It is important not to detach the miracles of Jesus from his teaching and the general course of his life. The discipline of apologetics studies the Gospel miracles as supernatural evidences of Jesus' divinity."[5] The Gospels indicate four categories of miracles performed by Jesus.

First, Jesus performed miracles of *healing.* Comprising the largest category of Jesus's miracles were personal healings. Jesus often took time to heal individuals of various infirmities so much that even skeptics readily accept Jesus's healing ministry. Marcus Borg, a prominent member of the ultra-skeptical Jesus Seminar, wrote, "Despite the difficulty which miracles pose for the modern mind, on historical grounds it is virtually indisputable that Jesus was a healer and exorcist."[6] A. M. Hunter adds that for the healing miracles of Jesus the "historical evidence is excellent."[7] Jesus healed the blind (Matt. 11:5), deaf (Mark 7:37), and physically disabled (Matt. 15:30). The first category of miracles demonstrated Jesus's power over sickness and disease.

Second, Jesus performed miracles of *exorcisms.* As noted earlier, even skeptics readily admit that Jesus was an exorcist. An exorcism is the casting out of a demonic spirit. One of the more humorous instances of Jesus's exorcist ministry occurred in Gadara. Two-demon possessed men had been living in the tombs and had become extremely violent because of their demonic possession. When the demons saw Jesus nearby, they begged that he not torment them before their time (Matt. 8:29). Instead, Jesus cast them into a herd of pigs (Matt. 8:30–32). The pig farmer became irritated at Jesus because he sent the pigs over a cliff. Instead of being joyous over the newfound freedom that the demon-possessed men had, the farmers sent Jesus away (Matt. 8:34) because he financially hurt their pig farming business. The second category of miracles illustrated Jesus's power over hell and the demonic realm.

Third, Jesus performed miracles of *resurrection.* By resurrection, it is meant that a person is raised from the dead. One of the most popular

---

5. Thomas D. Lea and David Alan Black, *The New Testament: Its Background and Message,* 2nd ed., 184.

6. Marcus Borg, *Jesus, A New Vision: Spirit, Culture, and the Life of Discipleship,* 61.

7. A. M. Hunter, *Jesus: Lord and Saviour,* 63.

examples of Jesus's resurrection ministry is his raising of Lazarus from the dead in John 11. A bit of semantics is in order here. There is quite a bit of difference between Jesus's own resurrection and his raising of the dead during his earthly ministry. By that, I mean to say that when Jesus raised individuals back to life, he did so with the full expectation that the person would die again physically. However, when Jesus was resurrected from the dead, he would never die again physically as his body had been glorified. Some have used the term *resuscitation* to refer to Jesus's ministry of raising the dead while on earth. Lazarus would eventually die again, but Jesus would not. When Jesus raises the dead at the end of time, it will be a resurrection in its purest form. The bodies of those raised will be changed into an incorruptible body. All of this illustrates Jesus's power over life and death. He has the authority to provide eternal life as it has been given to him by the Father (John 5:25–29). The literal resurrections performed by Jesus and ultimately his own verifies Jesus's authority over life.[8]

Finally, Jesus performed miracles over *nature*. This category of miracles is the most controversial among scholars. Quite honestly, such skepticism stems from a bias bent towards materialism and/or naturalism. These ideas hold that the physical world and the natural world is all there is. Therefore, nothing could supersede its ordinary functions. Yet, if one is to be truly open-minded, then the person needs to evaluate each historical and miraculous claim on a case by case basis. On several occasions, Jesus is said to perform works that override the natural physical laws. Jesus's first ministry was changing water into wine (John 2:1–12). Jesus is also said to have walked on water, confirmed by two Gospel accounts (Matt. 14:22–33; Mark 6:45–52). Jesus caused a fig tree to wither and die, also confirmed by two Gospel accounts (Matt. 21:18–22; Mark 11:12–14). Jesus also miraculously saves the disciples from an intense storm by speaking to the storm and calming it. This miracle is verified in three accounts (Matt. 8:23–27; Mark 4:35–41; and Luke 8:22–25). Jesus feeds 4,000 Gentiles[9] with seven loaves of bread and a few fish, confirmed in two accounts (Matt. 15:32–39; Mark 8:1–13).

Outside of the resurrection of Jesus, the only miracle recorded in all four Gospel accounts is the feeding of the 5,000 with five loaves of bread and two fish (Matt. 14:13–21; Mark 6:30–44; Luke 9:10–17; and John 6:1–15). These miraculous feedings were incredible especially when one considers that only men were counted in the group. By the time women were counted,

---

8. If you are looking for an evidential apologetic for Jesus's resurrection, it can be found on chapter 11 in unit 3.

9. Or at least a mix of Gentiles and Jews, probably predominantly Gentile.

the number escalates to over 10,000. When one considers that the average household had six children, the number of people fed by Jesus scales to over 20,000 individuals with leftovers to spare! Historically speaking, the fact that numerous Gospels report these nature miracles speaks well for the power of Jesus. Interestingly, the miracles related to a fish found with a coin in its mouth (Matt. 17:24–27); Jesus's turning the water into wine (John 2:1–11); and the first miraculous catch of fish (Matt. 5:1–11) are the only nature miracles that have singular verification by one Gospel account.[10]

Examples of Modern Miracles

Did the Gospel writers invent the miracles of Jesus? This is an objection that skeptics may pose. However, it must be asked if God continuously works miracles today. It could be that God worked miracles in the past and has ceased working them today. However, if it can be shown that God continues to perform miraculous tasks today, the authenticity for the biblical record of miracles performed in Jesus's name is further verified. All it takes to dismiss Hume's anti-supernatural bias is evidence for one miracle. This also discredits deism as well.

Craig Keener has written a two-volume work that records numerous modern-day miraculous accounts which he titles *Miracles: The Credibility of the New Testament Accounts*. Throughout the book, Keener provides various accounts of individuals who were healed of blindness, disabilities, and various ailments. There are even accounts of modern individuals being raised from the dead. While some of the hundreds of examples that Keener provides are more verifiable than others, the sheer volume illustrates the weakness of the arguments from both Hume and deism. One miracle is all it takes to dismiss such objections. It would not be surprising if the reader has experienced some form of miracle in his or her life.

Personally, I have experienced miracles firsthand. One of the more remarkable accounts occurred during my stay at Fruitland Baptist Bible College in Hendersonville, North Carolina where a woman was healed from an injury that caused her to temporarily go blind. She was playing baseball with her children. She ran to get a ball that had been hit into a field. As she reached down to retrieve the ball, she snagged her eye on a weed. The weed deeply entered her eye. The doctors told her that she would never regain sight because the weed had severed her optic nerve. The entire

---

10. However, the miraculous catch of fish is shown to have occurred a second time in a post-resurrection miracle recorded in John 21:1–14. So even the miraculous catch of fish has multiple eyewitness verification.

school prayed for the young woman. We left to go home for the weekend with somber hearts. The next week in chapel, her husband announced that over the weekend she began to see black and white images out of her eye. By Monday, she was seeing colored images out of her eye. By Tuesday's chapel service, the husband reported that his wife was seeing better out of her eye then than she had before since she was severely nearsighted. God had worked a miracle before us all.

Conclusion

As we have noted in this chapter, the skepticism of David Hume is not the challenge that many hold it to be when investigating miracles. We have seen that Hume's philosophy comes from circular reasoning and an anti-supernatural bias. Luckily, we have a multitude of reported miracles in the Bible and in modernity to show that God is very active in the world. While we only need one miracle to disprove deism, we have hundreds of cases reported in Keener's two volume book on miracles in addition to one of the greatest miracles of all time—the resurrection of Jesus of Nazareth.

Chapter 9

THEODICY

Can a Good, Powerful God Exist in a World of Evil?

This chapter will likely be one of the most emotionally charged of the entire book, and for good reason. When bad things happen to a person, regardless of whether that thing happens to the person in question, or a person's loved one; the individual wants answers. My professor Gary Habermas noted in class, "In my opinion, it is possible that seventy or even eighty percent of religious doubt could be driven in large part by people's emotions."[1] Previously, we noted that God was all-powerful and all-loving. If this is the case, then why does an all-powerful and all-loving God permit such horrible things to happen in life?

Questions like these bring up the issue known by theologians as *theodicy*. *Theodicy* comes from two Greek terms: *theos* meaning "God," and *dikē* meaning "justice" or "righteous punishment." In other words, the term relates to the question of God's goodness in a world full of evil. The late theologian Thomas Oden defines theodicy as "the attempt to speak rightly of God's justice (*theos-dikē*) under conditions of suffering and evil in which it is assailed. Theodicy is an intellectual discipline that seeks to clarify the hidden aspect of God's goodness despite apparent contradictions of that goodness in history."[2] Before we begin, it needs to be noted that the problem

---

1. Gary R. Habermas, "New Testament Creeds," Lecture, Lynchburg, VA, Liberty University, June 2019. Used with permission.
2. Thomas C. Oden, *The Word of Life: Systematic Theology*, Vol. II, 414.

of evil is not only an issue for Christianity, but it is a concern for every worldview. Different worldviews handle the issue better than others. As we shall see, different worldviews handle the problem of evil in numerous ways. It is in my estimation that classic orthodox Christianity provides the best answer available to the problem of evil.

The Question of God's Power and Goodness

Living in the third century BC, ancient Greek philosopher Epicurus asked, "Is [God] willing to prevent evil, but not able? Then he is impotent. Is he able, but not willing? Then he is malevolent. Is he both able and willing? Whence then is evil?"[3] In other words, God must not be all powerful to stop evil if he is loving, or he must not be loving if he is all-powerful and does not stop evil. Several have tried to respond to this issue in numerous ways.

First, some claim that the existence of evil must *deny the existence of any divine being.* How could a Being of any capable sort develop a world of parasitic animals that eat away their hosts from the inside-out, or a world where children are abused and neglected? Atheist such as Christopher Hitchens and Richard Dawkins often deny the existence of God on these grounds. However, they have not solved anything by denying God's existence. In fact, they have only made the problem worse. What do you say to a person who has been raped and whose offender was never caught in a godless universe? "I'm sorry. That's the way life goes." Or what would an atheist say to a child born with a terrible cancer that only permits him or her to live a few years? "Tough luck, kid. That's the way the cookie crumbles."

Even in a Buddhist or Hindu worldview, there is the chance for a better life when the person is reincarnated. While theodicy is a problem, at least in a theistic universe, there is the possibility for ultimate judgment for the uncaught criminal. Christians hold that God will judge each person for the good and evil that they have committed on this earth (Heb. 9:27). For the child born with a fatal disease, Christians have the hope for a better life in eternity for the child. Nothing like that is found in the atheist's worldview. There is no hope. There is no promise. There is nothing but meaningless heartache and meaningless pain. Injustice rules the day in a secularist's universe. How depressing, indeed!

Second, some worldviews hold that *God is not all loving* but is all-powerful. Like Viktor Frankl, Elie Wiesel was a Holocaust survivor. In his book *Night,* Wiesel recounts the horrors he experienced in the Nazi concentration

3. Epicurus, in Lactanius, *De Ira Dei (On the Wrath of God),* Kindle ed.

camps. Wiesel argues that God is powerful but is not always loving and good. Wiesel writes, "Never shall I forget those moments which murdered my god and my soul and turned my dreams to dust."[4] Wiesel lost his faith in God's goodness and justice while in the concentration camps. Wiesel, in a heartbreaking fashion, denotes, "Why should I bless his name? The eternal, lord of the universe, the all-powerful and terrible was silent. What had I to thank him for?"[5] For Wiesel, if one denies God's goodness, then the problem of evil disappears. Granted, suffering the horrors that any Holocaust survivor endured would easily lead one to lose all sense of God's goodness. I have personally looked into the eyes of individuals who were Holocaust survivors. Their eyes tell the story of the hell they endured. However, denying the goodness and/or justice of God does not answer the moral goodness found in the world and the need for a Moral Lawgiver. The only way to claim that the Holocaust was evil is to know that there must be a moral good. Losing trust in God's goodness and justice only leads to a similar fate that the secular worldview holds, if not even worse. At least in the secular worldview, death brings eternal nothingness to an individual.

In a universe where God is not good leaves the door open to the possibility that God may be morally evil. If God is evil, then good would be the absence of evil. But this is nonsensical. Evil can only be known if good is first acknowledged. For instance, HVAC professionals do not speak about cooling a home. They speak in terms of adding and removing heat. Why? It is because heat is energy. Cold is the absence of heat. Thus, you might think of air conditioners working to remove the heat (or energy) from a home. Just as cold is the absence of heat, so evil is the absence of good. Thus, denying God's moral goodness fails because you have removed the standard by which goodness can be known. Furthermore, how is one to trust God if he is not loving and kind? Yes, you may have questions as to why God allowed certain things to happen. But losing God's goodness leads to far more problems than solutions. This option has too many flaws.

Third, some argue that *God is not all-powerful* but is loving and kind. This is especially true in open theism which holds that God does not know future events, or at least some future events.[6] If God's power is restricted in some sense, then his moral goodness is redeemed. By claiming that God does not know the future, he is restricted by time and, thereby, cannot stop evil from taking place. The problem with this view is that there is no promise

---

4. Elie Wiesel, *Night*, 32.

5. Ibid., 31.

6. Gregory A. Boyd, *God of the Possible: A Biblical Introduction to the Open View of God*, 53–88.

that God could defeat evil in the first place. If God is overly restricted in his power, then it might be that he could become victorious in the end, but it is far from a certainty. Thus, no one has any hope that good will win in the end, especially in more extreme views of open theism. Furthermore, God would be unable to promise to bring all things to a good end for his children as he does in Romans 8:28. The best he could do is guess that everything will work out in the end.[7] In an attempt to defend God's goodness, the open theist has instead emasculated God which is nowhere close to solving the problem of theodicy—it actually worsens the problem as it could be that God won't win in the end! Thus, we are no better than Wiesel's argument or even the secularist argument because we are left with no promised hope.

Fourth, some contend that *good and evil do not exist*. Some will attempt to solve this problem by arguing that good and evil are merely illusions and are not real. Buddhism and many eastern religions hold this concept. By dismissing anything as good and evil, they have attempted to solve the problem by casting everything as an illusion. Therefore, pain and pleasure are not real. They are figments of your imagination. Did you stub your toe leading you to say a bad word? I'm sorry. You just think you're in pain because pain doesn't exist. Did someone steal your wallet? I'm sorry, you can't charge the criminal because there is no such thing as evil. It's all in your mind. Obviously, this logic doesn't work.

Furthermore, no real solution is given to the problem of evil. The advocate of this position merely hides his or her head in the sand pretending that the problem of evil does not exist. But try telling that to the survivors of the Holocaust (i.e., Frankl and Wiesel) or the victims of Pol Pot's killing fields. I am sure you will find yourself faced with a peculiar look staring back at you and perhaps some stern words accompanying them.

Finally, the Christian theist argues that *God is good and powerful and allows evil to bring about a greater good in the end*. This response is both biblically sound and philosophically valid. God allows evil to exist in order to allow human freedom. This will be further expounded in the next section. The position goes on to note that the good and powerful God will bless individuals in heaven and right all wrongs committed on earth. Evil will be judged. This position holds the least problems in the end. Justice becomes reality as does grace for the victims.[8] How does the Christian theist work

---

7. Granted, not all open theists hold to this position. I am admittedly using a bit of exaggeration at this point. Theological differences are often nuanced in several areas. Nonetheless, I am representing the more extreme views of open theism. Or rather, following the logic to its natural end.

8. See Jesus's Parable of the Rich Man and Lazarus in Luke 16:19–31 for an example of this upside-down kingdom.

through the problems of evil? This will be answered by the following two sections.

Good and Evil Defined and the Role of Human Freedom

Theologians divide the problem of evil into two categories: *moral evil* which describes the evil acts that people perform against one another, and *natural evil* which inquires as to why God would allow such destructive natural disasters to occur. First, let's examine moral evil. Why is it that God allows individuals to do great acts of violence toward others? As I write these words, I read a news report of two men who were caught in their quest to molest a three-year-old girl.[9] A three-year-old! If ever a person had thoughts about doing someone harm, it's after hearing about adults harming young children. You could probably think of several evil actions committed against another person, or perhaps those acts have been done to you. When especially considering the works done to us, the problem of evil becomes especially emotional. Many individuals suffer from post-traumatic stress disorder (PTSD) due to the trauma endured by intense tragedy that has incurred at some point in their life. So, why would a loving, powerful God allow such acts of evil?

God allows human beings to do such acts because of the freedom of the will that he has given to humanity. If God interjects himself every time an immoral act takes place, then people would not be free moral agents. Rather, they would be something comparable to automatons or androids. Consider John 3:16 which says, "For God loved the world in this way: He gave his one and only Son, so that everyone who believes in him will not perish but have eternal life." Notice the choice given in one's response to God's love.[10] So, why is human freedom important?

Freedom is necessary for a person to experience love. In illustrating the Triune nature of God, Norman Geisler compared the nature of God to love. Geisler explains, "love involves three elements: A lover, a beloved,

---

9. 10NewsStaff, "Men Accused of Plotting to Groom and Rape a 3-year-Old Girl," *WFMYNews2.com* (February 6, 2019), retrieved June 27, 2019, https://www.wfmynews2.com/article/news/crime/men-accused-of-plotting-to-groom-and-rape-a-3-year-old-girl/83-3eaea098-aa28-49d9-ae41-67375dc64302?fbclid=IwAR2cKky-dLfxyihxo8NZ9gFgvlXDKyLZv1ZUq2U_wLdOVeSc7fnMch16jSvs

10. It is interesting when one considers Pharaoh's hardened heart in the book of Exodus. While God says he will harden Pharaoh's heart, notice it was Pharaoh's choice to turn his heart from God once God showed mercy.

and a spirit of love."[11] The lover gives the love. The beloved is the recipient of the lover's love. The spirit of love is the love that freely exists between both parties. Think about a man asking out a girl for a date. The girl has the opportunity to accept or deny the boy's invitation. If she accepts, both individuals may come to love one another. But if one party forces the other person into the relationship, then love does not truly exist because it is one-sided and not reciprocated. Love must be freely given and must be freely received. Otherwise, it's not love.

The apostle John notes that God is love (1 John 4:16). If God is love, then the rejection of God leads to evil. Evil then becomes known as the absence of good or the absence of love. Think about the illustration of HVAC systems as mentioned previously. Cold is the absence of heat. Likewise, hate is the absence of love and evil is the absence of good. But if God is to create a world where individuals have the freedom to accept his love, then he must also allow the possibility that some will not receive that love. Therein, evil is a condition that stems from a person's rejection of God's goodness and love. But the possibility of evil must exist if love is to truly be given and freely received. Thus, evil is not created by God. Rather, it is the byproduct of human rebellion against God.

But one may ask, what of injustices committed where the criminal has not repented? Since God is just, then it stands to reason that he will judge those who harbor hate and do evil. Paul notes that every person will stand before God at some point (Rom. 14:12). Furthermore, the writer of Hebrews reminds that it is a fearful thing to fall into the hands of the living God without one's sins forgiven (Heb. 10:31). God will judge the evil of the world in due time. However, it must be remembered that when the moment that God switches from an age of grace to an age of judgment, it will be too late for a person to repent. The reason Jesus hasn't returned yet is to provide lost sinners a further chance to receive his grace and be saved. But a day will come when God brings an age of judgment. At that time, all wrongs will be made right.

Some may argue, how can God watch on while innocent people suffer? I'm not so sure that God is far apart from the suffering victim. In John 11, the apostle tells the story of Jesus's encounter with Martha and Mary. Martha and Mary had recently lost their brother Lazarus. Martha, Mary, Lazarus, and Jesus were all good friends. Even though Jesus knew the end result of what he was about to do—he knew Lazarus would rise from the dead—even still, "Jesus wept" (John 11:35). Jesus acknowledges that when a person gives a cup of water to someone in need, the person has done a good

---

11. Norman L. Geisler, *Systematic Theology: In One Volume*, 551.

deed for him, also (Matt. 10:42). I think it is quite possible that God suffers with those who suffer. God is not watching from afar. He is in the trenches with the victim. God will bring judgment in eternity and often in this life. Nevertheless, God will bring justice eventually.

Natural Evil

A brief word needs to be said about a second kind of evil: *natural evil*. Natural disasters are considered by theologians to be natural evil. When a person's home is destroyed, insurance companies will call the disaster an "act of God." However, it is not entirely clear that one could truly call such disasters evil. Yes, it is true that lives are destroyed by hurricanes, floods, tornadoes, and tsunamis. However, could one say that God had evil intent behind these events? Probably not, and we know this for a couple of reasons.

First, disasters cannot be called evil if they are part of God's *natural order*. That is to say, God has designed the world with certain cycles and patterns. Hurricanes may bring great destruction to an area; however, it may bring rain that is essential for crops in other areas. Living in North Carolina, we are prone to experience hurricanes and tropical storms. The coastline of North Carolina sits out in the ocean much like the chin of a boxer awaiting to get hit. However, there have been times when local farmers have hoped to get a tropical storm. When the land becomes dry from the hot, humid, summers; tropical systems may help the water table recover. Thus, while the tropical storm is a nuisance for coastal Carolinians, it is greatly beneficial for farmers living inland.

Volcanic eruptions serve as another example of how a destructive natural force can bring benefits to the earth. Volcanic eruptions provide nutrients to the soil in areas around the mountain. The ash may contain minerals that are beneficial to plants.[12] While the volcanic eruption may bring great destruction around the peak of the mountain, it may also bring great benefit to the earth in general.

The gazelle's death may seem tragic at first, however if the lion did not hunt the gazelle the gazelle population would increase so much that the gazelles would die of disease and famine. With no food, the lions would die. Thus, creation is designed with checks and balances in place.

The trouble comes when individuals build homes in areas prone to disasters (e.g., on the side of an active volcano, flood prone areas, and the like). God may allow disasters to take place for the good of the earth. However, if

---

12. See "What are some good things that volcanoes do?," *OregonState.edu,* http://volcano.oregonstate.edu/what-are-some-good-things-volcanoes-do.

a person builds a home in an area that is prone to experience such disasters, can we really blame God for the calamity? It would be like a person breaking into a neighbor's home, coming face to face with the homeowners' indoor Rottweiler, and then blaming the homeowner for the bite the intruder experiences on the backside while trying to escape. There is a price to pay for building a home in a perceived earthly paradise.

Second, natural disasters cannot be said to be evil if they are *intended to bring judgment*. While judgment may not be pleasant to consider, God is completely justified in destroying a civilization that is violent and depraved. Had the United States not joined the Allies in World War II and defeated Nazi Germany, many more deaths would have occurred in the concentration camps. Furthermore, it is possible that Germany could have invaded other nations leading to more lives being tortured and executed. It would be evil not to stop such a civilization. God cannot be said to be evil when bringing disaster. Thus, natural disasters are not a reason to deny God's goodness or power.

To some degree, it seems as if the antagonist builds himself into a corner. On the one hand, the antagonist blames God for not intervening when evil occurs. But, on the other hand, the antagonist blames God when he does intervene, accusing God of the evil. In such cases, the skeptic's antagonism shows a greater problem with the heart than it does the head.

When Christians Behave Badly

Before leaving the topic of theodicy, we need to deal with a problem that has faced Christians for some time. What do we do when the pain we experience comes from fellow believers? Even some pastors have rejected their faith because of pain experienced by the church.[13] For others, they may keep their faith but give up on the church forever. I, for one, am an individual who has been greatly hurt by the church while in active pastoral ministry. Pastoral ministry has not always been easy for me because I am listed as an INTJ according to Myers-Briggs, which means I am not always the most bubbly, extroverted person one will meet. I am not a recluse. In fact, I can sometimes be known as a blabbermouth especially when talking about theology and apologetics. Nevertheless, I have not always found myself in the "in crowd" in congregational life. Quite frankly, the pain I have experienced

---

13. Robert F. Worth, "From Bible-Belt Pastor to Atheist Leader," *NYTimes* (Aug. 22, 2012), retrieved July 15, 2019, https://www.nytimes.com/2012/08/26/magazine/from-bible-belt-pastor-to-atheist-leader.html.

from friendly fire has been far worse than that which I received from enemy lines. This has led me to deal with bouts of anxiety and depression.

The church's greatest enemy is not the atheist, the Muslim, or the progressive politician. The greatest enemy of the church is the church! Isn't it odd? The church is the devil's greatest enemy, but the church is often the devil's greatest tool. It is disheartening to hear about so many church splits. I was told of one church that had split over the choice of toilet paper. Yes, toilet paper! As one pastor eloquently noted, "That's the reason the church went down the toilet."

Experiencing church hurt as I have and the discouragements of hearing of churches that split over the most juvenile issues, it would be easy to throw up my hands and give up on my faith as I once did. However, these experiences have ironically strengthened my faith. Odd? Sure. But I have discovered five realities about Christianity that remain true no matter what other Christians may do or say.

1. Christianity is true even when the church is bad because *not all Christians are genuine in their faith.* We must remember that not everyone is what they claim to be. I could claim to be the President of the United States but that doesn't mean that I truly am. Not everyone who claims to be a Christian genuinely is a Christian. This shouldn't be surprising. Jesus taught that some people would act like they were sheep (one of God's children), but they would actually be wolves pretending to be sheep (Matt. 7:15). In the same message, Jesus notes that "Not everyone who says to me, 'Lord, Lord,' will enter the kingdom of heaven, but only the one who does the will of my Father in heaven" (Matt. 7:21). That statement is one of the scariest statements in all the Bible. Some who profess Christ are not really his followers.

    In his book *City of God,* Augustine of Hippo compares and contrasts two cities—the City of God which represents the genuine citizens of heaven (i.e., genuine believers) and the City of the Pagans (i.e., unbelievers). In Book I, chapter 35; Augustine provides the following evaluation, noting that the city is referencing the City of God:

    > But let this city bear in mind, that among her enemies lie hid those who are destined to be fellow-citizens, that she may not think it a fruitless labor to bear what they inflict as enemies until they become confessors of the faith. So, too, as long as she is a stranger in the world, the city of God has in her communion, and bound to her by the sacraments, some who shall not eternally dwell in the lot of the saints. Of these, some are not now recognized; others declare themselves, and

do not hesitate to make common cause with our enemies in murmuring against God, whose sacramental badge they wear. These men you may today see thronging the churches with us, tomorrow crowding the theatres with the godless.[14]

What a fascinating observation! Some of those who are of the world will eventually accept Christ. Even though a person may be in the depth of sin at the time you see them, he or she may eventually profess Christ and become part of the City of God. In contrast, the one who sits in church every Sunday and claims to be a Christian, may be no more of Christ than the person on the street that you deem a sinner.

2. Christianity is still true even when the church is bad because the *truth claims of Christianity are not dependent on the behaviors of its followers.* Generally speaking, the followers of a movement represent its founder. Unfortunately, this is not always true of Christianity. Christians often behave badly. Nevertheless, the claims of Christ are built upon objective facts which are independent of the actions of Christian adherents. At the end of the day, either Jesus rose from the dead or he didn't. If he did, then the bad actions of a few do not discredit the factual basis of the resurrection. When Christians are good, Christ is risen. When Christians are bad, Christ is still risen. Christianity remains true regardless of what Christians may do. I may not like the actions of those who follow a certain President of the United States. They may act horribly and arrogant. But it still doesn't change the fact that the person in office is still President whether I like him/her or not. This goes back to what we mentioned about the transcendent nature of truth. Truth is not based on emotional preference, but rather on objective fact. For this reason, I can still remain a Christian even when I may not like some of his followers.

How do we know who is truly of the City of God? On the one hand, only God knows for sure. But on the other hand, Jesus said that good trees will produce good fruit (Matt. 3:10; 7:17–19). There exist certain markers that identify the genuine saint of God. It may surprise you to note that church attendance and having one's name on the church roll are not markers of genuine Christianity. I do believe that church attendance is important. However, it is possible to attend church every Sunday and still be lost. The genuine markers of the child of God are found in the fruit of the Spirit. These fruits do not come

---

14. Augustine of Hippo, *The City of God* I.35., in *St. Augustine's City of God and Christian Doctrine*, 21.

from a person's attempt to be a Christian, but rather the manifestation of the Spirit of God working within the individual. The fruit of the Spirit are identified by Paul as "love, joy, peace, patience, kindness, goodness, faithfulness, gentleness, and self-control" (Gal. 5:22). If self-professed Christian has no love, no joy, no peace, and so on; then it is highly doubtful that the person holds a genuine relationship with Christ. Why? Because when God enters people's lives, he does not leave them the same. As I tell everyone I meet, I should have a construction sign on my head which says, "God at Work." I am not what I should be, but I am not what I used to be.

3. Christianity is still true even when the church is bad because *Christians do not escape judgment.* It is a popular myth that is propagated in some circles that Christians will not be judged. I have heard pastors quote from Psalm 103:12 claiming that a Christian's sins are removed as far as the east from the west to be remembered no more. The popular thinking is that the Christian will not have to face judgment. While it is true that a Christian's sins have been cleansed and the child of God is redeemed, it is not true that the Christian will not face judgment. The writer of Hebrews contends that every person will die once and then face the judgment of God (Heb. 9:27). Everyone means every person, including Christians. Paul also denotes that the child of God will stand before the Judgment Seat of Christ (Rom. 14:10; 1 Cor. 3:11–13; and 2 Cor. 5:10). When a person stands before the Judgment Seat of Christ, their actions will be judged. Their good deeds will be offered back as rewards and their bad deeds will be burned in the fire of God's judgment. So, don't think that Christians can do anything they want without any repercussion. Each person will give an account of themselves on the day of Judgment.

4. Christianity is still true even when the church is bad because *the changing culture has deeply influenced the church.* Many churches—especially in smaller, rural areas—have been impacted by the changing culture. Everything around them is changing and it scares them. The only sense of stability that many older congregants have is found in the church. So, when changes come to church, it is met with great hostility and obstinance. Why? Because the church is the only thing that hasn't changed for them. For that reason, I encourage young ministers to steer the church more like an ocean liner than a jet ski. An ocean liner must be turned slowly, otherwise it capsizes.

When people become frightened, they build defense mechanisms around themselves. If someone challenges those mechanisms, they lash out at the one trying to tear down the walls. Understand, we must be challenged as a church. But I believe the reason why many churches are experiencing increasing hostilities within their ranks is due to the fear that has come with a culture that is changing at an increasingly rapid pace. This doesn't make any hurt that is experienced acceptable and neither does this take away any pain that has been experienced. I am merely trying to explain one of the possible reasons behind some of the hostilities taking place in the modern church. We need be reminded that although the culture changes as quickly a rocket traveling to space, the God of all creation does not (Num. 23:19; 1 Sam. 15:29; and Heb. 13:8). Our sense of stability should not be found in the church. Rather, our sense of stability should be found in God.

5. Christianity is still true even when the church is bad because *salvation is based on grace and love and not on our good works*. Lastly, one must be reminded that a church is a place for the sick (Luke 5:31). Even the best Christian among us is nothing more than a broken sinner who has been saved by the grace of God. Salvation does not come by our goodness. It does not come by anything that is merited on our part. Salvation comes solely by the grace of God given to us (Eph. 2:8–10). So, we should realize that people are broken. We will get hurt because we are all broken people. But remember, it is not the good works of others that brought you to Christ, and it will not be the good works of others that keeps you in the faith. You are saved and sustained by God's grace though faith and nothing of yourselves. So, let our boasting be done in Christ. Let us be thankful for the grace of God that is working within us if we have professed faith in Christ. If you haven't professed your faith in Christ, now would be a good time to do so.[15]

Conclusion

This chapter is longer than most and for good reason. The issue of theodicy is one of the greatest challenges and one of the most frequently asked questions pertaining to Christian doctrine. All worldviews must deal with the problem of evil. Only Christianity offers an acceptable answer to the challenges brought forth by a world inundated with evil and despair. God allowed moral evil to occur because he allowed the existence of free will. He allowed human beings to be free in order that they might experience the fullness of his love. Love must be freely given and freely received for love

---

15. See Romans 10:9 for further information.

to exist. God the Lover offers his love to his creation. The beloved creation has the opportunity to respond or reject the love freely given by its Creator. When that love is rejected, evil is the natural byproduct.

For natural evil, we note that God has created the universe with certain systems with checks and balances ingrained. If someone builds in an area that is prone to suffer from the effects of natural disasters, then the person cannot really blame God in that sense. It would be just like someone stepping in front of an oncoming train and then blaming the engineer of the train for the collision.

Lastly, we also noted that the truth of Christianity is not based on the bad actions of its adherents. The truth of Christianity rises and falls on the historicity of Jesus's deity, his death, and his famed resurrection. If Jesus rose from the dead, then Christianity is still true regardless of what others do in his name.

Yes, there is evil in the world. Yes, we will get hurt. But, the wonderful news is that because Christianity is true, the child of God has a promise of better days ahead. The Christian has the promise that everything will work out in the end (Rom. 8:28) and that the child of God will experience the bliss of a new heavenly creation (Rev. 21 and 22). There is an answer to the problem of evil. The answer is found in the death, burial, and resurrection of Jesus.

Take a few moments to see how you would respond to the following objections.

1. There is no evidence for God's existence. Why do you believe in God?
2. Because there is evil in this world, God most certainly couldn't exist.
3. I believe in God, but I don't think he works in the world. He certainly doesn't do miracles.
4. I am an atheist. How can you Christians claim to be moral and good when you Christians led the Crusades and the Inquisition? Weren't there some Christians in favor of slavery?
5. I can be a moral and happy person without God.

UNIT 3

The Historicity of Jesus and the Veracity of Scripture

The final unit of the *Layman's Manual on Christian Apologetics* is devoted to what is often called "positive apologetics." Christianity is the only religion that can offer this. *Positive apologetics* presents an evidential defense for the worldview being given. That is, it offers reasons in favor of the worldview. In contrast, *negative apologetics* attacks other competing worldviews. The previous units have given explanations on how one can know truth and why one should believe in God's existence. It is in this unit where the rubber meets the road. For it is here where one ultimately finds reasons to believe in Jesus of Nazareth as God's Messiah. Whereas Unit 1 employed a bit of philosophy and Unit 2 involved theology, Unit 3 will use historical methodologies to show that Jesus of Nazareth was resurrected from the dead and that the New Testament is historically reliable.

Chapter 11 will center on the resurrection of Jesus focusing on Gary Habermas's minimal facts approach and my RISEN acronym. Chapter 12 will evaluate the manuscript evidence for the reliability of the New Testament's message. Chapter 13 will examine the rules of canonicity that were used to decide which documents made the New Testament canon. Chapter 14 will provide the latest and greatest archaeological finds verifying the biblical message, particularly the New Testament. Chapter 15 will discuss the debate over inconsistencies of Scripture. Are there inconsistencies in the Scripture or do individuals have a misunderstanding surrounding the biblical text? Chapter 16 will discuss the messianic prophecies of the Old Testament that relate to Jesus of Nazareth. Did Jesus fulfill these prophecies? This final unit is perhaps one of the most important in the book. For the lynchpin of Christianity is found in the resurrection of Jesus.

Chapter 10

HISTORICITY OF JESUS'S RESURRECTION

As mentioned in the unit review, only Christianity has positive arguments to give in its favor. That is to say, only the Judeo-Christian worldview can provide evidence for its truthfulness. The historical evidence for other world religious leaders is scant at best. The earliest biography we have of Muhammed dates to around 749 AD which was written around 118 years after Muhammed's death.[1] The biography for the Buddha did not appear until around 600–800 years after Siddharta Gautama lived. This led one biographer of the Buddha to concede that "there was no consensus across the various Buddhist traditions as to what constituted the canon, and the collections of texts became so large that they surpassed the comprehension of any single individual. Buddhism has therefore never had anything quite like the Bible or the Koran."[2] He goes on to say that the "first Buddhist works with named authors did not appear until the second century CE."[3]

Does Jesus of Nazareth enjoy better support for his teachings and, more importantly, his resurrection from the dead? This chapter will evaluate the evidence for Jesus's resurrection. The next chapter will examine the

---

1. Muhammed lived from 571–632 AD. Zohri wrote the earliest biography of Muhammed around 749 AD. Ibn Ishak wrote a biography of Muhammed in 773 AD. Other biographies of Muhammed are much later. Ibni Hisham wrote his biography of the Islamic leader in 835 AD and Tabari wrote is in 932 AD. Furthermore, the Hadith, a collection of these writings, are not fully accepted by Islamic leaders until 300 years after the death of Muhammed.

2. Edward Conze, *The Buddhist Scriptures*, Kindle ed.

3. Ibid. It must be remembered that Gautama died around 480 BC. This is an astounding 500 years after the historical Buddha lived.

manuscript evidence that is available for the core details of Jesus's ministry. So, can we know that Jesus rose from the dead? Let us look at two methods that illustrate how we can.

Minimal Facts Argument

Gary Habermas is the distinguished research professor at Liberty University and is one of the world's leading scholars on the resurrection of Jesus. Habermas uses a tactic he calls the *minimal facts approach*. This approach uses the information that a large body of historians accept from both liberal and conservative perspectives alike. While as many as twelve details about Jesus could be listed as minimal facts,[4] Habermas has condensed his list to six of the most accepted facts. These six facts concerning Jesus are incontrovertible, literally undebatable, among historical scholars. They are as follows:

1. Jesus died on a Roman cross.
2. The early disciples had experiences which led them to believe that Jesus had risen from the dead.
3. The disciples were willing to die for their belief in what they had seen.
4. The preaching of the resurrection was very early in the history of the church.
5. Paul the apostle was transformed after seeing Jesus alive.
6. James the brother of Jesus was transformed after seeing the risen Jesus.[5]

Let's explain these facts in further detail. The first minimal fact is self-explanatory. All reputable historians accept that Jesus died by Roman crucifixion. Even liberal Christians and unbelievers accept that Jesus died by crucifixion.[6] Jesus's death by crucifixion is as historically certain as any other established fact of antiquity. If any blogger suggests that the crucifixion never occurred, they have a tough hill to climb in order to prove their claim. The crucifixion of Jesus is as well established as any other historical event in antiquity.

4. Gary Habermas, *The Historical Jesus*, 158–167.
5. Gary Habermas, *Risen Jesus & Future Hope*, 26–27.
6. Bart Ehrman, *A Brief Introduction to the New Testament*, 136; John Dominic Crossan, *Jesus: A Revolutionary Biography*, 145; and James D. G. Dunn who says that "two facts in the life of Jesus command almost universal assent—baptism and the crucifixion, James D. G. Dunn, *Jesus Remembered*, vol. 1, 339.

The second minimal fact notes that nearly all scholars contend that the disciples had experiences that led them to believe that they had seen the risen Jesus. This does not mean that all scholars believe in the literal, bodily resurrection of Jesus of Nazareth. Rather, it only means that the only solution to the resurrection paradox is that the disciples really believed that Jesus had risen from the dead. The fact that scholars accept the early belief in the resurrection causes concern for those who hold that the resurrection message was a later legendary invention.

The third minimal fact holds that the disciples were willing to die for what they knew to be true. People die for false ideas all the time. Buddhists have lit themselves on fire for causes in which they believed. However, no one in their right mind would die for something that he or she knew to be false.

When I was a school bus driver, a little girl sat three seats behind me. She asked me when she stepped on the bus if she could eat a piece of chocolate cake that her teacher had given her. I said, "Honey, wait until you get home. The cake is messy, and you will get chocolate on the bus and yourself." Three-quarters the way through the bus route, another child said, "Mr. Bus Driver, she ate that cake you told her not to eat." I looked back and asked the young girl with the cake, "Did you eat the cake?" With chocolate smeared over her face, she initially said, "No." But when I quizzed her about the chocolate on her mouth, she started tearing up. I didn't have the heart to turn her over to the principal. However, she did readily confess when she was caught red-handed—or in this case, brown mouthed. No one in the early church ever confessed to inventing the story when threatened with persecution and/or death. Rather, the early church preached the resurrection of Jesus even stronger when met with hardship.

The fourth minimal fact states that the resurrection of Jesus was an early teaching of the church. This is known by numerous early creeds found throughout the New Testament. One of the most important of these creeds is 1 Corinthians 15:3–7. The creed is one that Paul received no later than 35 AD when visiting Jerusalem.[7] He passed on this creed to the Corinthian Church in 55 or 56 AD. The creed states:

> For I passed on to you as most important what I also received: that Christ died for our sins according to the Scriptures, that he was buried, that he was raised on the third day according to the Scriptures, and that he appeared to Cephas, then to the

---

7. Paul says in Galatians, "Then after three years I did go up to Jerusalem to get to know Cephas, and I stayed with him fifteen days. But I didn't see any of the other apostles except James, the Lord's brother" (Gal. 1:18).

Twelve. Then he appeared to over five hundred brothers and sisters at one time; most of them are still alive, but some have fallen asleep. Then he appeared to James, then to all the apostles (1 Cor. 15:3–7).[8]

Due to the nature of the creed, it should no longer be held that the resurrection of Jesus came by legendary development. In fact, many are now claiming that the creed could potentially date to within months after the crucifixion and resurrection of Jesus.[9] So, if you are a historian, which would you prefer: a story written about a person 300–800 years after the person lived, or information that comes months after the events being described? Obviously, the closer the material is to the event and/or person being studied, the more reliable the source generally is.

The fifth and sixth minimal facts describe the transformation of two individuals who were initially against Christ only to become strong advocates of the Christian movement after seeing the risen Jesus. Paul was initially an adversary of the church who wanted to eradicate Christianity. Paul was a well-educated man who was on his way to becoming a member of the Sanhedrin or may have already been a member of the council (Acts 26:10–11; Gal. 1:13–14). Paul held the coats of those who stoned Stephen (Acts 7:54–8:3) and drove out Christians from their homes (Acts 9:1–3). However, something drastically changed for Paul. Paul became a believer in Christ and one of the strongest evangelists of all time. What happened to change the mindset of Paul from a critic to a champion of Christianity? It was because Paul saw the risen Jesus.

James was not a believer of Jesus during Jesus's earthly ministry. James was Jesus's half-brother. In John's Gospel, we are told that Jesus's brothers did not believe in him either (John 7:5). However, James became a powerful leader of the Church of Jerusalem. He is believed to have written the New

---

8. Some translations include male and female witnesses as part of the number. However, the creed only lists men who saw the risen Jesus and not the women who were among the first to witness the risen Jesus. The ESV keeps the masculine only version of the text, saying that Jesus "appeared to more than five hundred brothers at one time" (1 Cor. 15:6, ESV). While the wording could indicate men and women who saw Jesus alive at one time, the creed only lists men which, in my estimation, seems to imply that only male witnesses are referenced. Either way, a large group of individuals are referenced in the creed. If the men only are mentioned, then the number of witnesses would be much higher since women and children are not included in the total.

9. James D. G. Dunn now holds that the 1 Corinthians 15 creed was formulated and distributed within months of Jesus's death and resurrection. Dunn, *Jesus Remembered*, 55. Anti-Christian Michael Goulder even admits that the creed "goes back at least to what Paul was taught when he was converted, a couple of years after the crucifixion." Michael Goulder, "The Baseless Fabric of a Vision," *Resurrection Reconsidered*, 48.

Testament letter that bears his name.[10] What happened to James? In the 1 Corinthians creed, James is listed as one of the individuals who saw the risen Jesus. The evidence for James and Paul's conversions is so strong that no reputable scholar denies it, or at least shouldn't.

A seventh fact can be added to the list. That is, the tomb was found empty three days after Jesus's death in Jerusalem. The seventh fact does not share the strength of consensus that the other six facts do. Nevertheless, the empty tomb is still held by a whopping 75 percent of historical scholars[11] including Michael Grant, James D. G. Dunn, and Thomas Torrance.[12]

While there are many reasons to accept the empty tomb theory, four defenses for the empty tomb are quite compelling. First, the *message of the resurrection was early*. The creedal material of 1 Corinthians 15:3–7 is extremely early, dating to within months of Jesus's crucifixion and resurrection. So, the resurrection message simply did not have enough time to become legendary. Thus, if Jesus was proclaimed to have been risen early in the life of the church, then one would think that people would have checked the tomb to see if the body of Jesus was still there. There would have been witnesses who could have been cross-examined to see whether the story held.

Second, one must consider the *Jerusalem factor*. The creedal material of 1 Corinthians not only holds the early message of the resurrection, but it also shows that the message stemmed from Jerusalem. Having the resurrection message begin in Jerusalem is unthinkable if someone were to be making up a story. All the inquirer would need to do is to check the tomb for himself or herself. That the tomb belonged to Joseph of Arimathea, a statesman of the time, only elevates the knowledge of where the tomb was located. For instance, I could say that the church I pastor has 20,000 members. However, individuals who live near me and who know the church where I serve can easily come to the church to evaluate the validity of my claims. By doing so, they will see that the church I serve, while large, is nowhere close to 20,000 members. It would be easier to believe that the empty tomb story was legendary if the story emerged in an area far removed from the events of Jesus's life. But, because the empty tomb was proclaimed

---

10. While James's authorship is often disputed, this writer sees no merit behind any of the critical claims against him penning the text. See Brian G. Chilton, "Who Wrote the Letter of James?," *BellatorChristi.com* (August 8, 2017), https://bellatorchristi.com/2017/08/08/who-wrote-letter-of-james/.

11. Gary R. Habermas and Michael R. Licona, *The Case for the Resurrection of Jesus*, 70.

12. Habermas, *Risen Jesus & Future Hope*, 45, fn127.

in the very city where the resurrection occurred and where the tomb could be evaluated removes any space for legend to occur.

Third, *the testimony of women* strengthens the case for the empty tomb as this would not have been something that the church would have invented. The testimony of women was an embarrassing factor for the resurrection story because a woman's testimony did not have the force of a man's testimony in first-century Israel (sorry, ladies). The women discovered the tomb to be empty. If the testimony of women strengthens the case for the resurrection due to the embarrassment factor, then it also increases the credibility for an empty tomb.

Finally, the *Jewish leaders' bribe* strengthens the case for the empty tomb. The Jewish leaders of the Sanhedrin paid the soldiers to tell everyone that the disciples had stolen the body of Jesus (Matt. 28:11–15). Their false allegations imply strongly that the tomb of Jesus was in fact empty. So, if we were to include the seventh minimal fact to Habermas's list, then the minimal facts would include the following:

1. Jesus died on a Roman cross.
2. The early disciples had experiences which led them to believe that Jesus had risen from the dead.
3. The disciples were willing to die for their belief in what they had seen.
4. The preaching of the resurrection was very early in the history of the church.
5. Paul the apostle was transformed after seeing Jesus alive.
6. James the brother of Jesus was transformed after seeing the risen Jesus.[13]
7. The tomb was found empty three days after Jesus's death in Jerusalem.

The minimal facts approach makes a persuasive case for the resurrection of Jesus by using historical details that are accepted by a large consensus of scholarship. The previous details are not controversial as the vast majority of reputable scholars accept these claims. The literal resurrection of Jesus is the best answer to explain why these facts are true.

R.I.S.E.N. Acronym

I have personally developed an acronym that uses some of the details found in the minimal facts approach along with other details of historical scholarship that are generally accepted. The acronym uses the term RISEN.

---

13. Habermas, *Risen Jesus & Future Hope*, 26–27.

R=Records of Jesus's Crucifixion and Resurrection.

Numerous biblical and non-biblical records note that Jesus lived, died by crucifixion, and was reported to have been seen alive on the third day after his crucifixion. These records include the four Gospels, the thirteen Epistles traditionally ascribed to Paul, Clement of Rome (95 to 96 AD), Ignatius's *Letter to the Smyrneans* (107-115 AD), Polycarp's *Letter to the Philippians* (110-140 AD), Justin Martyr's *On the Resurrection* (150-160 AD), Tacitus (64 AD), Josephus (80 AD), Suetonius (120 AD), Pliny the Younger (111-113 AD), Lucian of Samosota (165 AD), Thallus (55 AD), Celsus (175 AD), and Mara bar Serapion (70 AD). Some of these texts provide more evidence than the others, but they all add to the historical case for Jesus's existence, his burial, and resurrection. Note too that all these texts are much earlier than the earliest biography of Muhammed or Buddha, as was mentioned previously.

I=Irritating Details.

While it would be impossible to provide a full treatment of the issue here, there are a number of irritating, or embarrassing details, that prove to be of great historical significance within the passion narrative. As mentioned earlier, the testimony of women who were the first to see the risen Jesus was an embarrassing point that lends strong credence to its veracity (Mark 16:1-8). It was an embarrassing fact that the disciples were unable to give Jesus a proper burial, whereas Joseph of Arimathea, a member of the same Sanhedrin that killed Jesus, did (Luke 23:50-54) It was embarrassing that the male disciples ran and fled, with the exception of John (John 19:27), while the women stayed by the side of Jesus. Historically speaking, these details are not things that the disciples who lived in a patriarchal society would have concocted. It makes no sense for the disciples to elevate the women while emasculating themselves unless it were true. Embarrassing details adds strength to the resurrection account.

S=Sightings of the Risen Jesus.

The numerous sightings of Jesus illustrate that the disciples did not have a hallucination. Rather, large groups of individuals saw Jesus alive at one time. The Matthew 28 account seems to indicate a large group. The ascension of Jesus in Acts 1 seems to indicate another large group of individuals. The creedal material of 1 Corinthians 15 also denotes a group of 500 who saw

Jesus alive at one time. The 500 listing could address either the Galilean group of Matthew 28, the Judean group of Acts 1, or it may address another group of witnesses separate from either. It is intriguing that the 1 Corinthians 15 creed does not list women. Could it be that the 500 only references men? If so, the number could be far higher than the 500 listed. It could be that over 1,000 people witnessed Jesus alive if the women were not included in the 500 count.

E=Early NT Creeds.

As noted previously, the New Testament is chocked-full of early creeds that predate the New Testament writings. Most, if not all, of these creeds date to the earliest church. Due to the nature of the creeds, it is now generally accepted that the earliest Christology was the highest Christology.[14] The creeds include the sermon summaries of Acts; John 1:1–4 and 14 (possibly); Acts 17:3; Rom. 1:3–4; 4:24–25; 8:14–17; 8:34; 10:9; 1 Cor. 11:23–26; 12:3; 15:3–7; 2 Cor. 4:5; 13:13; Eph. 1:20–23; Phil. 2:5–11; Col. 1:16–20; 2:6–7; 1 Thess. 1:8b–10; 1 Tim. 3:16; Heb. 1:3; and 1 Pet. 3:18–20 to name a few. Many more are considered to be part of the larger body of received texts known as the *homologia*. The creeds are the more formalized version of the *homologia* which makes them easier to detect. Every book in the New Testament except the book of Revelation contains either the *homologia* or the creeds.[15]

N=Newfound Faith.

As mentioned earlier, the encounters people had with Jesus brought about a newfound faith that was so strong that the early disciples were willing to pay the ultimate sacrifice. When people met Jesus alive from the dead, they were never the same. The same holds true for people who have encounters with the risen Jesus today.

Conclusion

The resurrection of Jesus can be defended using the minimal facts argument. The minimal facts approach uses facts that are accepted by both conservative and liberal scholars who are both Christian and non-Christian

---

14. Richard Bauckham, *Jesus and the God of Israel*, x.
15. Even then, some of the hymns in Revelation *could* be creedal.

alike. These facts illustrate the power of the resurrection's historicity. Using another approach, the RISEN acronym provides a means to remember the core evidences surrounding the crucifixion, death, burial, and resurrection of Jesus of Nazareth.

Progressive theologians have often claimed that the resurrection came about by the evolutionary development of a legend. However, the creedal material indicates that the earliest church accepted the death, resurrection, and even the *deity* of Jesus of Nazareth![16] The only way to explain the data is to accept that the resurrection of Jesus is a historical fact. With this information, one can confidently say along with the first witnesses that Christ has risen, he is risen, indeed!

---

16. Colossians 1:15–20 and Philippians 2:5–11 are exemplary examples of the early church's belief in Jesus's deity.

Chapter 11

MANUSCRIPT EVIDENCE

How does one know whether something reported is historically true or not? You may have heard objections claiming that history has been written by the rich and powerful. While it is true that reports have been tainted due to political pressure, it is still possible for an individual to know whether certain events of history actually occurred or not. There is a field of research devoted to historical research known as *historiography* which is the study of historical writings. Historiographers have developed certain rules and criteria that they use to validate or invalidate a document's authenticity. Some of the rules of historiography include a determination on how many sources are available, whether the sources represent eyewitness testimony, how early the resources are,[1] whether oral traditions are unbroken, and enemy attestation. The same can be applied to the biblical texts as they are historical documents. Yes, they are theological documents, but they are still historical in nature, as are any theological documents, because they were written in space and time.

Before beginning this investigation, two caveats need to be given. First, this investigation will not seek to prove which Bible translation is best. That is not our concern here. Our concern is to demonstrate whether Jesus of Nazareth and his resurrection can meet the criteria for historical investigation. Thus, while one may or may not prefer the Codex Vaticanus (c. 300–325 AD), the Codex Sinaiticus (c. 330–340 AD), or the Codex Alexandrinus (c. 400–440 AD),[2] they are historically dated as the earliest com-

---

1. The closer the resource is to the event it describes, the greater reliability the resource holds.
2. Modern translators use Greek texts derived from these early sources. The *King*

pleted texts of the NT canon. Some extant NT manuscripts and fragments predate these texts, but these books hold the completed NT canon within one book which makes them important for historical Christian research.

Second, I hold to biblical inerrancy. That is to say, I believe the Bible is completely true in what it says. However, it is not my goal here to prove biblical inerrancy. Biblical inerrancy is an in-house discussion between Christians. Our apologetic goal is to deal with the historical validity of the testimonies being offered. Again, let me repeat that I am an inerrantist. However, even if the Bible were to have some errors in it, Christianity would still remain true if Jesus literally rose from the dead. At the end of the day, if Jesus's death, deity, and resurrection are true, then Christianity is true even if we only possessed scant information about him. So, with those issues out of the way, let's begin our investigation into the manuscript evidence.

Number of Early Manuscripts

The first historiographical question that must be asked is how many early manuscripts are extant, or in existence. Before the number of manuscripts are revealed, one needs to first consider the number of manuscripts available for other classical works. The number of early manuscripts for Homer's *Illiad* (c. 762 BC) is around 1,900 and the earliest manuscript available is dates to around 300 years after the original document was penned. We have 238 manuscripts of Plato's *Tetralogies* (c. 380 BC) with the earliest extant copy dating to around 100-200 years after the original. We have 251 copies of Caesar's *Gallic Wars* (c. 46 AD) with the earliest existing copies dating around 900 years after the original. For Tacitus's *Annuals* (c. 120 AD), we only have about 36 copies with the earliest copies ranging from 730-930 years after the original. So, how does the NT compare?

Starting with the number of texts, the NT has traditionally been known to have close to 24,000 early copies, with over 5,000 of them dating to the first three centuries. But, the latest count of NT manuscripts is quite astounding. According to Josh and Sean McDowell, the number of early Armenian NT manuscripts (MSS) total to over 2,000, 975 total Coptic MSS, 6 Gothic MSS, over 600 Ethiopian MSS, 110 Old Latin MSS, over 10,000 Vulgate MSS, over 350 Syriac MSS, 89 Georgian MSS, over 4,000 Slavic MSS, and 5,856 early Greek MSS which date to the first three centuries of the

---

James Version, New King James Version, and the more recent Modern English Version use the Textus Receptus which derives from the later dated Codex Byzantium. Answering which codex is best for modern translations is a conversation outside the boundaries of this investigation.

church.³ The total number of NT manuscripts rests at 23,986 with 5,856 dating to the first three centuries of the church's history which stands at slightly over 24 percent of the total MSS. By the time you add the OT scrolls and codices, you have the massive number of 66,286 biblical documents! That is astounding! But how early are the sources behind the NT? That will be the topic of the next section.

Sources Material for the Life of Jesus

Remarkably, the life of Jesus of Nazareth has excellent source material backing up both the historicity of the man and of key events in his life. Numerous sources in the New Testament canon as well as extra-biblical literature describe the key aspects of Jesus's life. For this sake of this study, the ten best available sources will be discussed. These ten sources will be ranked in order from the greatest to the least in regard to their historical value as it relates to the life of Jesus of Nazareth.

1. *Creeds (30–35 AD)*. Hidden within the New Testament mines are gemstones awaiting to be extracted. These gemstones are the early New Testament creeds. Creeds are statements of faith that are easily remembered so that they can be passed down to future generations. The creeds became part of the earliest oral and written traditions of the church.

    The creeds possess certain traits that make them more detectable. For instance, the creeds often possess Aramaisms. Jesus most likely taught in Aramaic since Aramaic was the common language of Galilee. When an Aramaic term is found untranslated (e.g., *Cephas, maranatha, eloi lama sabachthani,* etc.), the text comes from older material than is found in the Greek text. It's fascinating that even in the Gospels, 80 percent of Jesus's teachings in the Synoptic Gospels have Aramaic or poetic traits that mark early material.⁴ Poetic or rhythmic structure, along with the triple use of *kai hoti* (i.e., "and that"), parallelisms, rabbinic terms, a primitive Gospel message, and foreign terms are all additional markers of early creedal material.

3. McDowell and McDowell, *ETDAV,* 52.
4. Craig Keener contends that "80% of the Synoptic sayings material appears to fit a poetic or rhythmic form helpful for memorization. Jesus' common phrase 'Son of Man' . . . makes no more sense in Greek than it does in English, but a phrase makes perfect sense in Hebrew or Aramaic, where it frequently occurs." Craig S. Keener, *The Historical Jesus of the Gospels* (Grand Rapids: Eerdmans, 2009), 158. See also Ben Witherington, *Christology,* 16–17.

A few of the creeds include 1 Corinthians 15:3-7, the Philippians hymn of Philippians 2:6-11, Colossians 1:15-20, Romans 10:9, Philippians 2:5-11, and the sermon summaries of Acts. The general consensus is that 1 Corinthians 15:3-7 dates to within months of the crucifixion and resurrection of Jesus of Nazareth.[5] From the creeds, one has extremely early source material for the life of Jesus and the key events of his life, especially pertaining to his crucifixion, burial, and resurrection. Also, the creeds illustrate the early belief in the deity of Jesus. The creeds may be the closest material to the life of Jesus that could ever exist outside of someone taking a Polaroid picture of him or finding his personal memoirs.

2. *Five Gospel Sources (30-85 AD).* You probably read the title and asked yourself, "Five Gospel sources? I thought there were only four Gospels." You would be correct. However, critical scholars believe there may be five sources behind the four Gospels. These materials consist of the material behind Matthew's Gospel (M), Mark's Gospel (Mark), Luke's Gospel (L), John's Gospel (J), and the material shared by only Matthew and Luke (Q).[6] Even though I hold to the traditional understanding that Matthew and John were written by the apostles ascribed to them, that Mark was written by the student of Simon Peter, and that Luke was written by the physician who accompanied the apostle Paul; it is still possible that there are five or more sources behind the Gospels. These sources are independent which increase the strength in their combined witness of Jesus.

Who wrote Q? I think that Matthew most likely did. There is tradition that holds that Matthew wrote an early Gospel in Aramaic before the Greek version of his Gospel appeared. While the Gospel of Matthew does not appear to be a translation, it is possible that Q represents the early material documented by the former tax-collector which was later developed by Matthew or one of his disciples.

Mark and Matthew were most likely written in the 50s and the Gospel of Luke was written before 64 AD because the physician ends Acts (the sequel to Luke) with the first imprisonment of Paul which occurred that year. John's Gospel was written in 85 AD which is a mere 52-55 years after the life of Christ. This is still very early. It is

---

5. As noted previously, see Dunn, *Jesus Remembered*, 55 and Michael Goulder, "The Baseless Fabric of a Vision," *Resurrection Reconsidered*, 48.

6. "Q" is the first letter from the German word *quelle* which means "source." Critical scholars believe that the Q document, which would contain the sayings of Jesus and perhaps some of his miracles, was the earliest of the Gospels.

comparable to an individual at the time of this writing recounting the events of the Vietnam War. While I wasn't alive during the Vietnam War, my father-in-law is a Vietnam veteran as well as many of my friends. If Dan (my father-in-law) were to write an account of his time at Vietnam, he would play the part of a Matthew or John. If I were to interview individuals and to construct a history, I would play the part of Luke. If I were to recount the experiences of my father-in-law, I would play the part of Mark. Nevertheless, this experiment shows the early nature of the Four Gospels even including John. Having four Gospels stem from five sources provides a very good historical witness to Jesus.

3. *Clement of Rome (c. 90 AD)*. Clement of Rome (35–99 AD) became a follower of Christ before eventually becoming the Bishop of Rome from 88 AD until his death in 99 AD. Clement of Rome personally knew some of the original apostles. In his letter to the Roman church, Clement quotes from the Gospels (Matt. 18:6; 26:24; Mark 9:42; and Luke 17:2) in *1 Clement* 46. Clement's references to Jesus throughout the letter serves as an early source for the life of Jesus and adds further historical weight to the life and ministry of Jesus. While Clement of Rome is not as early as the New Testament Gospels and certainly not as early as the New Testament creeds, he still serves as an early source for the life of Jesus.

4. *Tacitus, "Annals" (c. 116 AD)*. Tacitus (56–120 AD) was a Roman Senator and a historian of the Roman Empire. Tacitus wrote his book *Annals* around 116 AD. In it, the historian recounts the fire of Rome and how the early Christians were used as a scapegoat for Rome's burning. Tacitus writes the following:

> But not all the relief that could come from man, not all the bounties that the prince could bestow, nor all the atonements which could be presented to the gods, availed to relieve Nero From the infamy of being believed to have ordered the conflagration, the fire of Rome. Hence to suppress the rumor, he falsely charged with the guilt, and punished Christians, who were hated for their enormities. Christus, the founder of the name, was put to death by Pontius Pilate, procurator of Judea in the reign of Tiberius: but the pernicious superstition, repressed for a time broke out again, not only through Judea, where the mischief originated, but through the city of Rome also, where all things hideous and shameful from every part of the world find their center and become popular.

Accordingly, an arrest was first made of all who pleaded guilty; then, upon their information, an immense multitude was convicted, not so much of the crime of firing the city, as of hatred against mankind.[7]

Tacitus's reference to Christ provides five historical points of contact regarding Jesus of Nazareth.[8] First, Christ is established as the founder of the Christian movement. Second, Christ is noted to have been executed by Pontius Pilate. Third, the followers of Christ held the belief that Christ had risen from the dead, which he terms as the "pernicious superstition." Fourth, the Christian message began in Jerusalem where the crucifixion and resurrection occurred. Finally, the early Christians were willing to die for what they knew to have been true. These five points of contact provide extrabiblical corroboration for the key points of Jesus's life.

5. *Josephus, "Antiquities of the Jews" (c. 94 AD)*. Flavius Josephus (37–100 AD) was a Jewish historian. Josephus's Hebrew name was Yosef ben Matityahu.[9] Josephus was born in Jerusalem and fought against the Roman Empire until he surrendered in 67 AD to Roman forces before the sack of Jerusalem in 70 AD. Josephus was met with mixed reactions by the Judean faithful as he became a Roman sympathizer after surrendering to them. In 75 AD, Josephus wrote his book *Jewish Wars* followed by *Antiquities of the Jews* in 94 AD. Josephus mentions Jesus of Nazareth twice in his latter book. The first reference, often called the *Testimonium Flavianum*,[10] recalls the life of Jesus, the wisdom attributed to him, the attention he received from the populace, his death, the reported resurrection, and the group that followed him. Josephus's testimony regarding Jesus is as follows:

> Now, there was about this time Jesus, a wise man, if it be lawful to call him a man, for he was a doer of wonderful works—a teacher of such men as receive the truth with pleasure. He drew over to him both many of the Jews, and many of the Gentiles. He was [the] Christ; and when Pilate, at the suggestion of the principal men amongst us, had condemned him to the cross, those that loved him at the first did not forsake him, for he appeared to them alive again the

---

7. Tacitus, *Annals* 15.44.
8. Note that *Christ* is a title given to Jesus of Nazareth.
9. That is, Joseph son of Matityahu (or Matthias).
10. Meaning "Flavius's testimony."

third day, as the divine prophets had foretold these and ten thousand other wonderful things concerning him; and the tribe of Christians, so named from him, are not extinct at this day.[11]

Skeptics often question why Josephus, who was not a Christian, mentions Jesus. Because Josephus was not a Christian, skeptics hold that the testimony is a Christian interpolation.[12] The skeptic, quite honestly, is left speaking out of both sides of their mouth. On the one hand, skeptics charge that no one records anything about Jesus. But on the other hand, they deny the records that do exist by claiming that no one would record anything about Jesus. If you're like me, this kind of logic shows more of a bias against Jesus rather than a focus on the evidence.

Nevertheless, a growing consensus of scholars accept that the testimony is genuine. Perhaps the wording was flavored a bit rosier than what Josephus originally wrote. However, early manuscripts of Josephus's *Antiquities* seem to have the testimony as it is currently found. Another reason to believe Josephus's testimony is a reference he gives to the death of James the brother of Jesus. Josephus recounts,

> Festus was now dead, and Albinus was but upon the road; so he assembled the Sanhedrin of judges, and brought before them the brother of Jesus, who was called Christ, whose name was James, and some others, [or, some of his companions]; and when he had formed an accusation against them as breakers of the law, he delivered them to be stoned.[13]

It is bizarre that Josephus would record the death of James the brother of Jesus without first identifying Jesus. Josephus's testimony is authentic in my estimation. The Jewish historian provided further historical verification for Jesus regardless of his intentions.

6. *Pliny the Younger, "Epistulae" (111–113 AD).* Pliny the Younger (61–113 AD) served several roles. He was a lawyer and magistrate of the Roman Empire. Pliny wrote extensively, primarily by letters. One of the more notable letters Pliny wrote was to Emperor Trajan who reigned from 98 to 117 AD. Since Christianity was illegal in Rome

---

11. Josephus, *Antiquities* 18.3.3.63–64, in Flavius Josephus, *The Works of Josephus: Complete and Unabridged*, 480.

12. A later addition falsely attributed to the author.

13. Josephus, *Antiquities*, 20.9.1.200.

at the time, Pliny describes his procedure when handling Christians. Pliny writes,

> They were in the habit of meeting on a certain fixed day before it was light, when they sang in alternate verses a hymn to Christ, as to a god, and bound themselves by a solemn oath, not to do any wicked deeds, but never to commit any fraud, theft or adultery, never to falsify their word, nor deny a trust when they should be called upon to deliver it up; after which it was their custom to separate, and then reassemble to partake of food—but food of an ordinary and innocent kind.[14]

Pliny the Younger notes the early worship of Jesus as divine. Early Christians held to the divine nature of Jesus as noted earlier. It wasn't until much later that heretics like Arius of Alexandria (256–336 AD) began questioning Jesus's divine nature. Ironically, the idea of Jesus's divinity did not arise by evolutionary development. Rather, heretical views arose by dilluting the message of Christ.

7. *Suetonius, "Lives of the Twelve Caesars" (c. 120 AD).* Suetonius (69–122 AD) was another Roman historian who writes that "As the Jews were making constant disturbances at the instigation of Chrestus, he expelled them from Rome."[15] The major issue with Suetonius's citation is the odd spelling of *Chrestus* which many hold to be a misspelling of *Christus*. Some hold that the misspelling probably refers to an association with an agitator in Rome who is not associated with Jesus.[16] However, others, like James D. G. Dunn, contend that Suetonius simply misheard the name *Christus* and erroneously spelled it *Chrestus*.[17] It would appear that Dunn is correct. However, the controversy surrounding the spelling lowers the historical standing of the reference on our list. Nevertheless, Suetonius's statement regarding Christ appears genuine despite the controversy. Thus, for our purposes, we have two Roman historians and one Jewish historian who verifies the life and ministry of Jesus of Nazareth.

8. *Mara bar Serapion (c. 75 AD).* Mara bar Serapion (mid to late first century) wrote a letter to his son around 73–75 AD. The letter begins

---

14. Pliny the Younger, *Epistulae*, 10.96.
15. Suetonius, *Life of Claudius*, 25.4.
16. Edwin M. Yamauchi, "Jesus Outside the New Testament: What is the Evidence?," in *Jesus Under Fire*, 215.
17. Dunn, *Jesus Remembered*, 141–143.

with the author mentioning the unjust deaths of Socrates, Pythagorus, and the wise king of the Jews. The third reference most likely speaks of Jesus. Here is Mara bar Serapion's citation.

> What else can we say, when the wise are forcibly dragged off by tyrants, their wisdom is captured by insults, and their minds are oppressed and without defense? What advantage did the Athenians gain from murdering Socrates? Famine and plague came upon them as a punishment for their crime. What advantage did the men of Samos gain from burning Pythagoras? In a moment their land was covered with sand. What advantage did the Jews gain from executing their wise king? It was just after that their kingdom was abolished. God justly avenged these three wise men: the Athenians died of hunger; the Samians were overwhelmed by the sea and the Jews, desolate and driven from their own kingdom, live in complete dispersion. But Socrates is not dead, because of Plato; neither is Pythagoras, because of the statue of Juno; nor is the wise king, because of the "new law" he laid down.[18]

Most likely, Jesus is Mara bar Serapion's "wise king." However, the lack of clarity in the passage does not hold as strong as the other references provided. Nonetheless, it does appear that the author refers to Jesus which would provide at least an indirect reference to Jesus of Nazareth.

9. *Lucian of Samosota (c. 165 AD)*. Lucian of Samosota (125–180 AD) was a satirical novelist who perfected the use of sarcasm. Lucian was highly critical of Christianity in his writings. Lucian notes that "that one whom they still worship today, the man in Palestine who was crucified because he brought this new form of initiation into the world."[19] He also states that

> The Christians, you know, worship a man to this day—the distinguished personage who introduced their novel rites, and was crucified on that account . . . You see, these misguided creatures start with the general conviction that they are immortal for all time, which explains the contempt of death and voluntary self-devotion which are so common among them; and then it was impressed on them by their

---

18. Referenced in Robert E. Van Voorst, *Jesus Outside the New Testament: An Introduction to the Ancient Evidence*, 53–55.

19. Van Voorst, *Jesus Outside the New Testament*, 50.

original lawgiver that they are all brothers, from the moment that they are converted, and deny the gods of Greece, and worship the crucified sage, and live after his laws. All this they take quite on faith, with the result that they despise all worldly goods alike, regarding them as common property.[20]

The *Lives of Peregrine* was written around 165 AD. It is clear that Lucian references both Jesus and the early church. This adds yet another extrabiblical reference to Jesus and the early church. However, the dating of the text is an issue. It dates to the second century which lowers the impact of the source. Lucian's references are important to explain the practices of the early church and the existence of Jesus. It is unique in that it provides further enemy attestation to Jesus and the church. Nevertheless, it does not pack the power that some of the other sources previously mentioned do.

10. *Thallus (c. 55 AD)*.[21] Thallus was a first-century historian. Most of Thallus's works have been lost. Most of what we have is fragmentary or is referenced in other works. As it pertains to the historicity of Jesus, Julius Africanus (c. 160–240 AD) quotes from Thallus's work. According to Africanus, Thallus writes,

On the whole world there pressed a most fearful darkness; and the rocks were rent by an earthquake, and many places in Judea and other districts were thrown down. This darkness Thallus, in his third book of his 'History', calls, as appears to me without reason, an eclipse of the sun.[22]

Thallus is low on our list for good reason. He does not specifically mention Jesus, nor does he mention the early church. However, Thallus does corroborate a key event of Jesus's life—the darkness and earthquakes that accompanied his crucifixion. For that reason, Thallus provides an implied reference to Jesus. His work is still important, but it does not have the impact that other sources do.

Conclusion

This chapter has shown the evidence supporting the historicity of Jesus of Nazareth. The evidence is so good that it is hard to imagine that we are

---

20. Lucian of Samosota, *The Death of Peregrine*, 11–13.
21. Add chain of command and enemy attestation to the book.
22. Julius Africanus, *Extant Writings, Fragment XVIII*.

talking about the evidence for a first century person who lived 2,000 years ago. Some cold-case investigations do not have the level of evidence in modern times that Jesus has going for him in 33 AD. Not only is there source material that dates to within months of his death and resurrection available, biographies were written about him coming from five independent eyewitness testimonies. In addition, Jesus's life has further historical endorsement from one Jewish, and two Roman historians! When considering the incredulous number of early manuscripts, the exceptionally early nature of the New Testament creeds, and the excessive amount of references to Jesus of Nazareth; we can say along with Norman Geisler and Frank Turek that "it takes a lot more faith to be a non-Christian than it does to be a Christian."[23]

---

23. Norman L. Geisler and Frank Turek, *I Don't Have Enough Faith to Be an Atheist*, 32.

Chapter 12

RULES OF CANONICITY, FAKE GOSPELS, AND THE UNIQUENESS OF CHRISTIANITY

Thus far, we have investigated the historical evidence for Jesus and his resurrection. Yet, there is another area where Christianity has been under attack. Unfortunately, some of the attacks have come from within the camp of evangelical Christianity, especially among those who are prone to accept conspiracy theories. I have encountered individuals—both of a scholarly and non-scholarly mindset—who claim that the New Testament canon is a byproduct of Constantine and should not include the 27 books traditionally placed in the New Testament. Rather, the conspiracists see the New Testament as one guided by the hand of the Emperor and so other books like the so-called *Gospel of Thomas* or the *Gospel of Judas* should also be included. How does the Christian apologist answer such claims? Can the New Testament be trusted?

This chapter will show that the New Testament is reliable by investigating the process by which the early church deemed which books were canonical and which were not. You will see that the inspired texts were discovered instead of invented. Also, the chapter will show that the other Gospels that are often noted by scholars and conspirators alike are ancient versions of fake news.

The Five As of Canonicity[1]

From the conversations I have had with individuals at Bellator Christi,[2] it is apparent that many are skeptical of the way that the New Testament canon was constructed. Perhaps this is due to the skepticism of early Christianity consisting of various competing worldviews as is popularly portrayed on many media outlets. Holland Lee Hendrix, President of the Faculty of Union Theological Seminary, contends that early Christianity was really "Christianities . . . [and that] . . . We really can't imagine Christianity as a unified coherent religious movement."[3] Skeptics will often argue that these Christianities were won over by the view that held prominence and political power. Constantine settled the matter, therefore what is deemed orthodox Christianity[4] was the version that won out.

However, rather than a social Darwinist endeavor, orthodox Christianity has remained the same throughout the centuries despite the changes that may have come with church polity. The Apostles' Creed has nearly always been regarded to hold the fundamentals of orthodox Christianity. That being said, what led to the formation of the New Testament canon?

We do not have the space to cover all the history leading to the formation of the finalized canon when considering all the nuances, twists, and turns that occurred over time. Nevertheless, a brief history will be given. One of the first names that should be known is Marcion of Sinope (85–160 AD). Marcion was not an orthodox Christian. He was somewhat anti-Semitic and rejected the Old Testament. He only accepted a few books of the New Testament as canonical which did not mention the Old Testament much. The books that made Marcion's canon were the *Gospel of Marcion* (closely resembling Luke), Galatians, 1 and 2 Corinthians, Romans, 1 and 2 Thessalonians, Laodiceans, Colossians, Philippians, and Philemon. Other canons were known which were more orthodox in nature. Origen of Alexandria (c. 250 AD) was the first to compile a canonical list of the 27 canonical books as we have them in the New Testament although they were not in the same order that is found in the current New Testament. He writes, using the story of Joshua as a backdrop,

---

1. A great deal of appreciation goes to Leo Percer who first introduced me to the five criteria of canonicity.

2. Found at https://bellatorchristi.com.

3. Holland Lee Hendrix, "Early 'Christianities' of the 2nd and 3rd Centuries," *PBS.org* (April 1998), retrieved April 25, 2019, https://www.pbs.org/wgbh/pages/frontline/shows/religion/first/diversity.html.

4. Christianity that is deemed true.

> But when our Lord Jesus Christ comes, whose arrival that prior son of Nun designated, he sends priests, his apostles, bearing "trumpets hammered thin," the magnificent and heavenly instruction of proclamation. Matthew first sounded the priestly trumpet in his Gospel; Mark also; Luke and John each played their own priestly trumpets. Even Peter cries out with trumpets in two of his epistles; also James and Jude. In addition, John also sounds the trumpet through his epistles [and Revelation], and Luke, as he describes the Acts of the Apostles. And now that last one comes, the one who said, "I think God displays us apostles last," and in fourteen of his epistles, thundering with trumpets, he casts down the walls of Jericho and all the devices of idolatry and dogmas of philosophers, all the way to the foundations.[5]

But note that Origen's list comes well before the Nicaean Council of 325 AD. So, one cannot argue that the canonical books were added to the New Testament by the decree of Constantine because Origen lists the canonical books some 22 years before Constantine was born![6]

Athanasius of Alexandria (296–373 AD) in his Easter Letter of 367 AD would later list the 27 books of the New Testament. He was the first to list the books in the order that they are positioned in modern Bibles. He writes,

> Again it is not tedious to speak of the [books] of the New Testament. These are, the four Gospels, according to Matthew, Mark, Luke, and John. Afterwards, the Acts of the Apostles and Epistles (called Catholic), seven, viz. of James, one; of Peter, two; of John, three; after these, one of Jude. In addition, there are fourteen Epistles of Paul, written in this order. The first, to the Romans; then two to the Corinthians; after these, to the Galatians; next, to the Ephesians; then to the Philippians; then to the Colossians; after these, two to the Thessalonians, and that to the Hebrews; and again, two to Timothy; one to Titus; and lastly, that to Philemon. And besides, the Revelation of John.[7]

The earliest mention of the New Testament canon from an orthodox position is the Muratorian canon (c. 170 AD) which consisted of all four Gospels, all thirteen letters of Paul, the three letters of John, Jude, Revelation, and also included two books not included in the New Testament canon: *The Apocalypse of Peter* and *The Book of Wisdom*. A Syriac New Testament canon called the Peshitta existed no later than the late second

---

5. Origen of Alexandria, *Homilies on Joshua*, 7.1.

6. Constantine was born in 272 AD.

7. Athansius of Alexandria, "Pascal Letters, 39.5," *Nicene and Post-Nicene Fathers*, 2nd Series, vol. 4, from *NewAdvent.org* (2017), retrieved April 26, 2019, http://www.newadvent.org/fathers/2806039.htm.

century (150–200 AD). It contained all the New Testament books except 2 Peter, 2 and 3 John, Jude, and Revelation. It may have also contained a harmony of the Gospels written by Tatian (120–190 AD) called the *Diatessaron*. It is important to remember that 85 percent of the New Testament canon was accepted as canonical no later than 125 AD, a mere 30 years after the last book of the Bible was written.

Fast forward to 325 AD. Constantine had become a Christian and established Christianity as an official religion of the Roman Empire. Contrary to popular belief, Constantine did not direct the Nicaean Council. He merely wanted the church to settle the controversial issues that they faced. The Council did not invent a canon. Rather, they confirmed the books that the church had already established as the official canon. Furthermore, the Nicene Council was not primarily concerned with the canon. They were concerned with a movement called Arianism[8] and the deity of Christ. It is even doubtful that the Nicaean Council discussed the canon as the council's documentation does not mention anything about the canon from what I can tell. With this in mind, what set of standards did the church use to identify which books were canonical as opposed to the books that were influenced by Gnostic teachings. Yes, they knew about the fake Gospels. The following five criteria were used to identify the books that were canonical.

Antiquity. Was the text old enough to have the endorsement of the earliest church? All of the canonical books of the New Testament were written in the first century. None of the Gnostic books, contrary to what *The DaVinci Code* would have you believe, were written in the first century. If a text was not old enough to enjoy the endorsement of the earliest church, then the book was dismissed as uninspired. This was part of the problem with the second and third letters of John, the second letter of Peter, Jude, and Revelation. They were written later and, therefore, drew more questions due to their later date.

Apostolicity. Was the text written by an apostle or did it have apostolic backing? As the church examined the lists of books within the early canons, those that were written by and apostle were included. The great church historian Eusebius notes the universal acceptance that Matthew and John wrote the Gospels that bear their name. He says, "Nevertheless, of all the disciples of the Lord, only Matthew and John have left us written memorials, and they, tradition says, were led to write only under the pressure of necessity."[9] Paul's letters were unanimously accepted as coming from the

---

8. Started by Arius of Alexandria. He was opposed by Athanasius of Alexandria who held that Christ was eternal, and God come in the flesh. Arius held a view comparable to the modern-day Jehovah Witnesses in that Christ was a created being.

9. Eusebius of Caesaria, "The Church History of Eusebius, 3.24.5," in *Eusebius: Church History, Life of Constantine the Great, and Oration in Praise of Constantine*, 152.

apostle. However, some writers were not apostles but had the backing of an apostle. For instance, Mark documented the teachings of Simon Peter, although not in chronological order. Luke compiled his Gospel in the most chronological order from eyewitness testimonies. Luke had the backing of Paul and the church. While the author of Hebrews is not known with any certainty, the author had the backing of the apostle Paul. For that reason, Hebrews was accepted.

Authenticity. Did the text represent the authentic teachings of Jesus and the early church? Contrary to what skeptics may lead you to believe, orthodox Christianity was fairly set from the earliest times. True, there were threats that often sought to change orthodox Christianity. But in the end, the church accepted the teachings that originated from Jesus of Nazareth and the first disciples. The church asked whether the document cohered with the teachings of the earliest church. If not, the document was cast aside. It is for this reason why the *Gospel of Thomas*, the *Acts of Andrew*, and so on were rejected.

Acceptance. Was the text accepted by the majority of the church? Different canons were found in the church with slight alterations. The texts were examined across the board. Those that held consensus across the church were accepted. Some good books were rejected on this basis. For instance, the *Didache* was an early document that found favor among early Christian groups. However, it did not find consensus across the board. Therefore, it was rejected.

Authoritative. Did the text possess divine authority? Was the power of God found in the text? Did the text show evidence of divine inspiration? Were lives changed by the power of the message? Did the text hold the wisdom of the Holy Spirit? If so, the text was accepted. If not, the text was rejected.

Hopefully, you have seen that the Nicaean Council did not dictate what books were accepted as canonical. The Council of Nicaea was more concerned with the conflict between Athanasius and Arius than they were the finalized canon. Instead, the church confirmed the books that were already accepted as authoritative. The New Testament canon was not dictated by Constantine, rather it was inspired by the Holy Spirit of God. But what about those books that were rejected?

Fake Gospels—Ancient Fake News

Modern politicians have coined the term "fake news" for news stories aired by the media that have no basis in fact, or stories that have greatly altered the truth to fit a certain political agenda. The term "fake news" was popularized during the 2016 Presidential election. It is amazing to watch the spin that takes place after an event occurs on both conservative and liberal news outlets. An event can occur that elevates conservatism and conservative news agencies will expound on the news, whereas progressive news channels will not, and vice versa. Each news agency has its own bias and bent. Sometimes, certain news agencies or bloggers will falsify an event to make their cause look legitimate.

In like manner, early church leaders recognized the existence of certain texts that were promoted as Christian, but really contained fake news. Eusebius of Caesarea acknowledged heretical books that were being passed off as Christian. They included the *Gospel of Peter*, the *Gospel of Thomas*,[10] the *Gospel of Matthias*,[11] the *Acts of Andrew*, the *Acts of John*, and "the other apostles, which no one belonging to the succession of ecclesiastical writers has deemed worthy of mention in his writings."[12]

In 1945, archaeologists discovered a treasure trove of Gnostic texts in what is called the Nag Hammadi Library. The storehouse of books included the *Gospel of Thomas* and numerous other texts. One may hear interesting titles including the *Gospel of Mary Magdalene*, the *Secret Gospel of Mark*, the *Gospel of Judas*, and so on. However, the following things must be remembered about these books.

1. *They were not quoted by the earliest leaders of the church.* In stark contrast, early church leaders quoted from the canonical New Testament texts voluminously. There are no references to the Gnostic texts, which is very telling.

2. *They do not contain orthodox teachings from the earliest church.* Some of the Gnostic Gospels do contain some truth which is interesting to consider. But they also warp the teachings of Christ. It is highly bizarre that progressive theologians promote the Gospel of Thomas even with the Gnostic text including the strange teaching that women should become men in order to be Christ's disciples.[13]

10. This is the same *Gospel of Thomas* that is promoted by progressive theologians and fictional writers (i.e., Dan Brown).

11. The *Gospel of Matthias* is also mentioned by Origen (*Homilies in Lucam*, I.) and Jerome (*Praef. In Matthew*). Clement of Alexandria references it in the *Stromata*, II.9; III.4; VII.13. He mentions that it had a high sense of morality and focused on asceticism.

12. Eusebius, *Church History*, III.25.6., 156.

13. "Simon Peter said to them, 'Make Mary leave us, for females don't deserve life.' Jesus said, 'Look, I will guide her to make her male, so that she too may become a living spirit resembling you males. For every female who makes herself male will enter the

3. *The Gnostic texts have no root in apostolic authority.* Contrary to the opinions of critical scholarship, there are strong reasons for believing that the apostles Matthew and John either wrote or dictated the texts to a scribe. Personally, the former option is quite reasonable considering that Galilee was far more intellectual than once thought. Luke had access to early testimonies.[14] Being a physician, one would most certainly think that he had the ability to read and write. Mark had the authority of Peter backing him. None of the Gnostic Gospel texts have any apostolic backing whatsoever! Rather, the ghost writers chose an apostle or early church member that they liked and falsely linked their chosen hero to the text.

Conclusion

Often, it's the case where rumors are started on social media and are eventually accepted as true by the general populace. This happens far more than one may like to think. For instance, I posted on social media a weather report which stated that the upcoming winter was anticipated to receive the most snow in history. While I am normally a snow lover, I was a bit concerned because I had started my PhD program and had to drive through the mountains of Virginia to get to my university for my seminars. A good friend of mine quickly pointed out that the weather report was a couple of years old and was put out by a fake news agency. I was thankful to hear that, but my son who was jumping with joy over the upcoming snow became quickly disappointed.

A small weight of research wards off a ton of speculation. When you are confronted by skeptics who claim that the Nicaean Council or emperor Constantine constructed the New Testament canon, lead them to the truth. Hopefully, this chapter has provided an ample amount of ammunition to fire against such erroneous onslaughts. The New Testament canon came out of the inspired teachings of the early church as guided by the Holy Spirit. Christ, not Constantine, was behind the canon. Furthermore, the church did not invent the canon. They discovered it.

---

domain of Heaven.'" The Gospel of Thomas, 114, in Robert W. Funk, Roy W. Hoover, and the Jesus Seminar, *The Five Gospels: What Did Jesus Really Say?*, 532.

14. There are good reasons for believing that Luke may have even interviewed Mary the mother of Jesus!

Chapter 13

ARCHAEOLOGICAL EVIDENCE FOR THE BIBLE

Archaeology is a fascinating science. I remember my first time watching *Indiana Jones and the Raiders of the Lost Ark*. I was completely fascinated by this historian who searched for ancient artifacts. Two of my professors, Randall Price and Chet Roden, along with my archaeologist friends Ted Wright and Scott Reynolds, are all individuals who do the work that Indiana Jones did, only they do it legally. I can neither confirm nor deny whether any of them carry whips with them on their archaeological digs or wear the fashionable hat that the fictional Indiana Jones wore. But all kidding aside, they explore biblical lands in hopes of discovering archaeological artifacts which correspond with biblical data.

As I have heard from many archaeologists, archaeology does not prove or disprove events in the Bible. Randall Price says it best in that "A common misconception is that the purpose of archaeology is to prove the Bible. However, since the Bible describes itself as the 'word of truth' (Ps. 119:43; 2 Cor. 6:7; Col. 1:5; 2 Tim. 2:15; Jas. 1:18), it cannot be proved or disproved by archaeology anymore than can God by the limited evidence of the world (cf. Eccl. 3:10-11)."[1] While archaeology can neither prove nor deny the truths of Scripture, it can better inform us of the times, events, and the people mentioned in the Bible.

Archaeology can also strengthen or weaken the probability that a historical event happened. When speaking of historical people, places, and events, the best the historian can do is to speak in probabilities as it is

---

1. Randall Price and H. Wayne House, *Zondervan Handbook of Biblical Archaeology*, 26.

difficult to hold 0 percent and 100 percent certainty that an event did or did not take place. Archaeology can increase or decrease the probabilities that such an event occurred. So, we could say that there is a 99.9 percent chance that George Washington was the first President of the United States, but that there is less than a ten percent chance that he cut down a cherry tree as a young boy, regardless of what the popular myth states.

It must be asked; how has archaeology impacted the historical probabilities, or certitude, of the biblical stories? When it comes to archaeology and the Bible, Rabbi Nelson Glueck noted that "As a matter of fact, however, it may be stated categorically that no archaeological discovery has ever controverted a biblical reference. Scores of archaeological findings have been made which confirm in clear outline or in exact detail historical statements in the Bible."[2] William Foxwell Albright, the American Dean of Biblical Archaeology, stated that "Discovery after discovery has established the accuracy of innumerable details, and has brought increased recognition of the Bible as a source of history."[3] Albright and Glueck are archaeological heavyweights. For them to give that form of credence to biblical history is quite telling. Edwin Yamauchi predicts that "it may take 8,000 more years of excavation, but eventually archaeology will prove the Bible to be true."[4]

This chapter will examine some of the archaeological discoveries that have best enlightened and further strengthened confidence in the biblical record. It should be noted that a complete examination cannot be given due to the space of this chapter. For further investigation into the archaeological evidence for Scripture, consider purchasing the *Zondervan Handbook of Biblical Archaeology* which is co-authored by Randall Price and H. Wayne House. Also, consider my friend Ted Wright's page *Epic Archaeology*.[5] For each of the following fifteen discoveries, a brief description will be given followed by the benefit of the find—that is, how the discovery benefits the veritability of the biblical record.

Dead Sea Scrolls

Perhaps the greatest archaeological discovery of all time was found by accident. In the mid to late 1940s, a Bedouin shepherd boy named Muhammed edh-Dhib—which means "Muhammed the Wolf" since he killed wolves that threatened his sheep—accompanied by his cousins Jum'a Muhammed

2. Nelson Glueck, *Rivers in the Desert,* 31.
3. William Foxwell Albright, *The Archaeology of Palestine,* 128.
4. Randall Price, *The Stones Cry Out,* 344.
5. Found at https://epicarchaeology.org.

and Khalil Musa, threw a rock into a cave at Qumran and heard something shatter. He and his cousins entered the cave to find jars that contained the Great Isaiah Scroll, a Habakkuk commentary, and the Community Rule. The young boys did not realize what they had discovered. They took them back to their community where it was thought that they were either stolen or worthless trash. In 1947, John Trever of the American Schools of Oriental Research compared the scrolls with other older biblical manuscripts. After the scrolls were identified to be ancient texts of the Hebrew Bible and community documents of Qumran, additional searches were undertaken to find more scrolls. All in all, eleven caves were discovered containing scrolls as old as the eighth century BC.

Recently, Randall Price of Liberty University and Oren Gutfield of Hebrew University made national news when they discovered a twelfth cave in February 2017. Broken vessels indicated that the cave had been looted. Their research revealed that there may be more caves which may yield further results in the future. It is highly possible that there are more Dead Sea Scrolls around the lonely caves of Qumran.

The Dead Sea Scrolls hold immense value for the Christian apologist. First, they show that the Old Testament has not changed over time. It remains quite the same as it existed in the eighth century BC. Second, the Dead Sea Scrolls pose a problem for those who hold that Isaiah was written by multiple people. The great scroll of Isaiah is a unified book which indicates that it may have come from one writer.[6] Third, some of the Dead Sea Scrolls boost the trustworthiness of messianic prophecies, showing that they were not later Christian interpolations. Fourth, the Dead Sea Scrolls unveil information concerning the Qumran community of the first century AD and a group known as the Essenes. It is possible that John the Baptist may have been an Essene although this is debatable. Finally, the literature of the Dead Sea Scrolls unveils the thinking of ancient Judeans. It was once thought that John borrowed from Greco-Roman symbols when utilizing the metaphors of light and darkness. However, the War Scroll (1QM) describes the sons of light battling the sons of darkness. The illustrations match those used in John's Gospel. John is revealed to be a thoroughly Jewish book.[7]

6. It still remains a possibility that the book could have undergone some redactions after its completion. Even still, this does not mandate multiple authorship.

7. Further research has indicated that even the Logos Principle of John 1 was not of Greco-Roman origin. John would not have traveled in the Alexandrian area where such views held prominence. Rather, John may have been borrowing from a Jewish understanding of the Memra (Aramaic term for "word") which described the Angel of Yahweh known as the Metatron in Jewish literature. This Being was one that was a creator, signer of covenants, revealer of truth, divine yet distinct from the Father, and eternal.

New Evidence for Destruction at Sodom

Research in the Dead Sea region unveiled another interesting find. Around where ancient Sodom would have been located, researchers have found evidence that suggests that a catastrophic incident took place around 3,700 years ago. A multi-disciplinary team of researchers found glazed potsherds in Jordan's Tall el-Hammam Excavation Project[8] that specified that the region experienced temperatures high enough to covert the potsherds to glass. According to the team, the heat was as hot as the surface of the sun.[9] The meteoric explosion would have disintegrated an area of around 15.5 miles turning what was once a lush, fertile area into a barren wasteland. The impact is comparable to the Siberian Stony Tunguska event of 1908.[10] The area would have been obliterated. This insight gives further evidence to the biblical story of Sodom and Gomorrah and should serve as a warning not to play games with God.

Caiaphas Ossuary

In November of 1990, an ossuary[11] was discovered in southern Jerusalem. The ossuary bore the inscription "Joseph, son of Caiaphas" and held the bones of a sixty-year-old male. It is believed that this burial box holds the bones of the high priest who tore his robes after hearing Jesus identify himself as the Son of Man of Daniel 7:13–14. Caiaphas later worked with Pilate to have Jesus executed. The benefit for the Christian apologist is quite evident. This provides tangible evidence that Caiaphas was not an invention of the church but was a real person of history.

---

8. Amanda Borschel-Dan, "Evidence of Sodom? Meteor Blast Cause of Biblical Destruction, Says Scientists," *TimesofIsrael.com* (Nov. 22, 2018), retrieved May 1, 2019, https://www.timesofisrael.com/evidence-of-sodom-meteor-blast-cause-of-biblical-destruction-say-scientists/.

9. Steve Warren, "'Temps as Hot as the Surface of the Sun': Did Scientists Find Evidence of the Destruction of Biblical Sodom?," *CBN.com* (Nov. 26, 2018), retrieved May 1, 2019, https://www1.cbn.com/cbnnews/cwn/2018/november/did-scientists-find-evidence-of-the-destruction-of-biblical-sodom-exploding-meteor-may-be-to-blame.

10. The Tunguska event may have been somewhat larger in that it covered 770 miles compared to 15 at Sodom and Gomorrah.

11. An ossuary is a burial box which contained the bones of individuals. In ancient Israel, people would wrap their dead loved ones in linens and anoint the body with spices and oils. Afterward, they would place the deceased loved one in a cave. After a year's time, the body would decompose. The bones of the loved one were collected and placed in a family burial box known as an ossuary.

Crucifixion Victim in Ossuary

Crucifixion was known to have occurred frequently in the Roman Empire as numerous evidences suggest. However, no one had ever discovered a trace of evidence from a crucified victim. Everything changed in 1968. The ossuary of one Yehohanan was discovered which contained his heel bone with a crucifixion nail still attached. Around 2,000 years ago, a young Jew in his twenties named Yehohanan was condemned by the Roman authorities.[12] While the nature of his crime has been lost in time, the means of his execution has been preserved.

This discovery indicates that crucifixion was indeed used by the Romans. It also indicates that nails were used to attach victims to the cross. Also, Yehohanan's ankle depicts the means by which the Romans used to nail their victims to the cross. In some instances, they may have nailed a person through the feet. But it seems that it was also common for them to nail a person through the ankle to the sides of the cross. This means of crucifixion would have placed intense pressure upon the chest cavity of Yehonanan which would have made it extremely difficult for him to breathe. He would have had little means to push himself up. In addition, the existence of Yehonanan's ossuary suggests that the Romans did sometimes allow the families of crucifixion victims to bury their loved one. Thus, it is not outside the realm of possibility that Joseph of Arimathea would have been granted permission to bury Jesus of Nazareth. While we know nothing of Yehonanan, he can be appreciated because of what he helps us to understand about the practice of Roman crucifixion.

Nazareth Decree

In 1878,[13] a profound piece of archaeological evidence was discovered which could, quite frankly, add additional weight to the resurrection of Jesus of Nazareth. A slab of stone was discovered in Galilee which held what has been called the "Nazareth Inscription," so named because a French scholar acquired it in Nazareth, Jesus's hometown.[14] The writing style indicates that

12. Matti Friedman, "In a Stone Box, the Only Trace of Crucifixion," Timesofisrael.com (Mar. 26, 2012), retrieved May 1, 2019, https://www.timesofisrael.com/in-a-stone-box-a-rare-trace-of-crucifixion/.

13. Norman L. Geisler, "Archaeology, New Testament," Baker Encyclopedia of Christian Apologetics, 48.

14. Ted Wright, "10 Significant New Testament Archaeological Discoveries," EpicArchaeology.com, retrieved May 1, 2019, http://epicarchaeology.org/archaeology-and-the-new-testament/10-significant-new-testament-archaeological-discoveries/.

it originated in the first half of the first-century AD, but cannot be dated any earlier than 44 AD since it was established in Galilee by order of Emperor Claudius who reigned from 41–54 AD. This is what the decree says,

> It is my decision [concerning] graves and tombs—whoever has made them for the religious observances of parents, or children, or household members—that these remain undisturbed forever. But if anyone legally charges that another person has destroyed, or has in any manner extracted those who have been buried, or has moved with wicked intent those who have been buried to other places, committing a crime against them, or has moved sepulcher-sealing stones, against such a person, I order that a judicial tribunal be created, just as [is done] concerning the gods in human religious observances, even more so will it be obligatory to treat with honor those who have been entombed. You are absolutely not to allow anyone to move [those who have been entombed]. But if [someone does], I wish that [violator] to suffer capital punishment under the title of tomb-breaker.[15]

Given that the Jewish authorities claimed that the disciples stole the body of Jesus (Matt. 28:13), this inscription gives evidence that the rumors of Jesus's resurrection must have been prominent and the authorities' claims of the disciples involvement in the disappearance of Jesus's body must have reached the Emperor's ears.

Pontius Pilate Inscription

Italian archaeologists discovered a stone in Caesarea Maritima in Israel which contained the name of Pontius Pilate. The stone reads, "To the Divine Augusti [this] Tiberieum . . . Pontius Pilate . . . prefect of Judea . . . has dedicated [this] . . ."[16] While Pontius Pilate is mentioned in several manuscripts, both biblical and non-biblical alike, the inscription gives concrete evidence that Pontius Pilate existed. This gives further weight to the notion that Pontius Pilate ordered Jesus to be crucified since he would have been the procurator in the region at the time of Jesus.

---

15. Clyde E. Billington, "The Nazareth Inscription: Proof of the Resurrection of Christ?," in *Artifax* (Spring 2005).

16. Wright, "10 Significant NT Archaeological Discoveries," *EpicArchaeology.com*.

Pool of Bethesda and Pool of Siloam

In the 1800s, liberal scholars dismissed the Gospel of John due to the details of the fifth chapter. John describes Jesus healing a man by the Pool of Bethesda (John 5:1–8). The pool is described as having five colonnades. Skeptics noted that no pool had been discovered that had five colonnades. Such an architectural design was not found in that period. In the late 1800s, the Pool of Bethesda was discovered and had, as one would imagine, five colonnades just as the Gospel of John described.

In 2004, archaeologist Eli Shukron discovered another pool, the Pool of Siloam which was mentioned in John 9:1–12, near where workers were working on a sewer line. The two pools together add weight to the notion that John reported what he had seen with great accuracy. Thus, the skeptic no longer has a reason to deny the Fourth Gospel based on archaeological issues with the pools described in the text.

Robinson's Arch

In 1838, Edward Robinson, a professor who taught at Andover Theological Seminary, discovered the remains of an ancient archway which held a staircase leading to the temple platform.[17] According to Ted Wright, Robinson, for whom the arch is named, became the "father of biblical geography."[18] Robinson's arch would have served as a major entry point to the temple and was likely used by Jesus and his disciples on numerous occasions.

Synagogue at Capernaum

One of the more famed areas outside of Jerusalem for Christian pilgrims to visit is the synagogue in Capernaum where Jesus would have taught on numerous occasions. The site was excavated in 1905 to 1921, and then again in 1969.[19] The synagogue that stands in white marble is from the late second to early third century. Virgilio Corbo dug trenches along the wall and discovered an older foundation with squared black volcanic basalt stones that dated to the first century.[20] While the earlier synagogue was constructed of black basalt rather than white marble, it is still thought to have

---

17. Ibid.
18. Ibid.
19. Price and House, *Zondervan Handbook of Biblical Archaeology*, 268.
20. Ibid.

been built in the same style as the current synagogue. The synagogue is also pointed in the direction of Jerusalem as it was in the first century. Further investigations in the area have revealed that Romans coinhabited the area with the Jews which would explain the presence of the Roman centurion in the area as noted in Luke 7:1–10.[21]

Peter's House in Capernaum

Virgilio Corbo made waves in 1968 by fully excavating an area that had begun in 1865. The house has related to Simon Peter due to the presence of a basilica which once covered the home. In 570 AD, Anonymous of Piacenza denoted the presence of such a basilica over Peter's home.[22] Furthermore, fishhooks were found in the home along with a particular room which was plastered and commemorated as the room of Simon Peter. Like the original synagogue in Capernaum, the home was built with black volcanic basalt stones. The home sits near the synagogue which may denote the respect that Simon Peter and his family had in the community even before becoming one of Jesus's chosen disciples. As it seems that families of prominence lived near the synagogue, Peter's family could have held major influence in Capernaum.

The "Jesus Boat"

Shelley Wachsmann of Texas A&M and members of the Israeli Antiquities Authority were able to bring an ancient fishing boat out of the water.[23] The boat was around 27 feet long, 7 ½ feet wide, and 4 feet deep. Great care was necessary to surface the boat out of the water as it was in extremely fragile condition. The boat had been repaired several times during its illustrious career. Despite its title, there is no precise evidence linking Jesus with the boat. However, radiocarbon testing indicated that the boat dates to 40 BC. Thus, the boat was most certainly in use during Jesus's day and potentially could have been used by Jesus and the disciples.

21. Ibid.
22. Ibid., 246.
23. Ibid., 263.

Stone Jar Factory

In 2016, a chalkstone cave was discovered in Kafr Kanna. Kafr Kanna has been identified as the biblical Cana of Galilee.[24] John 2:6 indicates that the water pots that Jesus used were made after the manner of the purification process of Judaism. At Kafr Kanna, archaeologists discovered that the cave was used as a manufacturing facility for these stone jars. It is quite likely that the water pots used by Jesus to turn water into wine were made at this very location.

Church of Holy Sepulchre

While Protestants prefer Gordon's Tomb over the Church of the Holy Sepulchre due to its irenic location, it is highly more likely that the Church of the Holy Sepulchre is the actual location of Jesus's crucifixion and burial sites. In 132 AD, Hadrian barred Jews from Jerusalem and tried to eradicate evidence of both Judaism and Christianity by building Roman temples over areas held sacred to both. Church historian Eusebius denotes that after Constantine legalized Christianity in 313 AD with the Edict of Milan, Constantine's devout mother, Helena, searched for and located the place of Christ's tomb. A statue of Venus had been place atop it. She immediately ordered for the statue's removal and ordered for the tomb to be cut out of the rock and to place a basilica over the entire area.

During an ongoing restoration project, researchers were allowed a limited amount of time to peer into the slab of marble said to cover the place where Jesus was buried. When the upper part of the marble was removed, they found an older bedding that dated to the first century covered with a broken piece of metal that had a Crusader's cross engraved on it which was placed on the same location that Helena believed to have been the stone bedding on which Jesus's body was lain. This proves that that tomb has been revered in the same location since the time of Helena. Also, the find adds additional strength that the tomb of Jesus was either within the Church of the Holy Sepulchre's Edicule, or at least in the general location.

Tomb of Simon bar Jonah

The Roman Catholic Church venerates a location known as St. Peter's Tomb. It is located at the base of the aedicula under the floor the basilica. In 1953,

---

24. Wright, "10 Significant NT Archaeological Discoveries," *EpicArchaeology.com*.

archaeologists extracted the bones and discovered that the tomb contained both human and animal bones. Another set of bones were transferred, without the archaeologists' knowledge from another location in the basilica. Radiocarbon testing indicated that the bones were from a 60-70-year-old man.[25] While it is impossible to know with certainty that the bones tested were those of the actual Simon Peter bar Jonah, it does indicate that the tomb of Simon Peter was venerated extremely early and at some point did house the body of Simon Peter.

Shroud of Turin

The Shroud of Turin is among one of the most controversial archaeological finds of all time. If genuine, it could be one of the most important artifacts in all of history. The Shroud of Turin is so named because it is kept in the Cathedral of Saint John the Baptist in Turin, Italy. The Shroud is a 14-foot, 5-inch by 3-foot, 7-inch linen cloth bearing a negative three-dimensional image of a crucified man in his thirties. The image bears red imprints that looks like blood around the back, arms, legs, and head. Heaps of blood are found under the right pectoral of the crucified man and around the wrists and feet. When a photograph is taken of the Shroud, the negatives afford a clearer view of the man on the cloth.

In 1988, a research team conducted a radiocarbon test on a lower strand of the linen. The test deemed that the cloth dated to around the 1300s. However, further research indicated that the Shroud had caught on fire in the 1532 and was repaired by some local nuns. When looking at the Shroud, one can see the burn marks indicated by two lines going up both sides of the cloth with burn marks in different locations. Water marks are also seen where the nuns tried to extinguish the flames. The strand of the cloth that had been tested probably originated from one of the nuns' weaves. A further strand of evidence that seem to indicate that the Turin Shroud could be the burial cloth of Jesus include the lack of paint pigment.[26] The blood on the Shroud is actual Type AB hemoglobin. The DNA is broken

---

25. Price and House, *Zondervan Handbook of Biblical Archaeology*, 250–251.

26. The STURP (Shroud of Turin Research Project) released its final report, saying, "We can conclude for now that the Shroud image is that of a real human form of a scourged, crucified man. It is not the product of an artist. The blood stains are composed of hemoglobin and also give a positive test for serum albumin. The image is an ongoing mystery and until further chemical studies are made, perhaps by this group of scientists, or perhaps by some scientists in the future, the problem remains unsolved." STURP, "A Summary of STURP's Conclusions," *Shroud.com* (1981), retrieved May 2, 2019, https://www.shroud.com/78conclu.htm.

down, but researchers can determine that the person was a human being and was male. Pollen particles have been found on the Shroud that date to the first century AD, including the *Zygophyllum dumosum* which only grows in Israel, Jordan, and Sinai.[27] Some of the flowers represented on the Shroud only bloom in spring. Thus, the Shroud is shown to have originated in Israel due to the plant particles.

Finally, the marks on the Shroud were caused by a high dosage of radiation. In his paper "Role of Radiation in Image Formation on the Shroud of Turin," Robert A. Rucker, a nuclear engineer who holds a Master of Science degree in nuclear engineering from the University of Michigan, wrote the following after leading a team to conduct research on the Shroud, "The best explanation for the evidence on the Shroud is that radiation was released by the dead body that was wrapped in the Shroud. As such, this event is outside of our current understanding of the laws of science."[28] While the Shroud is not necessary to prove the resurrection of Jesus, the mounting data concerning the Shroud seems to suggest that the Shroud might be Jesus of Nazareth's authentic burial cloth.

Conclusion

A few further notes need to be made about biblical archaeological discoveries before moving on to the next chapter. First, the 15 archaeological evidences presented in this chapter are just a small sampling of the large body of discoveries that have been made. It is estimated that of the near 20 percent of the biblical lands that have been excavated, some 80 individuals from the Old Testament and 40 individuals from the New Testament have been positively verified.

Second, archaeology only posits a very small sampling of what has existed in history with only a small portion of the discoveries making it to press. Randall Price has noted that only a fraction of what was made in history has survived; only a fraction of archaeological sites have been excavated; only a fraction of the explored sites have been excavated; only a fraction of excavated sites have been examined; and only a fraction of what has

---

27. Avinoam Danin, "Pressed Flowers: Where Did the Shroud of Turin Originate? A Botanical Quest," *Shroud.com* (1997), retrieved May 2, 2019, https://www.shroud.com/danin.htm.

28. Robert A. Rucker, "Role of Radiation in Image Formation on the Shroud of Turin," *ShroudResearch.net* (October 11, 2016), Kevin N. Schwinkendorf, ed, retrieved May 2, 2019, http://www.shroudresearch.net/hproxy.php/http:/role-of-radiation-in-image-formation.pdf?lbisphpreq=1.

been excavated have been reported and published.[29] So, while archaeology illuminates history, it does not provide a full picture. As more discoveries are made, the more ancient history will be illuminated. But it must be acknowledged that the absence of evidence is not necessarily evidence of absence, especially when realizing that much of biblical history lies beneath modern-day cities and structures. It is impossible to excavate around the Temple Mount in Jerusalem due to the sacredness the site holds to Jews, Muslims, and Christians alike.

Third, many more discoveries are yet to come. However, no discovery should be accepted at face value. A Christian needs to be discerning and resist the temptation to accept or reject any archaeological finding whether for or against the Bible until it is given proper research. For instance, many believed that a fragment of Mark's Gospel had been found that dated to the first century. Admittedly, I was one of them. However, it was later noted that the fragment dated to the second century. The fragment was still an amazing find. But it was not as early as once thought.[30] The same is true of finds that purportedly discount the Bible. Often, reports are sensationalized in order to sell books rather than a true quest for truth. A good example is found in the *Secret Gospel of Mark*. The so-called Gospel presented a homosexual version of Jesus championed by Morton Smith. The document was controversial from its inception. However, the document was later shown to be nothing more than a fraud.[31] This caused great embarrassment for the scholarly community as many, including John Dominic Crossan, had accepted its validity. While the book was sensationalized by the media, it was later dismissed by the scholarly community. Unfortunately, the press does not always publish the retraction of a discovery.

While archaeology cannot definitively prove or disprove the events described in the Bible, it is quite interesting to note that no discovery that has yet been made has ever successfully disproven anything in the Word of God. Yes, archaeology has raised specific questions concerning certain events. But archaeology has not given any reason to discredit the events described in the Bible. With more discoveries being made each year, it is truly an exciting time to be a child of God!

---

29. Price, *The Stones Cry Out*, 46–47.

30. A great deal of credit goes to Daniel Wallace for his honesty regarding the fragment of Mark's Gospel. His thoughts on the matter can be found at his blog. Daniel B. Wallace, "First-Century Mark Fragment Update," *DanielBWallace.com* (May 23, 2018), retrieved August 9, 2019, https://danielbwallace.com/2018/05/23/first-century-mark-fragment-update/.

31. Bruce Chilton, "Unmasking a False Gospel," *NYSun.com* (October 25, 2006), retrieved August 9, 2019, https://www.nysun.com/arts/unmasking-a-false-gospel/42197/.

Chapter 14

BIBLICAL AUTHORITY

Inconsistencies of Scripture or Misunderstanding?

One of the arguments that is often posited against Christians is that the Bible is full of inconsistencies or contradictions. Skeptics often accuse the Bible for being immoral because of the laws given in the Old Testament. As previously noted, Richard Dawkins wrote a scathing commentary filled with colorful adjectives describing his viewpoint of Yahweh in the Old Testament. After his diatribe, Dawkins states that "Thomas Jefferson—better read—was of a similar opinion, describing the God of Moses as a 'being of terrific character—cruel, vindictive, capricious and unjust.'"[1] It is interesting that people like Dawkins fail to see the many acts of grace and mercy displayed by Yahweh throughout the Old Testament. For instance, God illustrated his consistent grace given over to the people of God by the example of the prophet Hosea and his adulterous wife Gomer (Hos. 11:7, 9). Or consider the many times that Yahweh spared Israel throughout its history even though they constantly turned from him. This is not the depiction of a malevolent bully, but rather one of a compassionate friend.

Skeptics do not end with their charges of fouled morality in the Scripture. They also often point out inconsistencies within the text. For instance, the death of Judas Iscariot seems to be reported differently in the Gospels than in Acts. The hours of Jesus's crucifixion are seemingly reported differently in the Synoptic Gospels than in John's. Even within the evangelical Christian community, scholars debate as to whether the term *inerrancy*

---

1. Dawkins, *The God Delusion*, 51.

should be defended with such differences. However, extreme measures need not be taken. By using simple background information and understanding the nature of genre, the apologist will find that most, if not all, of the perceived inconsistencies stem from misunderstandings.

It is said that tellers are trained so well in knowing what a genuine dollar bill looks like that they automatically notice if a bill is fraudulent simply by looking at it. They don't need to know all the differences found in counterfeit bills. All they need is a thorough knowledge of the genuine dollar bill. Counterfeits are easily detected with such knowledge. In a similar manner, one is better served to understand how to best interpret the Bible rather than focusing on each claim of biblical inconsistency.

Understanding Genre

Many of the skeptics' accusations come from a misunderstanding of the writing style of the biblical text in question, particularly genre. For instance, I once encountered a skeptic who held that the descriptions of Jesus in Revelation proved that the resurrection was a hallucination. Because in Revelation, Jesus is described as having seven horns and seven eyes (Rev. 5:6). Certainly, this could not be literal! So, seeing that the disciple saw the risen Jesus in a hallucinatory manner in Revelation, that must have been the way that the disciples witnessed Jesus when they mistakenly thought that he had risen from the dead. I explained to the skeptic that Revelation is written in a different genre than the Gospels. In apocalyptic literature such as Revelation, symbols are used to describe a person or an event. In the case of Revelation 5:6, the number seven indicates perfection or completion. Horns represent strength and eyes represent wisdom. By understanding the nature of apocalyptic literature, we can then know that John describes Jesus having perfect strength and perfect wisdom. Rather than literally explaining the risen Jesus as he is viewed in heaven, John depicts the omnipotence and omniscience that Jesus holds being the glorified Son of God. Genre solved the problem.

Genre is a style or method of writing. Knowing the different genres in Scripture can help in resolving the so-called inconsistencies of Scripture as well as providing better understanding of the teachings of Scripture. It can prevent individuals from falling into theological pitfalls which comes by bad biblical interpretation. There are eight kinds of genre in the Bible.[2]

---

2. Understanding the differences in genre has helped me better understand Scripture than nearly any other hermeneutical device I have learned.

1. [NL 1–8]1. *Law.* The first genre in Scripture is *law.* Unsurprisingly, the first five books of the Bible (Gen. through Deut.) are written according to the legal genre. The law is arguably the most difficult areas of Scripture to find modern applications. Some laws have been overridden by the New Covenant of Christ. For instance, the dietary restrictions found in the Pentateuch do not have a bearing on New Covenant Christians, especially considering Peter's vision (Acts 10:9–16).

To find applications in the law, we need to note the kinds of legal codes in the biblical legal genre: civil, ceremonial, and moral. *Civil laws* are those that deal with the nation of Israel. This may include laws pertaining to the land and how the person was to behave in society. *Ceremonial laws* concern the religious and sacrificial practices related to the temple and/or tabernacle. This may also consist of Jewish holidays and the rituals associated with them. *Moral laws* are universal ethical codes of conduct concerning how one interacts with God (Deut. 6:4) and humanity (Lev. 19:17–18).

The ceremonial and civil laws have a moral law behind them. To interpret the law for modern contexts; first, evaluate the law; then, ask why it was implemented; and finally, see what a person can learn from the ancient law. Seek out the moral laws and evaluate what can be learned through the practice. Also, don't be quick to judge. On the one hand, it is unfair, and really anachronistic, to hold ancient cultures to the same standards of modern cultures. They faced different issues and with far more limited technology than we do today. On the other hand, while some of the laws may seem odd or even strange, realize the moral code of the Torah was vastly superior to other legislation in the Ancient Near East (ANE). Women also held a much higher status in Judaism than they did in any other ANE culture. In his book *Is God a Moral Monster,* Paul Copan argues that God works within an established patriarchal society to point to a better path while providing protections for women against abuse while living in substandard conditions.[3] Even with less than favorable legislation in the Old Testament, Copan holds that "we shouldn't consider these negative examples endorsements of oppression and abuse."[4] I believe that women are elevated far more in the pages of Scripture than any of us realize as are the oppressed and downtrodden. Understanding the legal genre affords a better understanding of the divine grace that was shown even when it is not always apparent.

3. Paul Copan, *Is God a Moral Monster?*, 102.
4. Ibid.

2. *Historical narrative.* Historical narrative composes the largest genre of the Bible, consisting of some 43 percent of the biblical text. Nearly half of the Bible reveals historical stories of people, places, and events that surround encounters with God in some fashion. The historical sections of the Old Testament along with the book of Acts in the New Testament are written using historical narrative. Biographies are historical narratives. The key difference between biographies and historical narratives is that biographies are only concerned with one person, whereas historical narratives tell the story of multiple people and nations. Nevertheless, for our purposes, the biographies of the New Testament will be discussed under a different category. Luckily, historical narrative is among the easiest of the genres to comprehend as they speak of colorful characters who face times of conflict within a historical space and time. However, there are three things that must be considered when interpreting the historical narrative genre.

   a. *Character.* First, the reader must understand the character and ask the following questions: Who is the character? What is his or her relationship with God? Who is/are the hero(es) known as the protagonist, and who is/are the villain(s) known as the antagonist? Also, investigate the person's name. For instance, Jesus's name in Hebrew is *Yeshua*, an abbreviation of the name *Yehoshua*. Yehoshua is transliterated as the name *Joshua*. Joshua and Yeshua both mean "God saves." In ancient cultures, a person's name indicated something of the person's character. Also, note that every character had flaws with the sole exception of Jesus of Nazareth. Each character in the Bible serves either as an inspiration (showing what you should be like or should do) or an example (showing what you should not be like and should not do). The genius of the biblical form of historical narrative is that the reader can identify with most characters in the Bible.

   For instance, I can identify with David because I am not tall like Saul. I am not a person's first choice when you think of a stately leader. Most successful preachers seem to be tall, slender, and eloquent of tongue. Meanwhile, I am short, stocky, and trip over my words. People desire leaders like Saul. But the problem with Saul is that he did not have a heart for God. David was not the people's first choice, but God used him to do far more than what Saul did. So already, we can discover two principles. First, we see how people can be led astray by appearances. Second, we see how God values the inner life of a person more than outer appearances. This is what makes the historical narrative genre so much fun. People love exciting stories. The Bible provides just that.

b. *Setting.* The setting of the story is the place where the event happens. This is where digging into history will be especially helpful. If the reader understands the culture, the socio-economic status of the area, the language, the nations, and national conflict; then the setting will become much more apparent.

A good example of how this information is beneficial is with the so-called inconsistencies of the Synoptic Gospels' time in comparison with John's. Mark says that Jesus was crucified at the third hour (Mark 15:25), whereas John says that Jesus was crucified about noon (John 19:14) or about the sixth hour. Is there a discrepancy between the Gospel writers? In reality, there is not. Some have argued that John may have been using the Roman time which would place the time of Jesus's crucifixion near 6 AM. For others, the idea of the sixth hour should not be pressed as John is giving an approximation rather than an exact hour. Jews and Romans often estimated the time as they did not wear Rolex watches or have smartphones to indicate the precise time that the event took place. In this case, the perceived discrepancy comes from a mere misunderstanding of the text. It is both impractical and unfair to hold ancient individuals to the same modern standards of precision. I would dare guess that if we did not have all of our technological gadgets and toys that we would have to estimate the same way that the ancients did. Understanding the setting and the practices of the time will go a long way to help better interpret the passages in question.

c. *Plot.* The plot is the flow of the story. When evaluating the story, examine what the problems were, what the climax of the story is, and what solutions were offered. The flow of the story will safeguard us from making faulty claims of error in the biblical text, and it will better help our understanding of the overall story. Other factors to consider are the patterns within the plot and how the plot of the story fits within the grander story of the Bible as a whole. Such is especially true when engaging the issue concerning biblical warfare and the commands to strike against enemy nations. What was the purpose behind God's command to attack them (Exod. 33:2)? In many cases, the cultures being attacked held barbarous practices such as infant sacrifice.[5] To attack these societies was morally just as it was for the Allies to attack Nazi Germany.

3. *Poetry.* Poetry makes up the next largest segment of Scripture. 33 percent of the Bible is poetic in nature. Poetry has sub-categories within it consisting of songs/psalms, wisdom literature, and prophecy. The prophets and wisdom genres will be discussed in separate categories. Job is considered a poetic book to a degree. The book uses long monologues as it asks why bad things happen to good people. Due to a limitation of space, our concern will primarily be with interpreting the Psalms.

Within the Psalms, you will find six categories of poetic literature. The first category consists of *lamentations.* The laments make up the largest portion of the Psalms as there are more than sixty psalms devoted to this category.[6] A lamentation is a sorrowful reflection on something bad that has happened. The lament identifies with a person's pain. The second category are psalms of *thanksgiving.*[7] The thanksgiving psalms are polar opposite to the lamentation psalms. Here, the psalmist is thankful for the goodness of God and for the blessings of life. The third category consists of psalms reflecting on the *salvation-history* of Israel. Only five psalms fit this category (Ps. 78, 105, 106, 135, and 136).[8] As the title of the category implies, these psalms evaluate the history of God's salvific plan with his people. As such, these psalms relate to historical events. Thus, the event needs to be evaluated when interpreting the passage. The fourth category of psalms is the *theological psalms.*[9] Psalm 2, 18, 20, 21, 24, 29, 45, 46, 47, 48, 50, 72, 76, 81, 84, 87, 93, 95–99, 101, 110, 122, and 144 all describe some theological aspect of God, his work, or his covenant

---

5. Copan notes that "infant sacrifice—whether to Yahweh or to Baal or Molech—is still detestable" and Yahweh called for the practices to end swiftly. Ibid., 98.

6. Gordon D. Fee and Douglas Stuart, *How to Read the Bible for All Its Worth,* 212.

7. Fee and Stuart distinguish psalms of thanksgiving and praise. Ibid., 212. However, the psalms are so comparable that I do not hold that a distinction between the two is necessary.

8. Ibid., 213.

9. Fee and Stuart call these psalms "Psalms of Celebration and Affirmation." Ibid.

with Israel.[10] *Wisdom psalms* comprise the fifth category. Only eight psalms (36, 37, 49, 112, 127, 128, and 133) are found in this category. The wisdom psalms read much like wisdom literature as they describe how God designed life to be, although life does not always follow such a pattern. Lastly, what Fee and Stuart call *"Songs of Trust"*[11] consist of the sixth category of psalms. These psalms denote the psalmist's trust in God no matter what difficulties he may encounter. Psalms 11, 16, 23, 27, 62, 63, 91, 121, 125, and 131 are considered to be within this sixth category.

4. *Wisdom.* While wisdom literature is found in various sections of Scripture, it is most prevalent in Proverbs. This section is distinguished from other areas of wisdom literature because proverbial writings are often misunderstood. Proverbs do not state the way things always are, but rather the way things are supposed to be in an ideal world. Proverbial statements are pithy declarations of moral and ethical standards exemplifying the *shoulds* of life. Life should be where the person who works the hardest is rewarded the greatest. Proverb 12:24 states that "the diligent hand will rule, but laziness will lead to forced labor." While this is generally true, anyone who has worked in blue collar industries as I have will quickly note that this is *not always* true. Sometimes, the person who plays political games while remaining lazy in their work is rewarded while the hardest workers who are faithful to their employers are often neglected. Psalm 12:23 also states that "A shrewd person conceals knowledge, but a foolish heart publicizes stupidity." Examining our society with all the posts posted on social media, either we are a generation of stupid people, or shrewd people sometimes publish knowledgeable information. Proverbial information does not tell of the way things always are, but the way things mostly are. So, for the former proverb, it is true in what it says. It is comparable to the modern proverb which says, "It is better to keep your mouth shut and let people think you are a fool, than to open your mouth and remove all doubt."

Another example is found in the proverb, stating, "Start a youth out on his way; even when he grows old he will not depart from it" (Prov. 22:6). While this is mostly true, is it always true? What of the prodigal son in Jesus's parable (Luke 15:11–32)? He was certainly trained in the way he should live. But did he always accept the wisdom

---

10. Fee and Stuart delineate these psalms into three subcategories: covenant renewal liturgies, enthronement psalms, and Songs of Zion. Ibid., 213–214.

11. Ibid., 214.

of his father? What of the sons of Eli the priest (1 Samuel 1–2)? Some may look at the proverb and claim that it is erroneous because it is not always true. But such an attitude comes from a misunderstanding of the nature of proverbs. Exceptions may exist with the proverbs. That's why in God's sovereignty he added Job and Ecclesiastes to the corpus of wisdom literature. Proverbially speaking, good and righteous people are blessed, and good things come to them. But Job shows the exception to the rule. Sometimes, good people suffer. Ecclesiastes shows the meaninglessness that comes to life without God. While success may bring happiness, Ecclesiastes indicates that nothing is of value without God (Ecc. 12:13–14). Altogether, the books of wisdom literature give a grand collective display on how the world works and how to live the best possible life. One gentleman noted after I taught through the book of Proverbs how amazed he was that the ancient proverbs are just as applicable today as they were then. I wholeheartedly agree.

5. *Prophecy.* Prophecy is perhaps the most difficult genre to interpret. The Bible has two sections of prophets: The *Major Prophets* and the *Minor Prophets*. The two classes of prophets are distinguished only by the length of their books and not by the level of their importance. When reading prophecy, it is important to mention that prophets were both forth tellers and foretellers. The prophets' *forth telling* ministry involved their preaching to the people of their own time. They warned of the culture's moral failure. Quite often, the culture of their time resembles the culture of our own. To properly interpret the passage in question, the reader must understand who the prophet was, the culture he was addressing, and people to whom he was speaking.

The *foretelling* ministry of the prophet included messages of future events that were to come. Some of the prophecies told of imminent judgments that were to come, messianic predictions of a future ruler, and eschatological messages of blessing and doom. To properly interpret the prophets, a person needs to read the passage of Scripture with the background information in mind. The prophets often used poetry and prose in their messages. As such, it is important to decipher through their genius use of wordplays[12] and the symbolism. Like the Epistles, one must remember that the prophets wrote primarily to

---

12. A good illustration of the prophets' wordplay is found in Amos 8:1–2. The Hebrew *qys* and *qs* are used. The text reads in the NRSV, "[God] said, 'Amos, what do you see?' And I said, 'A basket of summer [*qys*] fruit.' Then the LORD said to me, 'The time is ripe [*qs*] for my people Israel.'" See Gordon D. Fee and Douglas Stuart, *How to Read the Bible for All It's Worth,* 3rd ed (Grand Rapids: Zondervan, 2003), Kindle ed.

the people to whom they addressed in their prophecies. God, by his sovereignty and through the inspiration of the Holy Spirit, makes the texts applicable to us. But we must remember that the texts were not primarily written to us. Critics and Christians alike have misused the prophecies for their own cause without making an effort to understand the context of the prophecy.

6. *Bioi.* Scholars increasingly agree that the Evangelists[13] used the ancient *bios* genre (Gk., *bioi* is plural) to compose their Gospels. While it is generally accepted that the Evangelists wrote the Gospels according to the *bios* standards of the Greco-Roman period, it is hotly debated as to how much freedom this kind of literature gave the biographers in composing their work. Michael Licona argues that the Evangelists had substantial room to arrange material according to their audience's needs while remaining faithful to the historical facts and data of Jesus's life.[14] Lydia McGrew hotly contests Licona's claims. She holds that the Gospels can be defended using a centuries old tactic known as "undesigned coincidence" which is an unplanned historical fit between two or more texts.[15] While we don't have time in this section to go into all the nuances between the two views, we should explore both voices and note that both voices have a lot to offer.

On the one hand, it is quite apparent that some Gospels are arranged in better chronological order than others. Papias, writing in the first century as quoted by Eusebius, writes of John Mark, "Mark, having become the interpreter of Peter, wrote down accurately, though not indeed in order, whatsoever he remembered of the things said or done by Christ."[16] Thus, while Mark wrote accurately pertaining to the life of Christ, he did not necessarily write in chronological order. Of the three Synoptic Gospels,[17] Luke is written in the most systematic chronological order. Matthew is the second most chronological Gospel as he sometimes combines the teachings of Jesus with his miracles to show the connection between the two. Mark is the least chronological as he recounts Peter's eyewitness testimony. John only handles the

---

13. That is, the writers of the Gospels.

14. Michael R. Licona, *Why are There Differences in the Gospels? What We Can Learn from Ancient Biography*, 5–6.

15. Lydia McGrew, "Introduction to Part One," *Hidden in Plain Sight: Undesigned Coincidences in the Gospels and Acts*, Kindle.

16. Eusebius of Caesarea, *The Church History of Eusebius*, 3.39.15, 172.

17. *Synoptic* means seen through the same eyes. This term is used for Matthew, Mark, and Luke since they are all written in the same manner.

ministry of Jesus in Jerusalem and Judea. I am of the persuasion that John is fairly chronological in what he presents, but he does so with a different ministerial application of Jesus. The Synoptic Gospels focus on the Galilean ministry and John focuses on the Judean ministry of Jesus. So, the expositor must piece together John's information with the Synoptic texts. But why were the Gospels written in this fashion?

It must be remembered that the Evangelists wrote to different audiences. Matthew, an eyewitness and apostle of Jesus, wrote primarily for a Jewish audience. Thus, as previously noted, he linked together the teachings of Jesus with his miracles to show that Jesus was the new Moses bringing forth the New Covenant. John Mark recorded the teachings of Simon Peter. John Mark most likely wrote for the church in and around Rome. Therefore, he is writing to a Roman audience who was not concerned with details but wanted high volumes of action. It was not necessary for Mark to meticulously document every minute detail of Jesus's life. Such a Gospel would have lost his intended audience. Luke was a biographer par excellence. In contrast to Mark, he did meticulously record the life and teachings of Jesus in an orderly fashion (Luke 1:3). Luke's Gospel was written for the Greeks who were more intellectuals and placed a higher value on historical detail. It is also interesting that Luke, being a physician, places more emphasis on medical issues than any other Gospel writer does.

John's Gospel is also written in a historically accurate manner following the *bios* genre. John, the beloved apostle of Jesus and an eyewitness of the post-resurrected Jesus, was probably a teenager when he began to follow Jesus. According to the best traditions available, John served as a pastor in Ephesus later in life. If John was 20 when Jesus died in 33 AD, he would have been in his 70s when he composed the Fourth Gospel.

If the traditions concerning John are correct and John of Zebedee truly is the author of the Fourth Gospel, then John writes his Gospel for the future generations of the church. He realizes that Jesus is most likely not going to return in his lifetime. Thus, he writes so that future generations of the church can follow Christ. Because of this, John composes the most theologically rooted Gospel of the four. The Gospel includes explanations of Jesus's teachings and deep theological truths such as the prologue of the Fourth Gospel (John 1:1–14).[18]

18. There is some debate as to whether John 3:16–21 records the words of Jesus or John's explanation of Jesus's teaching in John 3:10–15. While this writer believes that the words are from Jesus, the words are inspired and infallible either way.

It bears repeating that John focused on the Judean ministry of Jesus, whereas the Synoptic Gospels focused on the Galilean ministry of Jesus. When reading John's Gospel in correlation with the Synoptics, this fact must be considered. Most of what may be considered an inconsistency or inaccuracy between the Gospels can be resolved when one understands the *bios* genre, the audiences to whom the Evangelists were writing, while also acknowledging the undesigned coincidences that arise when a careful reading is given to the Gospel texts.

7. *Epistles.* The epistles are like letters in that they are written by a person and directed toward a specific audience in mind. Epistles differ from traditional letters only by the audience and the nature of the document. Epistles are written to a group of people, whereas letters are normally written to only one person. Epistles normally come from a religious perspective and offer a treatise on a particular topic, whereas letters may address numerous issues. As with prophecy, the interpreter of Scripture must remember that the epistle was not originally intended for them. At times, the writer may have in mind a specific issue or problem that needed to be addressed. Any pastor knows that churches have problems. The purpose behind the writing is some church or theological problem that needed to be resolved. More times than not, the specific issue or problem will not be explicitly obvious. Some of the apostles' teaching will hold individual or cultural implications for the church in question. At other times, the teachings are universal in scope. Distinguishing between specific/cultural and universal teachings is done in three ways—context, context, context. Like other genres, it is important to remember the background information when interpreting the passage.

8. *Apocalyptic literature.* Finally, one of the most intimidating genres of all is the genre of apocalyptic literature. Primarily, apocalyptic literature includes the book of Revelation.[19] Some parts of Daniel and Ezekiel are also apocalyptic. Apocalyptic literature is distinguishable from prophecy in five ways. First, apocalyptic literature exclusively speaks of the end times, whereas prophecy primarily speaks of the times in which the book was written.

Second, apocalyptic literature primarily communicates by the usage of a vast array of symbolic images to teach about certain nations,

---

19. Revelation is singular and not plural. It is called the book of Revelation and not the book of Revelations.

people, or entities, whereas prophetic literature uses symbolism in a secondary role.

Third, apocalyptic literature is by and large positive in its overall message, whereas the prophets are often negative. This is not always true as Habakkuk, Amos, Hosea, and Isaiah all have positive outlooks of extended history. But even then, their immediate outlook is negative. The Lamentations of Jeremiah are much more depressing because of its limited scope as he looks at the impending judgment of the nation.

Fourth, the overall message of apocalyptic literature calls for the faithful to persevere until the end, whereas prophecy addresses the current sins of the nation and calls for a message of repentance because imminent judgment is near. As such, the prophets call for immediate action to prevent the judgment to come. Apocalyptic writers teach that bad things are coming despite the people's faithfulness. Therefore, they must take heart and trust in God.

Finally, apocalyptic literature primarily consists of visions that convey the overall plan of God throughout history, whereas prophetic literature primarily comprises oracles that communicate the will of God in clear and unmistakable terms. Apocalyptic literature requires the reader to decode the symbolism used to understand a literal event to come.

To properly interpret apocalyptic literature, one must seek to always keep the text in context. In addition, always seek to understand the symbols being used. Even then, it may not always be clear where symbolism ends, and literal language begins. The best tactic is to study the symbols as used in other passages of Scripture. It is remarkable how much Revelation uses symbols and concepts found in the Old Testament.

Pastors have told me that they never preach or teach from Revelation. This is sad. Revelation and apocalyptic literature offer great hope for a church facing chaotic times. Don't become too bogged down with the scary aspects of Revelation. The primary message is that God is sovereignly directing the course of history. In the end, we win!

Contextual Understanding

From the study already presented in this chapter, one should already see the significant importance of keeping Scripture in its proper context. Most of the so-called inconsistencies and/or discrepancies of Scripture fade away when the text is understood in light of the overall message of the book and the Bible as a whole. For instance, some people have read Isaiah 45:7 and thought that God was the creator of evil. In the text, Yahweh is speaking. He says, "I form light and create darkness, I make success and create disaster; I am the LORD, who does all these things" (Is. 45:7). Another rendering of the text reads, "I form the light, and create darkness: I make peace, and create evil: I the LORD do all these things" (Is. 45:7, KJV). The prophet used the term *ra' ah* which can indicate calamity, some disaster, or evil. When keeping the verse in context of Isaiah 45:1–7, Yahweh is speaking of some disaster that was yet to come and not evil. He speaks of disarming the kings (45:1), leveling the uneven places (45:2), shattering the bronze doors (45:2), and cutting the iron bars in two (45:2). The passage is Yahweh's address to Cyrus the king of Persia. He was promising that Cyrus would be raised up to a prominent position and that everything that stood in his way from accomplishing the goals that Yahweh had set for him would be cleared. The text illustrates God's sovereignty over all of history. He is not bringing about evil. Rather, he is bringing judgment to the rebellious.

Keeping the context in the overall scheme of the Bible's message is also key. Can God do evil? Well, God is said to be "light, and there is absolutely no darkness in him" (1 John 1:5). If light is understood to be a symbol for holiness and dark a symbol for evil, then the apostle is saying that God is not in the least bit evil. He is completely holy. God is the absolute good. The psalmist proclaims that God is holy and that there was no one like God (Ps. 77:13). Paul notes that it is impossible for God to lie, thus indicating the absolute righteous nature of God (Titus 1:2). Isaiah notes the holiness of God earlier in the book by noting how the "holy God shows that he is holy through his righteousness" (Is. 5:16). Finally, God is called holy three times which indicates his absolute and undeniable righteous nature (Is. 6:3; Rev. 4:8).

Conclusion

This chapter may seem a bit out of place for some. It may seem that the chapter belongs more in a hermeneutics book which instructs on proper biblical interpretation rather than in an apologetics book. However, we must understand that biblical illiteracy rates are at an all-time high for both believers and unbelievers alike. Many charges of biblical inconsistences or inaccuracies come from the skeptic's misunderstanding of the text, which in turn originates from faulty interpretations regarding the genre of the text, the historical background of the text, and the context of the biblical passage in which it is found. This is not to say that there are not some problem passages that must be ironed out. Some do deserve attention. But such an exploration is for another time and for another book. So, to cover the largest swath of the skeptics' charges, we have dealt with proper biblical interpretation. To keep the skeptic at bay, always interpret the right way.

Furthermore, it is good practice to never develop your theology from one obscure verse as a general rule. You can make the Bible say anything you want by taking a verse out of context. For instance, you can force the Bible say, "there's no God." The Bible does say those words in Psalm 14. However, if you keep the text in its proper context, you'll find that the verse says, "The fool says in his heart, 'There's no God'" (Ps. 14:1). Keeping the text in its proper context reveals the truth behind what the biblical author intended.

Good biblical interpretation also reduces faulty criticisms concerning the nature and being of God. Christians must do their part to properly interpret the Word of God and present the biblical theistic view of God. This can be done by always keeping a verse in the context of the paragraph, in the context of the chapter, in the context of the book, and in the context of the entire biblical canon. If you don't understand a verse, read the paragraph. If you don't understand the paragraph, read the chapter. If you don't understand the chapter, read the book. If you don't understand the book, keep the text in the context of a systematic biblical understanding. The point is, don't read Bible verses independently. Read Bible passages.

Chapter 15

MESSIANIC PROPHECY

Among some of the most intriguing biblical characters are the prophets. The prophets were literary geniuses, wordsmiths if there ever were any. They used poetic, colorful language to both forthtell and foretell. Their forthtelling ministry was to the current generation. The prophets would warn the people of their own time of their sin and encourage them to repent of their sins. Forthtelling was the primary objection of the prophet. However, God also used the prophet to foretell future events. Of the events the prophets foretold, the most important of their prophecies were messianic. *Messianic prophecies* are proclamations that foretell a future, eschatological Messiah who was to come and set up a new covenant, redeem the people of God, and to establish a new Garden of Eden—a place where God and humanity lives in harmony—which was lost at the fall of humankind.

While critical scholars are often skeptical of the foretelling ministry of the prophets and especially of messianic prophecy, their skepticism shows nothing more than an anti-supernatural bias which speaks more of their own naturalism than it does in following the biblical evidence.[1] As one might tell, I am sometimes critical of the claims of critical scholarship. Problematically, the skepticism from critical scholarship is beginning to creep into conservative evangelical circles leading some to abandon the enterprise.

It may surprise you to discover that messianic prophecy was one of the chief apologetic tools of the early church because messianic interpretations of the Old Testament prophecies are among the earliest of interpretations. In the Talmud, it is said that "None of the prophets prophesied except of

---

1. Granted, there are exceptions. But overall, this seems to be the case.

the days of Messiah."[2] Alfred Edersheim notes that "the passages in the Old Testament applied to the Messiah or to messianic times in the most ancient Jewish writings . . . amount in all to 456, thus distributed: 75 from the Pentateuch, 243 from the prophets, and 138 from the Hagiographa, and supported by more than 558 separate quotations from the rabbinical writings."[3] Let it be repeated: the most ancient and enduring of interpretations pertaining to the Hebrew Bible is that several of the prophecies are messianic in nature. Many of the oldest messianic interpretations predate the birth of Jesus of Nazareth. Thus, such messianic interpretations cannot be Christian interpolations since Christianity did not yet exist!

With that in mind, let us look at some of the more prominent messianic prophecies in the Hebrew Bible (i.e., Old Testament). We will examine five messianic prophecies in the Pentateuch, ten from the Major Prophets, and five in the Minor Prophets. Understand that this is only a small sampling of messianic prophecies which are available. By the time one counts them all, conservative estimates are that there are around 181 prophecies that relate to the coming Messiah, not counting messianic allusions.[4]

The Messiah in the Pentateuch

Normally, when individuals think about messianic prophecy, their minds gravitate toward Isaiah or another prophet. However, a close examination of the Pentateuch—the first five books of the Bible—demonstrates that at least five messianic prophecies are present in the Law.

Genesis 3:15—Seed of a Woman

I will put hostility between you and the woman,
and between your offspring and her offspring.
He will strike your head,
and you will strike his heel (Gen. 3:15).

In this passage of Scripture, Yahweh is talking to the Serpent who is classically understood to be Satan. Yahweh tells the Serpent that his

---

2. b. Sanhedrin 99a.
3. Alfred Edersheim, "Appendix 9," *Life and Times of Jesus the Messiah*, 980.
4. We need to add a caveat to our exploration into messianic prophecy. The following messianic prophecies hold varying levels of confidence among modern scholars. However, as I previously mentioned, early interpreters accept most, if not all, of the texts discussed in this chapter.

seed—that is, descendants—would be in hostility with the seed—that is, descendants—of the woman. The term *zera* describing the offspring is a critical term in the text as it describes the enmity between those who follow after Satan and those who are of God.[5] However, at some point, a particular descendant of Eve's will arise. He will strike the head of the Serpent while the Serpent strikes the Descendant's heel. The term "strike" is translated from the Hebrew term *shuwph* which can mean a bruise or a break. In the context in which it is used, *shuwph* indicates a fatal blow which is delivered to both parties. This future Descendant would break the curse brought forth by the Serpent. For this reason, many theologians have called Genesis 3:15 the *protoevangelium*—the Gospel before the Gospel.[6]

Genesis 22:18—Seed of Abraham

And all the nations of the earth will be blessed by your offspring because you have obeyed my command (Gen. 22:18).

Yahweh tells Abraham that all the world, which includes all the nations of the world, would find their blessing by his offspring. While some would find a fulfillment in the people of Israel, a more traditional understanding, even among early rabbinic scholars, was to see the Messiah being the vessel by which God would bless the world. He would bring salvation to the world through One particular offspring—the Messiah of God.

Genesis 49:8–12—Coming of Shiloh

Judah, your brothers will praise you.
Your hand will be on the necks of your enemies;
your father's sons will bow down to you.
9 Judah is a young lion—
my son, you return from the kill.
He crouches; he lies down like a lion
or a lioness—who dares to rouse him?
10 The scepter will not depart from Judah
or the staff from between his feet
until he whose right it is comes

---

5. This is indicated in the story of Cain and Abel where Cain kills Abel over his sacrifice to Yahweh (Gen. 4:1–16).

6. Tremper Longman III, *How to Read Genesis*, 166.

and the obedience of the peoples belongs to him.
11 He ties his donkey to a vine,
and the colt of his donkey to the choice vine.
He washes his clothes in wine
and his robes in the blood of grapes.
12 His eyes are darker than wine,
and his teeth are whiter than milk (Gen. 49:8–12).

This messianic prophecy is hidden unless you read the Hebrew text. Due to a desire to keep from interjecting personal theological convictions and/or interpretations in the text, most biblical translations choose to translate the term *Shiloh* as "he whose right it comes." The text literally reads as follows, "The scepter shall not depart from Judah and the ruler's staff from his feet until Shiloh comes and the obedience of the nations belongs to him."[7] The oddity of the passage is that the term *Shiloh* in the Hebrew text is used as a personal name. According to ancient Jewish midrashic interpreters,[8] *Shiloh* was a descriptive name for the Messiah. The name indicates peace and tranquility. Thus, the Messiah is not only identified with the royal lineage stemming through Judah and the eternal kingdom what would come to him, he is also shown to be an ultimate peacemaker.

Numbers 24:14–19—Rule of the Messiah

Now I am going back to my people, but first, let me warn you what these people will do to your people in the future."

15 Then he proclaimed his poem:
The oracle of Balaam son of Beor,
the oracle of the man whose eyes are opened;
16 the oracle of one who hears the sayings of God
and has knowledge from the Most High,
who sees a vision from the Almighty,
who falls into a trance with his eyes uncovered:
17 I see him, but not now;
I perceive him, but not near.
A star will come from Jacob,
and a scepter will arise from Israel.

---

7. Translation my own.
8. *Gen. Rab.* 98:9, b. *Sanhedrin* 98b, and even Rashi.

> *He will smash the forehead of Moab*
> *and strike down all the Shethites.*
> *18 Edom will become a possession;*
> *Seir will become a possession of its enemies,*
> *but Israel will be triumphant.*
> *19 One who comes from Jacob will rule;*
> *he will destroy the city's survivors (Num. 24:14–19).*

Despite Balak's attempts to dissuade Balaam from preaching the truth, Balaam delivers a message from God. In this oracle, one of Jacob's descendants would come and destroy the enemy nations. He would rule from on high and would hold a global dominion. There is no king that has come close to fulfilling this prophecy except Jesus the Messiah. This prophecy has yet to be completely fulfilled. When Christ returns, every person on earth will be subdued and will proclaim that Jesus is Lord to the glory of the Father (Isa. 45:23; Rom. 14:11; and Phil. 2:10).

Deuteronomy 18:15–19—Prophet Like Moses

> *The Lord your God will raise up for you a prophet like me from among your own brothers. You must listen to him. 16 This is what you requested from the Lord your God at Horeb on the day of the assembly when you said, 'Let us not continue to hear the voice of the Lord our God or see this great fire any longer, so that we will not die!' 17 Then the Lord said to me, 'They have spoken well. 18 I will raise up for them a prophet like you from among their brothers. I will put my words in his mouth, and he will tell them everything I command him. 19 I will hold accountable whoever does not listen to my words that he speaks in my name (Deut. 18:15–19).*

Moses prophesies a time when God would send a prophet much like him. On one hand, God would send multiple prophets. God warned the people not to accept the teaching of false prophets (Deut. 18:20). On the other hand, the prophet mentioned in verses 15–19 would provide the complete revelation of God as he would speak nothing but what the Father had told him. This future eschatological prophet would be the Messiah.

The Messiah in the Major Prophets

Not only does one find messianic prophecies in the Pentateuch, messianic prophecies are also found in the Major Prophets. The Major Prophets (Isaiah, Jeremiah, Ezekiel, and Daniel) are called "major" because of the length of their written work. These writing prophets spoke and wrote frequently. Isaiah is so important regarding messianic prophecy that he is quoted by Jesus more often than any other prophet in Scripture. Due to the volume of the prophecies in this section, only a brief description of their messianic nature will be provided.

Jeremiah 23:5–6—Messiah the King

> *Look, the days are coming"—this is the Lord's declaration—*
> *when I will raise up a Righteous Branch for David.*
> *He will reign wisely as king*
> *and administer justice and righteousness in the land.*
> *6 In his days Judah will be saved,*
> *and Israel will dwell securely.*
> *This is the name he will be called:*
> *The Lord Is Our Righteousness (Jer. 23:5–6).*

Throughout the Hebrew Bible, the term *tsemach*, which means "branch," is used for the Messiah. The Branch is a shoot from the Davidic lineage who is God's future Anointed King. In Jeremiah 23, the Righteous Branch from David's ancestry will come and reign as king. This future King would provide safety and security for Israel and Judah. In many cases, such references will be ultimately fulfilled at Christ's future millennial reign.

Isaiah 7:1–16 - The Birth of the Messiah

> *This took place during the reign of Ahaz, son of Jotham, son of Uzziah king of Judah: Aram's King Rezin and Israel's King Pekah son of Remaliah went to fight against Jerusalem, but they were not able to conquer it.*
>
> *2 When it became known to the house of David that Aram had occupied Ephraim, the heart of Ahaz and the hearts of his people trembled like trees of a forest shaking in the wind.*

> 3 The Lord said to Isaiah, "Go out with your son Shear-jashub to meet Ahaz at the end of the conduit of the upper pool, by the road to the Launderer's Field. 4 Say to him: Calm down and be quiet. Don't be afraid or cowardly because of these two smoldering sticks, the fierce anger of Rezin and Aram, and the son of Remaliah. 5 For Aram, along with Ephraim and the son of Remaliah, has plotted harm against you. They say, 6 'Let us go up against Judah, terrorize it, and conquer it for ourselves. Then we can install Tabeel's son as king in it.'"
> 7 This is what the Lord God says:
> It will not happen; it will not occur.
> 8 The chief city of Aram is Damascus,
> the chief of Damascus is Rezin
> (within sixty-five years
> Ephraim will be too shattered to be a people),
> 9 the chief city of Ephraim is Samaria,
> and the chief of Samaria is the son of Remaliah.
> If you do not stand firm in your faith,
> then you will not stand at all.
> 10 Then the Lord spoke again to Ahaz: 11 "Ask for a sign from the Lord your God—it can be as deep as Sheol or as high as heaven."
> 12 But Ahaz replied, "I will not ask. I will not test the Lord."
> 13 Isaiah said, "Listen, house of David! Is it not enough for you to try the patience of men? Will you also try the patience of my God? 14 Therefore, the Lord himself will give you a sign: See, the virgin will conceive, have a son, and name him Immanuel. 15 By the time he learns to reject what is bad and choose what is good, he will be eating curds and honey. 16 For before the boy knows to reject what is bad and choose what is good, the land of the two kings you dread will be abandoned (Isa. 7:1–16).

This passage of Scripture has become quite controversial, especially since the Revised Standard Version infamously translated *almah* as "young woman" rather than "virgin." A full treatment of this issue would take up more space than what we currently have. I have written a fuller treatment on this issue elsewhere.[9] However, it is clear from the context of Isaiah 7 and in correlation with the rest of Isaiah that a miraculous event was to take place with the birth of the Messiah. Isaiah asked Ahaz to ask for a sign. Ahaz refused. So, there are two prophecies occurring in this Scripture. Isaiah uses

---

9. See Brian G. Chilton, "Is Isaiah 7:14 a Messianic Prophecy?," *BellatorChristi.com* (Dec. 10, 2018), retrieved May 10, 2019, https://bellatorchristi.com/2018/12/10/is-isaiah-714-a-messianic-prophecy/.

singular language when directing his prophecy towards Ahaz and plural language when directing his prophecy to the House of David. This prophecy is plural with a singular sign coming from the Messiah's birth. The most reasonable interpretation is to accept the traditional view in that Isaiah prophesies the virgin birth of the Messiah.

Isaiah 9:6–7—The Nature of the Messiah

For a child will be born for us,
a son will be given to us,
and the government will be on his shoulders.
He will be named
Wonderful Counselor, Mighty God,
Eternal Father, Prince of Peace.
7 The dominion will be vast,
and its prosperity will never end.
He will reign on the throne of David
and over his kingdom,
to establish and sustain it
with justice and righteousness from now on and forever.
The zeal of the Lord of Armies will accomplish this (Isa. 9:6–7).

Isaiah 9 comes on the heels of Isaiah 7:14. It appears that the prophet Isaiah is referencing the child who was born of a virgin when describing the child that would be born. The titles used of the child reference a divine person. The term *pele* (i.e., "Wonderful") is almost exclusively used for God. The term *el gibbor* (i.e., "Mighty God") also denotes a divine person, as does *ad avi* ("Eternal Father") which is odd to use of a child unless a connection is made to the Father. The dominion of this child will be global and eternal. Thus, by far the best interpretation is to accept this as a Messianic prophecy referring to the divine nature of the coming eschatological King.

Isaiah 11:1–16—The Stump of Jesse

Then a shoot will grow from the stump of Jesse,
and a branch from his roots will bear fruit.
2 The Spirit of the Lord will rest on him—
a Spirit of wisdom and understanding,

a Spirit of counsel and strength,
a Spirit of knowledge and of the fear of the Lord.
3 His delight will be in the fear of the Lord.
He will not judge
by what he sees with his eyes,
he will not execute justice
by what he hears with his ears,
4 but he will judge the poor righteously
and execute justice for the oppressed of the land.
He will strike the land
with a scepter from his mouth,
and he will kill the wicked
with a command from his lips.
5 Righteousness will be a belt around his hips;
faithfulness will be a belt around his waist.
6 The wolf will dwell with the lamb,
and the leopard will lie down with the goat.
The calf, the young lion, and the fattened calf will be together,
and a child will lead them.
7 The cow and the bear will graze,
their young ones will lie down together,
and the lion will eat straw like cattle.
8 An infant will play beside the cobra's pit,
and a toddler will put his hand into a snake's den.
9 They will not harm or destroy each other
on my entire holy mountain,
for the land will be as full
of the knowledge of the Lord
as the sea is filled with water.
10 On that day the root of Jesse
will stand as a banner for the peoples.
The nations will look to him for guidance,
and his resting place will be glorious (Isa. 11:1–10).

Isaiah continues speaking about a future eschatological Messiah. This future descendant would be a branch, or shoot (Heb., *netzer*) which is a term used for the Messiah. This Branch would come from the lineage of Jesse. This Messianic figure would have the Spirit of God (Heb., *ruach YHWH*) resting on him and abiding with him (11:2–3). His judgment would be just (11:4) and would provide peace to the point that the animal kingdom is affected where predatory wolves will lie down with their prey (11:6). The latter part of the prophecy will come about in the end times.

Isaiah 40:3–5; 42:1–7—The Herald of YHWH

A voice of one crying out:
Prepare the way of the Lord in the wilderness;
make a straight highway for our God in the desert.
4 Every valley will be lifted up,
and every mountain and hill will be leveled;
the uneven ground will become smooth
and the rough places, a plain.
5 And the glory of the Lord will appear,
and all humanity together will see it,
for the mouth of the Lord has spoken (Isa. 40:3–5).
This is my servant; I strengthen him,
this is my chosen one; I delight in him.
I have put my Spirit on him;
he will bring justice to the nations.
2 He will not cry out or shout
or make his voice heard in the streets.
3 He will not break a bruised reed,
and he will not put out a smoldering wick;
he will faithfully bring justice.
4 He will not grow weak or be discouraged
until he has established justice on earth.
The coasts and islands will wait for his instruction."
5 This is what God, the Lord, says—
who created the heavens and stretched them out,
who spread out the earth and what comes from it,
who gives breath to the people on it
and spirit to those who walk on it—
6 "I am the Lord. I have called you
for a righteous purpose,
and I will hold you by your hand.

> *I will watch over you, and I will appoint you*
> *to be a covenant for the people*
> *and a light to the nations,*
> *7 in order to open blind eyes,*
> *to bring out prisoners from the dungeon,*
> *and those sitting in darkness from the prison house (Isa. 42:1-7).*

The first part of the prophecy may relate to John the Baptist being the Messiah's forerunner. But the greater part of the prophecy relates to the Messiah himself. These passages indicate that the Messiah would speak the truth as he receives it from the Father. In Isaiah 42, it is of great interest to note that the Messiah would be a light to the nations. It should not have been surprising to early Christian believers that individuals from Gentile nations would enter the fold since the was prophesied by Isaiah many years prior.

Isaiah 49:1–13—The Servant of YHWH

> *He said to me, "You are my servant,*
> *Israel, in whom I will be glorified" (Isa. 49:3).*
> *And now, says the Lord,*
> *who formed me from the womb to be his servant,*
> *to bring Jacob back to him*
> *so that Israel might be gathered to him;*
> *for I am honored in the sight of the Lord,*
> *and my God is my strength—*
> *6 he says,*
> *"It is not enough for you to be my servant*
> *raising up the tribes of Jacob*
> *and restoring the protected ones of Israel.*
> *I will also make you a light for the nations,*
> *to be my salvation to the ends of the earth."*
> *7 This is what the Lord,*
> *the Redeemer of Israel, his Holy One, says*
> *to one who is despised,*
> *to one abhorred by people,*
> *to a servant of rulers:*
> *"Kings will see, princes will stand up,*
> *and they will all bow down*

The Servant in this prophecy describes the work of the Messiah. The New Testament writers indicated as much in their writings (Matt. 8:17; 12:17-21; John 12:38; and Acts 8:30-35). The Messiah was prophesied to restore Israel to its former glory. Here again, the Messiah is noted to be a light for all nations (Isa. 49:6). Before the Messianic ruler, all the world's kings would bow before he who was bestowed the title "King of Kings and Lord of Lords" (Rev. 19:16). The remainder of the prophesy denotes the peace that comes to God's people and the judgment facing those who deny the Messiah's reign.

Isaiah 52:13–53:12—The Suffering Servant

But he was pierced because of our rebellion,
crushed because of our iniquities;
punishment for our peace was on him,
and we are healed by his wounds.
6 We all went astray like sheep;
we all have turned to our own way;
and the Lord has punished him
for the iniquity of us all.
7 He was oppressed and afflicted,
yet he did not open his mouth.
Like a lamb led to the slaughter
and like a sheep silent before her shearers,
he did not open his mouth.
8 He was taken away because of oppression and judgment;
and who considered his fate?
For he was cut off from the land of the living;
he was struck because of my people's rebellion.
9 He was assigned a grave with the wicked,
but he was with a rich man at his death,
because he had done no violence
and had not spoken deceitfully.
10 Yet the Lord was pleased to crush him severely.
When you make him a guilt offering,

> he will see his seed, he will prolong his days,
> and by his hand, the Lord's pleasure will be accomplished.
> 11 After his anguish, he will see light and be satisfied.
> By his knowledge,
> my righteous servant will justify many,
> and he will carry their iniquities.
> 12 Therefore I will give him the many as a portion,
> and he will receive the mighty as spoil,
> because he willingly submitted to death,
> and was counted among the rebels;
> yet he bore the sin of many
> and interceded for the rebels (Isa. 53:5–12).

Of all messianic prophecies, the Suffering Servant prophecy of Isaiah 53 is king. In this prophecy, all the major details of the Messiah's life are brought forth. The Messiah is noted as being a powerful ruler (53:13; 53:1), a man of humility (53:2), and a suffering Servant who would die among criminals and buried in a rich man's tomb (52:14; 53:3–9). But what is most fascinating in this prophecy is that the resurrection of the Messiah was predicted. Notice verses 9 and 10. In verse 9, the Servant died. The Servant was "assigned a grave with the wicked, but he was with a rich man at his death." Yet, verse 10 holds that Yahweh would "prolong his days, and by his hand, the LORD's pleasure will be accomplished." Verse 12 also notes that because the Servant was willing to submit himself to a vicarious death, Yahweh would "give him the many as a portion, and he will receive the mighty as spoil." Answer me this. How does a dead man receive anything? How does a dead man see his days prolonged? It can only come by a resurrection event. Even the Messiah's resurrection was prophesied!

Isaiah 61:1–3—The Mission of the Servant

> The Spirit of the Lord God is on me,
> because the Lord has anointed me
> to bring good news to the poor.
> He has sent me to heal the brokenhearted,
> to proclaim liberty to the captives
> and freedom to the prisoners;
> 2 to proclaim the year of the Lord's favor,

and the day of our God's vengeance;
to comfort all who mourn,
3 to provide for those who mourn in Zion;
to give them a crown of beauty instead of ashes,
festive oil instead of mourning,
and splendid clothes instead of despair.
And they will be called righteous trees,
planted by the Lord
to glorify him (Isa. 61:1–3).

This prophecy relates to the Messiah's healing ministry on earth. He came to heal those who were broken and to proclaim freedom to those who were oppressed. The Messiah would truly be loving and compassionate in his earthly ministry. Jesus fulfilled that aspect of his Messianic ministry to a tee. The Spirit of God would be upon the Messiah in a powerful and demonstrative fashion. It is no mistake that Jesus read this text in the synagogue (Luke 4:18). Most likely, synagogues read Scriptures in progression. So, it was by the providence of God that Jesus would stand to read the passage of Scripture when it was at the time that Isaiah 61 was to be read. The Scripture truly was fulfilled before everyone that day.

Daniel 7:13–14—The Son of Man

I continued watching in the night visions,
and suddenly one like a son of man
was coming with the clouds of heaven.
He approached the Ancient of Days
and was escorted before him.
14 He was given dominion,
and glory, and a kingdom;
so that those of every people,
nation, and language
should serve him.
His dominion is an everlasting dominion
that will not pass away,
and his kingdom is one
that will not be destroyed (Dan. 7:13–14).

Daniel begins recording his night visions in seventh chapter of his book. Chapters 1–6 contain historical narrative, whereas Daniel's visions are found in the later chapters. The book of Daniel is unique in that more than half of the text is written in Aramaic. It is held that the Hebrew portions of Daniel relate only to the Jewish community while the Aramaic text is issued to a global audience. The Son of Man passage in Daniel 7 is written in Aramaic. Of special interest is that the "Son of Man" (Aram., *kebar enash*) does not say that the being is a human being. Rather, the being is one *like* a son of man. The person holds a humanlike appearance. The being is one who could boldly approach the Ancient of Days, a name for Yahweh. The Son of Man character relates to the divine nature of the Messiah. The earliest Jewish interpreters, even prior to the times of Jesus, held that this passage was thoroughly messianic.[10]

Daniel 9:25–27—The Messianic Timetable

Know and understand this:
From the issuing of the decree
to restore and rebuild Jerusalem
until an Anointed One, the ruler,
will be seven weeks and sixty-two weeks.
It will be rebuilt with a plaza and a moat,
but in difficult times.
26 After those sixty-two weeks
the Anointed One will be cut off
and will have nothing.
The people of the coming ruler
will destroy the city and the sanctuary.
The end will come with a flood,
and until the end there will be war;
desolations are decreed.
27 He will make a firm covenant
with many for one week,
but in the middle of the week
he will put a stop to sacrifice and offering.
And the abomination of desolation

---

10. For instance, see Sanhedrin 98a.

> *will be on a wing of the temple*
> *until the decreed destruction*
> *is poured out on the desolator (Dan. 9:25-27).*

This prophecy is so complex that a scant commentary on the text as I am providing is nearly offensive. The Seventy Weeks prophecy holds many different interpretations as one might expect. However, the best interpretation is to interpret each week as seven years. The result for the entirety of the prophetic times for all seventy prophetic weeks relates to a period of 490 years. Yet, there is a gap of time between the sixty-ninth and seventieth week. It would be sixty-nine weeks before the Messiah, or "Anointed One" would be cut off. The sixty-nine prophetic weeks equates to 483 years. If the timeline begins when Cyrus gives the decree to rebuild Jerusalem and the temple which was March 5, 444 BC, then 483 years from that point leads to the date March 30, 33 AD. Most likely, Jesus was crucified on Friday, April 3, 33 AD and resurrected on Sunday, April 5, 33 AD. So, if this timeline is correct, then the prophecy falls to the time that Jesus entered Jerusalem riding a donkey on Palm Sunday, March 30th, 33 AD. The prophecy would relate to Jesus being cut off from society by way of his betrayal and crucifixion later that week. If this is true, not only does prophecy relate to the person, the work, and the mission of the Messiah, it also provides a timetable for the Messiah's arrival!

The Messiah in the Minor Prophets

As previously noted, the Minor Prophets are so named due to the small size of the prophetic books. Most likely, the Minor Prophets were collected into a singular work called the *Book of the Twelve*. If so, each prophet would have written his own work. However, their books were collected and place on a singular scroll to preserve their writings and to protect the works from getting lost. While the prophets are called "Minor," they are anything but insignificant. Their messages are among the most powerful in all the Scripture![11] The Minor Prophets also present many messianic prophecies. Let's examine five of them.

Zechariah 9:9–10—The Humble King

> *Rejoice greatly, Daughter Zion!*

---

11. If you want a good treatise on God's solution to the theodicy problem, read the book of Habakkuk! It is an easy, yet profound read.

> *Shout in triumph, Daughter Jerusalem!*
> *Look, your King is coming to you;*
> *he is righteous and victorious,*
> *humble and riding on a donkey,*
> *on a colt, the foal of a donkey.*
> *10 I will cut off the chariot from Ephraim*
> *and the horse from Jerusalem.*
> *The bow of war will be removed,*
> *and he will proclaim peace to the nations.*
> *His dominion will extend from sea to sea,*
> *from the Euphrates River*
> *to the ends of the earth (Zech. 9:9-10).*

This prophecy relates to Jesus's entrance into Jerusalem riding a colt, the foal of a donkey. Many people would have identified Jesus's entrance as a fulfillment of this prophecy. However, the latter part of the prophecy is yet to be fulfilled when Christ returns. His domain would be global and eternal. That's exciting to consider given the current political scene in America.

Zechariah 11:1–17—The Two Shepherds

> *Throw it to the potter," the Lord said to me—this magnificent price I was valued by them. So I took the thirty pieces of silver and threw it into the house of the Lord, to the potter. 14 Then I cut in two my second staff, Union, annulling the brotherhood between Judah and Israel.*
>
> *15 The Lord also said to me: "Take the equipment of a foolish shepherd. 16 I am about to raise up a shepherd in the land who will not care for those who are perishing, and he will not seek the lost or heal the broken. He will not sustain the healthy, but he will devour the flesh of the fat sheep and tear off their hooves.*
>
> *17 Woe to the worthless shepherd*
> *who deserts the flock!*
> *May a sword strike his arm*
> *and his right eye!*
> *May his arm wither away*
> *and his right eye go completely blind (Zech. 11:13-17).*

This prophecy shows the rejection of the Messiah. The people of God would choose a worthless shepherd over the One True Shepherd of God. They would sell the Shepherd for the price of thirty pieces of silver. Woes are pronounced to the worthless shepherds who led the people astray. In this sense, the worthless shepherds were the religious authorities of the day who crucified Jesus. In a modern sense, people still choose worthless shepherds over the faithful Shepherd of God. For that reason, many churches choose to have speakers who preach falsehoods who tickle the ears, thereby filling the congregation with enormous crowds. In contrast, many faithful churches choose trustworthy preachers who preach the truth of God before a half-filled building. Times change, but the rebelliousness of the human heart does not.

Zechariah 12:10; 13:7—Messiah as a Suffering Shepherd

Then I will pour out a spirit of grace and prayer on the house of David and the residents of Jerusalem, and they will look at me whom they pierced. They will mourn for him as one mourns for an only child and weep bitterly for him as one weeps for a firstborn (Zech. 12:10).

Sword, awake against my shepherd,
against the man who is my associate—
this is the declaration of the Lord of Armies.
Strike the shepherd, and the sheep will be scattered;
I will turn my hand against the little ones (Zech. 13:7).

This prophecy relates to the previous one in Zechariah's prophecy. The people had rejected God's Messiah. They chose for themselves a worthless shepherd. In turn, they would pierce the faithful Shepherd. Once the people realized what they had done, they would mourn and weep over the Shepherd whom they pierced. When the Shepherd was struck, his own sheep scattered which may reflect on the status of the early disciples during the trial and crucifixion of Jesus the Nazarene.

Malachi 3:1–4—Messenger of the Messiah

See, I am going to send my messenger, and he will clear the way before me. Then the Lord you seek will suddenly come to his temple, the Messenger of the covenant you delight in—see, he is coming," says the Lord of Armies. 2 But who can endure the day of his coming? And who will be able to stand when he appears? For he will be like a refiner's fire and like launderer's bleach. 3 He will be like a refiner and purifier of silver; he will purify the sons of Levi and refine them like gold and silver. Then they will present offerings to the Lord in righteousness. 4 And the offerings of Judah and Jerusalem will please the Lord as in days of old and years gone by (Mal. 3:1–4).

This prophecy concerns the Messiah's forerunner which was fulfilled by John the Baptist. The Messiah is then discussed. The Messiah would be one who would refine individuals by a refiner's fire. John the Baptist noted that Jesus would baptize with water and fire (Matt. 3:11). God is often identified as fire, light, or by clouds. In this sense, fire represents the Holy Spirit of God. The Messiah would purify the people with the power of the Holy Spirit.

Micah 5:1–4—The Birthplace of the Messiah and His Future Rule

Now, daughter who is under attack,
you slash yourself in grief;
a siege is set against us!
They are striking the judge of Israel
on the cheek with a rod.
2 Bethlehem Ephrathah,
you are small among the clans of Judah;
one will come from you
to be ruler over Israel for me.
His origin is from antiquity,
from ancient times.
3 Therefore, Israel will be abandoned until the time
when she who is in labor has given birth;
then the rest of the ruler's brothers will return
to the people of Israel.
4 He will stand and shepherd them
in the strength of the Lord,
in the majestic name of the Lord his God.
They will live securely,
for then his greatness will extend
to the ends of the earth (Micah 5:1–4).

This prophetic passage is intriguing because it describes the birthplace of the Messiah. While Bethlehem was small and insignificant among the cities of Israel, it would give birth to the greatest leader of all time. His greatness would be known across the world. Isn't it amazing how God used a small, rural, insignificant area to be a blessing to the entire world? That's the power of God and that's the significance he places on each of his children.

The Odds of Fulfillment

Could it be that Jesus simply fulfilled the prophecies concerning the Messiah by happenstance? Could he not have merely made things come about by naturalistic means? Considering the odds of these prophecies being fulfilled, any natural explanation begins to substantially lose its rationale. Consider this: The odds of fulfilling just eight of the prophecies written about the Messiah is the same as filling the state of Texas with dimes, marking only one of the dimes with a black mark, and then blindfolding an individual with the expectation that the person would find the one marked dime in Texas while remaining blindfolded! That's an impossibility.

But it gets even worse when considering the odds that Jesus fulfilled forty-eight prophecies. The odds of one person fulfilling forty-eight messianic prophecies is 1 in 10^{157} or 1 in 10 sextillion! That's 1 in 10,000,000,000,000,000,000,000,000,000,000,000,000,000,000,000,000,000! Mathematicians say that it is impossible to explain anything past fifty zeroes by chance alone. The number presented has fifty-two zeroes in case you haven't counted.

But it gets even worse for the skeptic! According to J. Barton Payne, Jesus fulfilled 191 prophecies.[12] The odds increase to 1 in 10 with something like 625 zeroes behind it! According to Floyd Hamilton, Jesus fulfilled over 332 distinct predictions.[13] There is literally no way to explain away the prophetic fulfillment of the Messiah by any other means than divine agency.

Conclusion

It thoroughly amazes me how little attention is placed on Messianic prophecy. Prophecy was among the chief apologetic arguments that the disciples used in addition to the evidence for Christ's resurrection. When the context of the Hebrew Bible's Scriptures is kept intact, it becomes increasingly clear that the entirety of the Hebrew Bible (i.e., the Old Testament) is thoroughly

---

12. J. Barton Payne, *Encyclopedia of Biblical Prophecy*, 665–670.
13. Floyd E. Hamilton, *The Basis of Christian Faith*, 160.

messianic. As it has been said before concerning biblical interpretation, the plain sense is the best sense unless it becomes nonsense. Messianic prophecy was generally held by the majority of Christians and adherents of Judaism until the time of Rabbi Rashi (1040–1105 AD) in the medieval ages, a man who opposed Christian missionary movements, and the skepticism of critical scholars who were influenced by the anti-supernatural biases of Bultmann and other. It is telling that Jewish rabbis prior to the first century AD viewed many of the Old Testament texts we mentioned in messianic light.

It is my hope that the brief explanations of the selected messianic prophecies in this chapter has spurred you on to consider the great power from prophetic apologetics. Only God could have fulfilled the prophecies that he has through Jesus the Nazarene. For that, we can all be appreciative.

POSTLUDE

Now that our journey has come to an end, you may be asking, "Where do I go from here?" You have just been exposed to the core essentials of apologetics, but this is only the beginning. There is much more territory for you to cover. I would suggest the following.

First, love the Lord your God with your mind. Don't settle for mediocrity in your understanding of God's Word. The Bible is simple enough that a child can understand its message, but it is so deep that not even the greatest minds can understand all of God's truths.

Never stop learning about God and his Word. Dr. Daniel Mitchell, Professor of Theology at Liberty University, once said, "The more you learn about God, the bigger God becomes."[1] That does not mean that God literally becomes bigger. It means that you learn about just how big God really is. Theology and apologetics hold real-life applications. They are not just heady material only suitable for the ivory towers of academia and the upper echelons of intelligentsia. When a person realizes that God is whom he said he was, that Jesus truly has risen from the dead, and that heaven is a reality; then death loses its impact. Yes, a person still grieves over the loss of their loved one and faces fear when one looks down the hallway into eternity. But there is newfound power when one realizes that substantial evidence backs up Christian beliefs.

Second, specialize in a particular area. My area of focus is primarily in historical apologetics. This area specializes in the historical evidence for Christ's resurrection and for the validity of the Bible. However, multiple areas of specialization are needed. For instance, I have a friend in seminary who concentrates his attention on scientific apologetics. He has a background in neurology, so he is especially a powerhouse when it comes to defending

---

1. Daniel Mitchell, "Systematic Theology I," lecture, Lynchburg, VA, Liberty University.

the existence of the soul. You may have found an area that was mentioned which you would like to learn much more. Apologetics is best employed as a community endeavor. When the people of God who specialize in different genres come together as a team, the saints become much stronger. The power of the Avengers and the Justice League pales in comparison to the punch that can come from the Christian apologetic community when unity in the essentials is found.

Third, engage the lost. I would recommend Gregory Koukl's book *Tactics*. This book describes various useful strategies when witnessing to the lost. After going through this program, you have the basics to handle most objections to the faith. Use it! But remember, the job of the apologist is not to win arguments. It is to win souls for Christ. As you discuss issues with the lost, always remember to have a heart of compassion and love.

Fourth, remember that most doubts stem from emotional issues coming from some past hurt or an unrepentant sin. Be sure to listen to what the person says. Learn to be a good listener. It may be that by showing compassion and granting a listening ear that the skeptic may be far more willing to hear your case. If you aren't willing to listen to them, then they won't be willing to listen to you.

Fifth, learn to ask good questions. Don't think that you must always be on the defense. Force the skeptic to evaluate his or her own worldview. Ask questions like, "What do you mean by that?" Ask them who they understand God to be. Jesus used the rabbinic method of answering questions with questions. This is a wonderful practice. As we learned previously, have them define their terms and state their points clearly so that you can evaluate their arguments.

Lastly, when engaging with the lost, don't be embarrassed if you don't have the answer. Be honest and tell the person that you don't know and that you'll be willing to investigate the question further. But don't just say it. Do it. Look it up. Study the material and then go back to the person with your answer. As you look up answers and engage the lost, always be in prayer. Be confident. But also, be humble enough to ask other apologists for help when you need it.

Apologetics is my passion and the primary drive of my ministry. Feel free to look through my website at https://bellatorchristi.com. Many of the articles and podcasts on the site stem from questions I have received while in ministry. If you have any questions, you can submit questions through the website at https://bellatorchristi.com/submit-a-question-to-bellator-christi/.

For too long, Christians have sat on the sidelines without engaging the culture. Now, equipped by the evidence and empowered by the Spirit, Christians have access to reach more people than at any point in history.

Instead of posting cute little pictures on your social media account, become an apologetic warrior who posts evidences that force the skeptically inclined to second guess their skepticism. You have the power. You now have the ability. But, do you have the willingness? That is a question that only you can answer.

Appendix 1

THEODICY CENTERED IN THE CROSS[1]

by Daniel Merritt

Without question "theodicy" is a complex word. The word has been clothed with a variety of meanings, but a concise definition this writer gives for reflection of the term—proposing an adequate response that preserves the truth of the omnipotence, goodness and righteousness of God in a world where evil, suffering and pain are prevalent. The pursuit to present such a "defense" of God is often viewed as merely an intellectual endeavor that has little practical implications for everyday life. However, developing a theodicy that is practical in nature is one of the best ways to give one hope and strength even in the face of the evil and suffering that is present in the world. A proper theodicy can aid in helping undergird one with resolve and fortitude when traumatic events occur.

It is recognized when one seeks to develop a philosophical and theological theodicy, one undertakes a daunting task. The first question that needs to be asked, "Where does one begin in seeking to justify God in the face of evil?" For the answer to this all-important question, one theologian whom this writer has turned to for theological insight in this matter is P.T. Forsyth (1848–1921). A Scottish theologian, Forsyth is largely forgotten in the twenty-first century, yet his vision into the mysteries of theodicy are filled with sparkling diamonds of wisdom that seek to wed both the human and the divine. He seems to do so with the wisdom of a prophet. His

---

1. This article was used with permission by the author. It was originally written as class notes for a class in apologetics concerning the issue of theodicy.

eloquence and spiritual insights need to be revisited. While it would be impossible to cover in detail his views on theodicy in a few pages, it is hoped the readers thirst will be wetted enough to continue to search Forsyth's vast goldmine of insights.

Now to answer the question in the previous paragraph, "Where does one begin in seeking to justify God in the face of evil?" In justifying the goodness and righteousness of God in a world of evil and suffering one must begin with God's act of atonement on the cross as His self-justification. When the center of one's theodicy is the historical event of the cross, one realizes the bed-rock on which the unanswered questions of life rest are anchored not in man's finite thoughts, but in an historical event in which God has acted. Forsyth states, "No reason of man can justify God in a world like this. He must justify Himself, and He did so in the cross of His Son ... [the cross being] God's own theodicy."[2] How does God defend His love and goodness in the face of evil and suffering? According to Forsyth, "He does so through the cross; the supreme theodicy is atonement."[3]

Forsyth contends that the only way one can reconcile God's righteousness and goodness with the horrors of sin and suffering is to consciously place at the center of any theodicy the cross of Christ. It is in the cross where we find the supreme revelation of God. In the cross we don't have to justify God, for the cross justifies God. In the cross "God shows Himself to be righteous and good in spite of the existence of evil in our world."[4]

For Forsyth, the cross must be at the heart of any biblical approach to theodicy. It is at the cross we see God in Christ interacting with and becoming involved with man and suffers with him. God's interactions with human sin and suffering culminate in the cross where the Creator took upon Himself the burden of and suffering with those He has created. Forsyth writes, "[Christ] brings God's providence to the bar of God's own promise. In Christ, God is fully justified by Himself. If any man thinks he has anything to suffer in the flesh, God more. In all their afflictions He was more afflicted."[5] Echoing Forsyth's summation, Milton Crum writes, "Portraying God as fully in Christ portrays God as suffering all that Christ suffered on the cross, but it implies more than that. It implies that God suffered and has always suffered all that humanity suffers."[6] Yet through it all Christ was victorious over the

---

2. Peter Taylor Forsyth, *The Justification of God*, 14, 122.
3. Ibid., 174.
4. Ibid., 122.
5. Ibid., 174.
6. Milton Crum, *Evil, Anger, and God*, 185.

worst man sought to do to God's best. Forsyth's theodicy is "an extension of the doctrine of the atonement" whereby Christ was victorious.

Of theodicy's mystery Forsyth writes, "The tactics of Providence cannot be traced, but in the cross His purpose we have, and His heart. We have Him."[7] God's own theodicy is a theodicy of reconciliation and relationship that comes through the victory won on the cross, a theodicy that enables trust in God in spite of unanswered questions, which in His time will be answered and every wrong righted. Though man's worst was done to Christ, He was triumphant over sin and evil upon the cross and emerged from the grave victoriously, ensuring victory has been won forever and for humanity.

Karl Barth hitched his wagon to Forsyth's theodicy, writing that "the unaided mind of man cannot devise a theodicy that establishes the idea of the goodness of God."[8] Like Forsyth, Barth contended that what human theodicies could not do, on the cross God in Christ "gave Himself that He might bear and suffer what man himself had to suffer."[9] In the cross Barth saw a twofold justification, as he interpreted the cross as both our justification and "the justification in which God justifies Himself."[10]

In Christ's atoning work on the cross, it was an act that was not only triumphant over evil, it was God's self-justification as He vindicated His holiness in the face of sin. The cross revealed God's holy hatred of sin, and, as well, satisfied the heart of God in regard to the demands of His "wounded holiness." This could only be accomplished by one who was both human and divine...that Person was Christ. Because Christ was the Representative of humanity, we are one with Christ not only on the cross but in His resurrection. The cross was clearly God's answer to the dilemma of man's sinfulness and man's doubt of God's goodness. The cross of Christ proleptically announces God's unfathomable ways with sinful humanity and creation.

In the event of the cross, followed by the resurrection, humanity finds the solution to a proper theodicy whereby one gains confidence that God has and will take action to right all wrongs and vindicate all underserving victims of evil. It was holy God's holy-love and grace that brought Christ to the cross, and the goal of God is the establishment of divine holiness within and throughout the human race and creation, the triumph on the cross foreshadowing this historic consummation already accomplished in "the supreme theodicy of the atonement."[11] One can be assured that God

7. Ibid., 23.
8. Karl Barth, *Church Dogmatics*, III.1., 368.
9. Ibid., II.2., 165.
10. Ibid., IV.1., 564.
11. Forsyth, *Justification*, 125.

through His self-justification in the Christ Event (the cross), is moving all history towards His glorious goal, which the victory on the cross foreshadows. While with faith and hope we await its full actualization, the cross assures us of its certainty.

Appendix 2

THIRTY-THREE LOGICAL FALLACIES EVERYONE SHOULD KNOW[1]

As the late Norman Geisler once noted, "Logic deals with the methods of valid thinking."[2] (Geisler 1999, 427). Logical fallacies, then, are errors in the way one thinks or presents an argument. Logical fallacies are important for everyone to know, but it is especially important for Christians to know since they are called to promote truth. Paul writes that the Christian should be in the practice of "laying aside falsehood, speak truth each one of you with his neighbor, for we are members of one another" (Ephesians 4:25, NASB). So, the Christian should know how to speak the truth and to avoid any fallacy of thinking. Unfortunately, many sites devoted to logic promote an atheist agenda. One might think that the atheist has a stranglehold on logic, but nothing further could be the case. Therefore, this article will provide 33 logical fallacies that every Christian, in fact every person, should know.

Ad Hominem: This fallacy means literally "against the man." This is a classic debate tactic. Instead of attacking an argument's validity, the debater will instead attack one's opponent. For example, some atheists have attacked the character of William Lane Craig instead of dealing with Craig's cosmological arguments. This is an ad hominem fallacy because not only does Craig have wonderful character, his arguments are strong, as well.

---

1. This selection is a revision to the article "33 Logical Fallacies Everyone Should Know" which was originally posted at BellatorChristi.com. Brian G. Chilton, "33 Logical Fallacies Everyone Should Know," *BellatorChristi.com* (July 28, 2014), https://bellatorchristi.com/2014/07/28/33-logical-fallacies-everyone-should-know/.

2. Geisler, "Logic," *Baker Encyclopedia of Christian Apologetics*, 427.

Attacking a person's character without engaging the argument is an ad hominem fallacy.

Ambiguity: The fallacy of ambiguity is used when the debater uses vague language that could be taken in a variety of ways. This is also known as someone speaking "out of both sides of their mouth." Politicians are normally the worst culprits of this fallacy. When posed with a particular problem, the politician may claim that he or she may not have known about the issue when it is clear that the politician did. Or, it could be demonstrated by a politician presenting a bill without directly expressing the contents of the bill. All of these are examples of ambiguity.

Anecdotal: The anecdotal fallacy is found when one uses one's experience instead of a sound argument when making a case. For instance, one could argue that one person benefited from taking a particular medicine; therefore, everyone should take that medicine. It could be that not everyone would benefit from that kind of medicine due to the differences in each person's body. It is for this reason that the Christian should not only rely upon their experience with Christ when making a case for Christianity. Rather, provide the evidence for Christianity in addition to providing one's experience. If one relies only on their experience, one could be found guilty of committing the anecdotal fallacy. A good example was found when I had severe digestive issues. I heard many anecdotes as to what would cure my ailing stomach. Nothing worked. It wasn't until I went to the doctor and discovered that I had severe acid reflux that I found a solution.

Appeal to Authority: This fallacy is often used in the atheist community, but is often used in the theist community, as well. The appeal to authority fallacy is committed when one uses the beliefs of one in authority (scientist, archaeologist, theologian, philosopher, etc.) instead of dealing with the argument itself. It may be that the authority in question is correct. However, just because one is in authority does not make the authority figure correct. Consider the fact that at one time; many scientists and theologians believed that the world was flat. Thus, an appeal to authority would have been flawed in those days.

Appeal to Consequences: In this fallacy, one uses consequences without providing any real evidence that a consequence would follow the antecedent. Mothers forgive me. But this is normally used by mothers when they tell their children that if they do not eat their Brussel sprouts, they will not grow up big and strong. It may be that the children will grow up big and strong without eating Brussel sprouts. The mother has not provided a clear link between the consumption of Brussel sprouts and growing up big and strong. (Note to children: I would not use this against your mothers, or you may find yourself the victim of the appeal to force.)

Appeal to Emotion: This fallacy is found in the classic "guilt trip." In this fallacy, the debater will manipulate an emotional response from the listener without providing any clear evidence for the debater's claim. For instance, atheists will appeal to the atrocities performed by Christians as an argument against the resurrection of Christ. It could be that Christ has risen and that Christians have performed atrocious acts, but their atrocities do not deny the validity of Christ's resurrection. Grandparents are good at the "appeal to emotion." For instance, a grandmother may claim, "You never come see me. You must not love me anymore." In fact, it could be that the grandchild loves the grandparent very much but was not able to see the grandparent as they wish they could. Nonetheless, this is an appeal to emotion.

Appeal to Force: The appeal to force is also known by its Latin name *argumentum ad baculum*. This fallacy is committed when a person, or institution, forces their beliefs upon another by issuing threats. The person or institution has not proven its case but forces others to believe or accept their claim by force. In certain regimes of the past, if one did not become an atheist and adhere to the government's new system of control, the person could lose his/her occupation, could be ostracized, or could be executed. Another example may be found in a company's charge that if the men of the company do not shave their beards, they will be fired. The company offered no reason as to why they wanted the bearded men cleanshaven. Rather, they appealed to force.

Appeal to Nature: This fallacy claims that just because something is "natural" it must be good. For instance, some will argue that men are drawn to have multiple relationships with other many other women. Therefore, infidelity must be okay. One can find the falsehood in such a claim. Just because something comes "natural" does not make it right. Unfortunately, this fallacy is made by many trying to cover up their misdeeds.

Appeal to Novelty: This fallacy assumes that just because something is new that the thing, or idea, must be better. For instance, many believed that Windows Vista was going to be better than Windows XP because it was newer. It was later found that Windows XP was far better since Vista had many programming flaws. Therefore, just because something is new does not make it better unless it is demonstrated to be better. Some people believe that newer refrigerators are better. However, I have known people who have owned refrigerators that dated back to the fifties that worked just as good, if not better, than newer models. The merit of a claim is not based on its novelty. Rather, it should be based on the merit of the claim.

Appeal to Poverty: This fallacy occurs when one assumes that just because a view is held by the poor that it must be true. This is the opposite of the appeal to wealth fallacy. A poor person may believe that he or she is poor because the government is oppressing them. The view may or may not be true. However, such a view cannot be accepted on the merits that the poor hold it without any other evidence. The merit must be tested by its claim rather than by the poor economic status of the one purporting it. It is possible that the poor person is poor because he or she made many bad life decisions. Each claim must be evaluated by its merit and not by the monetary status of the person promoting it.

Appeal to Tradition: This fallacy is the opposite of the appeal to novelty fallacy. In this fallacy, one holds that just because a viewpoint is old that it must be true. For instance, a Calvinist may hold that their view is true because it correlates with the view held by Augustine. It could be that the view is true. However, one cannot gauge the accuracy of the view by its antiquity alone. The claim must be based upon the evidence for the claim itself and not because of its age. While Aristotle was correct about many things, he was also incorrect in many of his views concerning physics. So, to claim that Aristotle was correct in everything he said about physics because he wrote a long time ago is to commit the appeal to tradition fallacy.

Appeal to Wealth: This fallacy is opposite of the appeal to poverty fallacy. In this fallacy, one holds a view as true because its adherents are wealthy. For instance, one might claim that global warming must be correct because wealthy people claim that the earth is warming. The validity of global warming is not based on the wealth of those proposing its truth. Rather, the claims must be verified by its own merit. Wealthy people might be correct in what they say, or they might be incorrect. To claim otherwise is to commit the appeal to wealth fallacy.

Bandwagon Fallacy: This fallacy is based upon an appeal to popularity. One claims that something is good based only on the fact that everyone else thinks that it is good. For instance, a young lady may ask her parents if she can have her tongue pierced because all of her friends are piercing their tongues. The problem is that a view can be popular and be incorrect. Therefore, the bandwagon fallacy should be avoided.

Begging the Question/Circular Reasoning: Circular reasoning is performed when the conclusion is presented in the argument. For instance, a Christian may be asked, "How do you know that the Bible is true?" The Christian responds, "I know the Bible is true because the Bible says that it is true." This provides absolutely no evidence whatsoever. Such a form of defense should be wholeheartedly rejected.

Black or White: This fallacy is committed when only two options are presented when more options may be available. For instance, some claim that one can only have faith or reason. However, it can be that one can hold faith and reason. Another example of this fallacy would be to think that only a Democrat or a Republican are viable options in an election when there are other candidates running by way of an independent ticket. Advertisers may make you think that you must buy their product to be happy. Their ads are often guilty of the black and white fallacy. It is quite possible that you could live a life of great contentment without their product in hand.

Burden of Proof: This fallacy is committed when one assumes that they do not have to provide evidence for their claim and that the burden is upon the one trying to prove them wrong. For example, the atheist may desire to have 100% certainty that God exists in order to believe. Therefore, the atheist will declare that the Christian must provide this level of evidence or the Christian's view is wrong, or vice versa. Therefore, it could be said that a person that desires more evidence than is necessary to believe/disbelieve. Nevertheless, the burden of proof is passed, and the person does not prove his or her case.

Composition/Division: The composition fallacy assumes that what is true of a part is true of the whole. The division fallacy assumes that what is true of the whole is true of the parts. Someone might claim that since North Carolina has islands offshore and is one of the states of the United States of America, that all states in the United States of America must have islands offshore. This is impossible since many states are not aligned along an ocean. Therefore, this is the composition fallacy. Someone could also claim that since the United States is one nation, all the states of the nation must experience the same weather. While the United States possesses fifty states, those fifty states experience much different weather. My friends in Montana may experience snow and cold while I experience heat and humidity in North Carolina. We are all still citizens of the same nation. Such a claim has committed the division fallacy.

False Cause: This fallacy occurs when someone finds a correlation and assumes a cause. For instance, one may view a chart to find that the crime rate in a particular community is rising while the immigration rate in the community is also rising. One may assume that the rise in immigration caused the rising crime rate. However, there may be other causes afoot than just the rise in immigration. For instance, it may be that a drop in employment in the area caused the rise in crime rather than immigration.

Gambler's Fallacy: This fallacy has ties to Las Vegas. This fallacy occurs when one attributes a run of events to independent events. For instance, a gambler may claim to have a "run" on the roulette wheel. In fact, there is no run but a series of independent events. For instance, assuming that nine red cards have been consistently taken from a card deck that a black card will be drawn next is committing the gambler's fallacy. Or, assuming that a flipped quarter will show heads after seven times of showing tails would also commit the gambler's fallacy. It may be that the flipped quarter will once again show tails.

Genetic Fallacy: This fallacy is committed when one's argument is considered good or bad only based upon the advocate's ancestry. For instance, a theologian from Nigeria may not have his arguments taken seriously because he is dark-skinned and comes from a third world nation. The person not listening to the Nigerian theologian's arguments would have committed the genetic fallacy. Or, a Christian scientist may not have her experiment considered as viable because she is a Christian. This is also a genetic fallacy.

Loaded Question: This fallacy is committed when one asks a question with a presumption built into it. This is performed so as to side-track the particular person in question. For instance, one may ask a Christian apologist, "Since a belief in God is primitive and superstitious, wouldn't that make your arguments primitive and superstitious?" Or if one were to ask another, "Do you need help with your drug problem" when there is no evidence of a drug problem; this would be an example of a loaded question. Another example is a case that happened to me. I once asked a woman, "When is your baby due?" I assumed because her belly protruded that she must be pregnant. Unfortunately for me, the lady was not pregnant. I had committed a form of the loaded question fallacy which lead to loaded embarrassment on my part.

Middle Ground Fallacy: This fallacy assumes that a "middle ground" between two extremes is always true. Or, this fallacy can be conducted when assuming that a middle ground exists when it does not. You may have heard it said that each person has a case and the truth is found somewhere in the middle. While this is sometimes true, it is not always true. For instance, some may try to find a middle ground in the debate on the existence of God. However, there are only two options: God exists, or God does not exist. No middle ground can exist in such a case. If one is true, then the other must be false.

Moralistic Fallacy: This fallacy is the opposite of the appeal to nature fallacy. In this fallacy, one assumes that because something should be a certain way, something is that way. For instance, one may claim that all parents will take care of their children because all parents should take care of their children. Unfortunately, not all parents do take care of their children. Churchgoers are guilty of this fallacy when they say, "We should not implement security measures because it would be immoral for someone to attack a church." While it is greatly immoral to attack a place of worship, that is not to say that someone would not attack a church. In some sense, this fallacy is guilty of the "it can't happen to me" form of thinking.

No True Scotsman: This fallacy is somewhat difficult to describe. To simplify, this fallacy avoids criticism by changing the dynamic of the argument so present the case unfalsifiable. The tenets are changed to avoid scrutiny. Suppose that Bob speaks to Chris concerning his use of a fanny pack. Bob says, "Chris, no American man uses a fanny pack!" Chris replies, "Bob, I am an American male and I use a fanny pack." Bob angrily and with increased volume declares, "No American man uses a fanny pack!" Bob has not proven his point. Rather, he presents his case with great emotion so as to convince Chris that American males should not use fanny packs, but he cannot provide any real evidence to back his claim. Bob has committed the no true Scotsman fallacy.

Personal Incredulity: This fallacy is committed when one passes off difficult concepts as inherently false because one does not understand the concept. For instance, Jimmy does not think that Thomism is a valid theological system because he does not understand the writings of Thomas Aquinas. Jimmy thinks that Thomism is false because he does not understand it. This is fallacious because it may be that Thomism is true regardless of Jimmy's ability to understand its concepts.

Another example is found with Betty and light years. Betty does not believe in the distance of light-years because she cannot understand how light can travel at 186,000 miles per second. Since she denies that light travels at 186,000 miles per second, she also denies that a light travels 5,865,696,000,000 a year. Therefore, a light-year must not exist. However, light does travel at 186,000 miles a second. Just because Betty doesn't understand how light travels that fast does not mean that light doesn't travel that fast. Betty's denial is based on fallacious thinking.

Post Hoc Fallacy: This fallacy is committed when one assumes that things happen after an unrelated experience. For instance, athletes participate in certain rituals before they take the field. They believe these rituals will help them perform in the game. In reality, there is no correlation. Note: some sites have claimed that the efficacy of prayer is a post hoc fallacy. However, this claim is committing several fallacies including the anecdotal and black-or-white fallacy. The author who claims that prayer is superstitious is abiding by their own preconceived notions that God does not exist. If God does exist, then it is entirely logical to expect an answer to one's prayer. It is just as logical as expecting a person on the other end of the telephone line to respond to one's question. Beware of sites that promote a genetic fallacy in designating that people of faith are automatically wrong because they believe in the power of God.

Red Herring: The red herring fallacy came from fox hunters who sent out their dogs to chase foxes only to find that their dogs were distracted by red herrings (perhaps purposely placed by opposing hunters) which led them off the trail of the fox. This is a tactic used to get a person off their point. For instance: a Christian apologist is addressing the evidence for God's existence. Someone then asks, "What about the crusades? Don't the evil acts performed by the Crusaders in the name of God negate God's existence?" Obviously, the Crusades have nothing to do with the plausibility of God's existence.

Slippery Slope: This fallacy assumes that just because a person does one thing that the person will eventually do something else. For instance, some would claim that if one listens to rock music then one will become a delinquent. Or others assume if one reads any other translation other than the King James Version, one will become a flaming liberal. Obviously, the consequents do not proceed from the antecedents with the slippery slope fallacy.

Special Pleading: This fallacy is similar to the No True Scotsman fallacy. In this fallacy, one refuses to accept that one is wrong by inventing ways in which to hold to old notions. For instance, it has been demonstrated that the Alexandrian codex is a better than the Byzantium codex for use in translating the Bible. However, for those who desire to hold to the Byzantium texts, one will claim that the Alexandrian texts were modified by cults when there is no evidence to back up such a claim. If science demonstrates something to be true, one will claim that science is faulty. These are cases of special pleading.

Strawman: Strawman fallacies are among one of the more popular fallacies that are employed. This fallacy misrepresents someone's argument to make the argument easier to attack. Unfortuately, this happens far more than this writer would like to imagine. For instance, Bill might claim that Sally is a tree-hugger because she believes in global warming. Or, Brent makes Hugh out to be a Darwinist because Hugh believes in an old-earth interpretation of Genesis. These are examples of the strawman fallacy.

The Fallacy Fallacy: This fallacy accuses a claim to be false because it is poorly argued or another fallacy has been committed. In other words, the claim is not evaluated on its own merits but by the way it was presented. Since Susan presented a poor presentation on the nutritional value of blueberries, Barbara believes that blueberries should never be eaten. Barbara has committed the fallacy fallacy.

The Texas Sharpshooter: Picture a self-professed sharpshooter who claims he can hit the bullseye each time he shoots. He then proceeds to shoot a barn and draws a bullseye around the bullet hole after his shot has been made. In like fashion, the person committing this fallacy will choose data that only suits one's arguments or presumptions. For instance, a drug company may only choose positive data that supports a drug that they are promoting without considering the negative data. Or, Zane, a statistician, evaluates the educational systems of various states. He only chooses the best schools to evaluate in his state, while choosing the worst schools in other states, in order to demonstrate that his state's educational system is better than any other system. Zane has committed the Texas Sharpshooter fallacy.

Tu Quoque: Pronounced (too-kwoo-kee), this fallacy is committed when one turns criticism back upon the critic instead of dealing with the criticism itself. It's also called "passing the buck." For instance, Christine's theory is challenged by Cassandra because of a mathematical error. Christine retorted, "Oh yeah, well your last theory had two mathematical errors in it, and you didn't hear me say anything about it." In this case, Christine was guilty of the tu quoque fallacy because she did not deal with the criticism but instead dealt with the criticism by offering criticism against her critic. Many politicians use this tactic in full force especially during debates.

Conclusion

One may find that they have engaged in these fallacies more than on one occasion. While these logical fallacies are certainly not the unpardonable sin, they should be avoided by the one promoting truth. The Christian's faith is built upon fact and reality. The Christian has nothing to hide. Therefore, these fallacies should be avoided as much as possible. Remember the words of Paul, "Instead, speaking the truth in love, we will grow to become in every respect the mature body of him who is the head, that is, Christ" (Eph. 4:15, NIV). On a final note, a person may wonder how to avoid making fallacious points. If a person focuses on the data and cogently deals with the evidence while remaining fair in his or her evaluation, then most fallacies will be avoided.

Appendix 3

RESPONDING TO FOUR APOLOGETIC OBJECTIONS[1]

When I entered into the apologetics ministry, I realized that I would meet criticism and scorn due to the nature of apologetics in general. It is not surprising when a person defends the Christian worldview that one would receive pushback from those defending other worldviews. However, what took me by surprise was the level of opposition that apologetics receives from the church. I had the idea that the apologist would be something like a superhero, flying into assist those whose faith has been attacked. Yet, many firing bullets at the caped crusaders come from Christians.

One particular ministry leader once said to me, "It's my experience that people are not brought to faith by arguments." The statement was shocking enough. However, I was even more bewildered by some who seemed to agree with him. I replied, "What do you say of Josh McDowell, Lee Strobel, and J. Warner Wallace who were former atheists and became believers because of the evidence for the Christian faith?" The conversation quickly moved to a different topic. I will be the first to admit that nothing is possible to bring a person to faith without the moving of the Holy Spirit. But still, if a person dismisses apologetics, would the person not also dismiss evangelism?

I do not tell this story to demonize or demoralize anyone. The person who voiced opposition to apologetics was a *good, caring* individual who

---

1. This is a revised edition of the article that first appeared at Bellator Christi. Brian G. Chilton, "People Do Not Come to Faith by Arguments!" 4 Objections to Apologetics," *BellatorChristi.com* (August 30, 2016), https://bellatorchristi.com/2016/08/30/people-do-not-come-to-faith-from-arguments-4-objections-to-apologetics/.

loved the Lord and the people he served. However, we must engage the question he presented. Do logic and argumentation bring people to faith or are such disciplines useless endeavors? The mission statement of Bellator Christi is that it takes up the sword of Christian theology and the shield of Christian apologetics in order to take Christian truth into the arena of ideas. But if people cannot be convinced of the truths of the Christian faith, this ministry would seem a bit futile, at least in the latter portion of the mission statement. The 200 pages of this book would have been meaningless if people cannot be convinced of the truths of Christianity. So, are apologetic argumentations necessary? This article will review four common objections given to apologetics by the modern church. Each objection will contain an explanation and an appropriate reply.

Objection #1: Arguments Do Not Bring People to Faith.

The ministry leader I mentioned posed the first objection against the use of Christian apologetics. This objection claims that arguments do not really bring people into faith. Faith is a matter of the heart, not of the mind.

One could provide several replies to the first objection. To keep the post brief, I will present only two. First, objection 1 is in reality a self-defeating statement. How so? Well, the objector is presenting an argument to persuade others that arguments do not persuade. The objection is much like someone claiming to be a married bachelor or saying "I cannot speak a word of English" in English. If someone can be convinced that arguments do not convince someone of truth claims, then how could one place faith in the objection being made?

Second, the Bible presents several examples where people came to faith or were persuaded to faith by various argumentations. For instance, the miracles and teachings of Jesus provided a case for His claim to be Messiah. The miracles served as a sign. Why were such signs offered? Signs were provided to present an argument for the Messianic claims of Jesus of Nazareth. Jesus argues that "the works that the Father has given me to accomplish, the very works that I am doing, bear witness about me that the Father has sent me" (John 5:36).[2] In addition, Jesus challenged His adversaries to "search the Scriptures because you think that in them you have eternal life; and it is they that bear witness about me" (John 5:39). Other examples could be offered such as Paul's defense of the faith before various groups of people,

---

2. Unless otherwise noted, all Scripture in this article comes from the *English Standard Version* (Wheaton: Crossway, 2001).

including the Athenians. Consider Philip's argumentation to the Ethiopian that Isaiah 53 referred to Jesus of Nazareth. All such arguments were used to bring people to faith.

Objection #2: The Holy Spirit Brings People to Faith, So Argumentation is Useless.

Some people have objected to the use of Christian intellectual arguments due to the assumption that the Holy Spirit leads people to faith only by experience. If the Holy Spirit leads people to faith, then why should one worry about intellectual argumentation.

Let me first say, I wholeheartedly agree that the Holy Spirit leads people to faith. Jesus noted that when the Holy Spirit comes that He would "convict the world concerning sin and righteousness and judgment: concerning sin, because you do not believe in me; concerning righteousness, because I go to the Father, and you will see me no longer; concerning judgment, because the ruler of this world is judged" (John 16:8–11). While the Holy Spirit convicts, we are told that we have a part to play in the evangelism process. Jesus also told the disciples before His ascension, "But you will receive power when the Holy Spirit has come upon you, and you will be my witnesses in Jerusalem and in Judea and Samaria, and to the end of the earth" (Acts 1:8). Using the same logic posed against apologetics, one could also ask: If the Holy Spirit brings people to faith, then why evangelize? Christians evangelize because God commanded us to do so. Through the preaching of the Word, people are convicted by the Holy Spirit to come to faith. The Holy Spirit uses our evangelistic efforts to save people. The same is true for apologetics. Intellectual argumentation is often used by the Holy Spirit to bring people to faith. While the majority of Athens did not follow Christ after hearing Paul's intellectual defense of the faith, the book of Acts states that "some men joined him and believed, among whom were Dionysius the Areopagite and a woman named Damaris and others with them" (Acts 17:34). If the apologetics endeavor could lead just one person to faith, would it not be worth it?

Another problem I have with this mentality is that it stems from the spirit of laziness that exists in some modern Christians. A congregant once told a pastor, "You don't have to study to preach. Just follow the Holy Spirit." While I wholeheartedly agree that a person should follow the Holy Spirit, I also accept that the Scripture tells us the "test the spirits" (1 John 4:1). How does a person test a spirit? One tests a spirit against the Word of God. Testing spirits require study. The Old Testament is replete with commands for the believer to study the word of God and to make it part of their lives. I truly believe that it is the increased biblical illiteracy and lack of study that has led the modern church into many great heresies.

Objection #3: No One Has Ever Come to Faith Through Argumentation.

Anti-apologetic apologists argue that no one comes to faith through intellectual argumentation. Why bother if no one comes to faith through argumentation?

This is an easy objection to answer. The claim is false. Many have come to faith through intellectual argumentation for the faith. Among such converts include: C. S. Lewis (famed English professor and writer), Josh McDowell (author of countless Christian books), Lee Strobel (former legal editor of the *Chicago Tribune,* atheist turned Christian pastor and writer), Fazale Rana (Christian biologist), and J. Warner Wallace (former Los Angeles cold-case homicide detective turned Christian apologist). These individuals only scratch the surface of those who have come to Christ because of the evidence for Christianity. Also, it was through Christian apologetics that I came back to faith.

Objection #4: If Someone is Argued into Faith, Then They Could be Argued Out of Faith.

Lastly, objectors to Christian apologetics often claim that if it is by evidential argumentation that one comes to faith, then one could be easily led astray by some other persuasive argumentation. That is, if arguments lead a person to faith, then they could lead someone away from the faith that they accepted.

This objection holds two problems in my estimation. First, the objector does not understand the power of the Holy Spirit. If Christianity is true and a person comes to faith in Christ, then the Scripture states that the Holy Spirit will abide with the repentant person (John 14:15–16). Jesus notes that the Holy Spirit would lead a believer in truth (John 15:26–27). Thus, it would appear that the objector places less value on the power of the Holy Spirit than the advocate of Christian apologetics.

Second, the objector must consider the following point. If Christianity is true, then it will always remain true. The truthfulness of Christianity will never change. Truth is unchangeable. Thus, if a person is truly convicted of the claims of Christianity and truth does not change, then the person (although doubts may come) will not leave the faith due to the truth claims.

Conclusion

While I respect the objections made and the people who make them, it cannot be said that such objections hold any merit or value. Christianity is true. Period. If Christianity is true, then it is worth defending. If Christianity is true, eternity is at stake. Some people do come to faith when given the evidences for Christianity. It may be true that some people do not require the same level of evidence that other people require. But, refusing apologetics to the one who needs it is like refusing insulin to a diabetic because not everyone needs insulin. It is, to a degree, a categorical mistake. Remember, Peter tells us, as has been noted several times before, that we must "honor Christ the Lord as holy, always being prepared to make a defense to anyone who asks you for a reason for the hope that is in you; yet do it with gentleness and respect" (1 Peter 3:15).

BIBLIOGRAPHY

"Drive-In Movie Ads: Drive in Intermission 1960's." Video. YouTube (August 6, 2009), https://www.youtube.com/watch?v=26pQNKEOXjo.

"What Science Can't Prove: Dr. William Lane Craig explains to Dr. Peter Atkins." Video. YouTube (October 18, 2010). https://www.youtube.com/watch?v=BQL2YDY_LiM.

10NewsStaff. "Men Accused of Plotting to Groom and Rape a 3-year-Old Girl." *WFMYNews2.com* (February 6, 2019). https://www.wfmynews2.com/article/news/crime/men-accused-of-plotting-to-groom-and-rape-a-3-year-old-girl/83-3eaea098-aa28-49d9-ae41-67375dc64302?fbclid=IwAR2cKkydLfxyihxo8NZ9gFgvlXDKyLZv1ZUq2U_wLdOVeSc7fnMch16jSvs

Albright, William Foxwell. *The Archaeology of Palestine*. London, UK: Penguin, 1954.

Aquinas, Thomas. *A Summa of the Summa: The Essential Philosophical Passages of St. Thomas Aquinas' Summa Theologica*. Edited by Peter Kreeft. Translated by the Fathers of the English Dominican Province. San Francisco: Ignatius, 1990.

———. *Summa Theologica*. Edited by Robert Maynard Hutchins. Translated by the Fathers of the English Dominican Province. Chicago: William Benton, 1952.

Athansius of Alexandria. "Pascal Letters." In *Nicene and Post-Nicene Fathers*. Second Series. Volume 4. Edited by Philip Schaff and Henry Wace. Buffalo: Christian Literature, 1892. *NewAdvent.org* (2017). http://www.newadvent.org/fathers/2806039.htm.

Augustine of Hippo. *The City of God*. In *St. Augustin's City of God and Christian Doctrine*. Volume 2. A Select Library of the Nicene and Post-Nicene Fathers of the Christian Church. Edited by Philip Schaff. Translated by Marcus Dods. Buffalo, NY: Christian Literature Company, 1887.

Baggett, David, and Marybeth Baggett. *The Morals of the Story: Good News about a Good God*. Downers Grove: IVP, 2018.

Barth, Karl. *Church Dogmatics*. London, UK: T&T Clark, 1957.

Bauckham, Richard. *Jesus and the God of Israel: God Crucified and Other Studies on the New Testament's Christology of Divine Identity*. Grand Rapids: Eerdmans, 2008.

Billington, Clyde E. "The Nazareth Inscription: Proof of the Resurrection of Christ?" In *Artifax* (Spring 2005).

Borg, Marcus. *Jesus, A New Vision: Spirit, Culture, and the Life of Discipleship*. San Francisco: HarperSanFrancisco, 1991.

Boyd, Gregory A. *God of the Possible: A Biblical Introduction to the Open View of God*. Grand Rapids: Baker, 2000.

Borschel-Dan, Amanda. "Evidence of Sodom? Meteor Blast Cause of Biblical Destruction, Says Scientists." *TimesofIsrael.com* (Nov. 22, 2018). https://www.timesofisrael.com/evidence-of-sodom-meteor-blast-cause-of-biblical-destruction-say-scientists/.

Bryson, Bill. *A Short History of Nearly Everything*. New York: Broadway Books, 2004.

Bultmann, Rudolf. *New Testament Mythology and Other Basic Writings*. Minneapolis: Fortress Press, 1984.

Calvin, John, and Henry Beveridge. *Institutes of the Christian Religion*. Volume 1. Edinburgh: The Calvin Translation Society, 1845.

Chilton, Brian G. "Is Isaiah 7:14 a Messianic Prophecy?" *BellatorChristi.com* (Dec. 10, 2018). https://bellatorchristi.com/2018/12/10/is-isaiah-714-a-messianic-prophecy/.

———. "Who Wrote the Letter of James?" *Bellator Christi.com* (Aug. 8, 2018). https://bellatorchristi.com/2017/08/08/who-wrote-letter-of-james/.

Chilton, Bruce. "Unmasking a False Gospel." *NYSun.com* (October 25, 2006). https://www.nysun.com/arts/unmasking-a-false-gospel/42197/.

Conze, Edward. *The Buddhist Scriptures*. London, UK: Penguin, 1959. Kindle Edition.

Copan, Paul. *Is God a Moral Monster? Making Sense of the Old Testament God*. Grand Rapids: Baker, 2011.

Craig, William Lane. *On Guard: Defending Your Faith with Reason and Precision*. Colorado Springs: David C. Cook, 2010.

Cross, F. L. and Elizabeth A. Livingstone, eds. *The Oxford Dictionary of the Christian Church*. New York: Oxford University Press, 2005.

Crossan, John Dominic. *Jesus: A Revolutionary Biography*. New York: HarperOne, 1995.

Crum, Milton. *Evil, Anger, and God*. Livermore, CA: WingSpan, 2008.

Danin, Avinoam. "Pressed Flowers: Where Did the Shroud of Turin Originate? A Botanical Quest." *Shroud.com* (1997). https://www.shroud.com/danin.htm.

Dawkins, Richard. *The God Delusion*. New York: First Mariner, 2008.

Dembski, William. *Intelligent Design*. Downers Grove: IVP, 1999.

Dunn, James D. G. *Jesus Remembered*. Volume 1. Grand Rapids: Eerdmans, 2003.

Edersheim, Alfred. *Life and Times of Jesus the Messiah*. Peabody, MS: Hendrickson, 1993.

Ehrman, Bart. *A Brief Introduction to the New Testament*. Oxford, U.K.; Oxford University, 2008.

Epicurus. In Lactanius. *De Ira Dei (On the Wrath of God)*. Kindle Edition.

Erickson, Millard J. *Christian Theology*. Third Edition. Grand Rapids: Baker Academic, 2013.

Eusebius of Caesaria. "The Church History of Eusebius." In *Eusebius: Church History, Life of Constantine the Great, and Oration in Praise of Constantine*. Edited by Philip Schaff and Henry Wace. Translated by Arthur Cushman McGiffert. Volume 1. A Select Library of the Nicene and Post-Nicene Fathers of the Christian Church. Second Series. New York: Christian Literature Company, 1890.

Fee, Gordon D., and Douglas Stuart. *How to Read the Bible for All It's Worth*. Third Edition. Grand Rapids: Zondervan, 2003. Kindle Edition.

Forsyth, Peter Taylor. *The Justification of God*. London, UK: Independent Press, 1917.

Frankl, Viktor E. *Man's Search for Meaning*. Boston: Beacon, 2006.

Friedman, Matti. "In a Stone Box, the Only Trace of Crucifixion." *TimesofIsrael.com* (Mar. 26, 2012). https://www.timesofisrael.com/in-a-stone-box-a-rare-trace-of-crucifixion/.
Funk, Robert W., Roy W. Hoover, and the Jesus Seminar. *The Five Gospels: What Did Jesus Really Say?* New York: HarperSanFrancisco, 1993.
Geisler, Norman L. *Baker Encyclopedia of Christian Apologetics*. Baker Reference Library. Grand Rapids, MI: Baker Books, 1999.
———, and Frank Turek. *I Don't Have Enough Faith to Be an Atheist*. Wheaton, IL: Crossway, 2004.
———. *Systematic Theology: In One Volume*. Minneapolis: Bethany, 2011.
Glueck, Nelson. *Rivers in the Desert: A History of the Negev*. New York: Farrar, Straus, and Cudahy, 1959.
Goulder, Michael. "The Basic Fabric of a Vision." In *Resurrection Reconsidered*. Edited by Gavin D'Costa. Oxford, U.K.: Oneworld, 1996.
Groothius, Douglas. "Jesus: Philosopher and Apologist." *Christian Research Journal* 25, no. 2 (2002): http://www.equip.org/article/jesus-philosopher-and-apologist/.
Gundry, Stanley N., and Steven B. Cowan, eds. *Five Views on Apologetics*. Grand Rapids: Zondervan, 2000.
Habermas, Gary R. *Risen Jesus & Future Hope*. Lanham, MD: Rowman & Littlefield, 2003.
———, and J. P. Moreland. *Beyond Death: Exploring the Evidence for Immortality*. Eugene, OR: Wipf & Stock, 2004.
———, and Michael R. Licona. *The Case for the Resurrection of Jesus*. Grand Rapids: Kregel, 2004.
———. "New Testament Creeds." Lecture. Lynchburg, VA. Liberty University. June 2019. Used with permission.
Hamilton, Floyd E. *The Basis of Christian Faith: A Modern Defense of the Christian Religion*. New York: Harper & Row, 1964.
Hawking, Stephen, and Leonard Mlodinow. *The Grand Design*. New York: Bantam, 2010.
Hendrix, Holland Lee. "Early 'Christianities' of the 2nd and 3rd Centuries." *PBS.org* (April 1998). https://www.pbs.org/wgbh/pages/frontline/shows/religion/first/diversity.html.
Hume, David. *An Enquiry Concerning Human Understanding*. London: A. Millar, 1777.
Hunter, A. M. *Jesus: Lord and Saviour*. Grand Rapids: Eerdmans, 1976.
Josephus, Flavius. *The Works of Josephus: Complete and Unabridged*. Translated by William Whiston. Peabody: Hendrickson, 1987.
Julius Africanus. *Extant Writings, Fragment XVIII*.
Kant, Immanuel. *The Critique of Practical Reason*. Translated by Thomas Abbott. Mineola, NY: Dover, 1954.
Keathley, Kenneth. *Salvation and Sovereignty: A Molinist Approach*. Nashville: B&H Academic, 2010.
Keener, Craig S. *Miracles: The Credibility of the New Testament Accounts*. Grand Rapids: Baker, 2011.
———. *The Historical Jesus of the Gospels*. Grand Rapids: Eerdmans, 2009.
Kelly, Stewart E. *Truth Considered and Applied: Examining Postmodernism, History, and the Christian Faith*. Nashville: B&H, 2011.
Krauss, Lawrence M. *A Universe from Nothing*. New York: Atria, 2013.

Kreeft, Peter, and Ronald K. Tacelli. *Handbook of Christian Apologetics: Hundreds of Answers to Crucial Questions*. Downers Grove, IL: InterVarsity Press, 1994.

———. *Socratic Logic: A Logic Test Using Socratic Method, Platonic Questions, and Aristotelian Principles*. Edition 3.1. South Bend, IN: St. Augustine's, 2014.

Lea, Thomas D., and David Alan Black. *The New Testament: Its Background and Message*. Second Edition. Nashville: Broadman & Holman Publishers, 2003.

Licona, Michael R. *Why are There Differences in the Gospels? What We Can Learn from Ancient Biography*. Oxford, UK: Oxford University, 2016.

Longman III, Tremper. *How to Read Genesis*. Downers Grove: IVP Academic, 2005.

Lucian of Samosota. *The Death of Peregrine*.

Mangum, Douglas, et. al., eds. *Lexham Theological Wordbook*. Lexham Bible Reference Series. Bellingham, WA: Lexham Press, 2014. Logos Bible Software.

McDowell, Josh, and Sean McDowell. *Evidence that Demands a Verdict: Life-changing Truth for a Skeptical World*. Nashville: Thomas Nelson, 2017.

McGrew, Lydia. *Hidden in Plain Sight: Undesigned Coincidences in the Gospels and Acts*. Chillicothe, OH: DeWard, 2017.

Mitchell, Daniel. "Systematic Theology I." Lecture. Lynchburg, VA: Liberty University.

Moreland, J. P. *The Soul: How We Know It's Real and Why It Matters*. Chicago: Moody, 2014.

Oden, Thomas C. *The Word of Life: Systematic Theology*. Volume 2. San Francisco, CA: HarperSanFrancisco, 1992.

Origen of Alexandria. *Homilies on Joshua*, 7.1.

Paley, William. *A View of the Evidences of Christianity*. n.g.,: Palala Press, 2015.

Payne, J. Barton. *Encyclopedia of Biblical Prophecy*. Grand Rapids: Baker, 1980.

Plantinga, Alvin. *Warranted Christian Belief*. Oxford, UK: Oxford University, 2000.

Plato. *Theaetus*. In *Plato in Twelve Volumes*. Volume 12. Translated by Harold N. Fowler. Medford, MA; Cambridge, MA: Harvard University Press; William Heinemann, 1921. Logos Bible Software.

Pliny the Younger. *Epistulae*, 10.96.

Powell, Doug. *Holman QuickSource Guide to Christian Apologetics*. Nashville: Holman Reference, 2006.

Price, Randall. *The Stones Cry Out: What Archaeology Reveals about the Truth of the Bible*. Eugene, OR: Harvest, 1997.

———, and H. Wayne House. *Zondervan Handbook of Biblical Archaeology*. Grand Rapids: Zondervan, 2017.

Rainer, Thom S. "Hope for Dying Churches." *Facts & Trends* (January 16, 2018). https://factsandtrends.net/2018/01/16/hope-for-dying-churches/.

Rucker, Robert A. "Role of Radiation in Image Formation on the Shroud of Turin." *ShroudResearch.net* (October 11, 2016). Edited by Kevin N. Schwinkendorf. http://www.shroudresearch.net/hproxy.php/http:/role-of-radiation-in-image-formation.pdf?lbisphpreq=1.

Ryrie, Charles Caldwell. *Basic Theology: A Popular Systematic Guide to Understanding Biblical Truth*. Chicago, IL: Moody Press, 1999.

STURP. "A Summary of STURP's Conclusions." *Shroud.com* (1981). https://www.shroud.com/78conclu.htm.

Suetonius, *Life of Claudius*, 25.4.

Tacitus, *Annals* 15.44.

Turek, Frank. *Stealing from God: Why Atheists Need God to Make Their Case.* Colorado Springs: NavPress, 2014.

Van Voorst, Robert E. *Jesus Outside the New Testament: An Introduction to the Ancient Evidence.* Grand Rapids: Eerdmans, 2000.

Wallace, Daniel B. "First-Century Mark Fragment Update." *DanielBWallace.com* (May 23, 2018). https://danielbwallace.com/2018/05/23/first-century-mark-fragment-update/.

Warren, Steve. "'Temps as Hot as the Surface of the Sun': Did Scientists Find Evidence of the Destruction of Biblical Sodom?" *CBN.com* (Nov. 26, 2018). https://www1.cbn.com/cbnnews/cwn/2018/november/did-scientists-find-evidence-of-the-destruction-of-biblical-sodom-exploding-meteor-may-be-to-blame.

"What are some good things that volcanoes do?" *OregonState.edu.* http://volcano.oregonstate.edu/what-are-some-good-things-volcanoes-do.

Wiesel, Elie. *Night.* New York: Hill and Wang, 2006.

Witherington III, Ben. *Christology of Jesus.* Minneapolis, MN: Fortress, 1990.

Worth, Robert F. "From Bible-Belt Pastor to Atheist Leader." *NYTimes* (Aug. 22, 2012). https://www.nytimes.com/2012/08/26/magazine/from-bible-belt-pastor-to-atheist-leader.html.

Wright, Ted. "10 Significant New Testament Archaeological Discoveries." *EpicArchaeology.com.* http://epicarchaeology.org/archaeology-and-the-new-testament/10-significant-new-testament-archaeological-discoveries/.

Yamauchi, Edwin M. "Jesus Outside the New Testament: What is the Evidence?" In *Jesus Under Fire.* Edited by Michael J. Wilkins and J. P. Moreland. Grand Rapids: Zondervan, 1995.

www.ingramcontent.com/pod-product-compliance
Lightning Source LLC
Chambersburg PA
CBHW070741160426
43192CB00009B/1523